ALSO BY EUGENE EHRLICH

Amo, Amas, Amat and More

The Highly Selective Dictionary for the Extraordinarily Literate

The Highly Selective Thesaurus for the Extraordinarily Literate

Les Bons Mots

Mene, Mene, Tekel

Veni, Vidi, Vici

what's in a
Name?

EUGENE EHRLICH

what's in a

Name?

How Proper Names Became Everyday Words

henry holt and company

new york

Henry Holt and Company, Inc.
Publishers since 1866
115 West 18th Street
New York, New York 10011

Henry Holt® is a registered trademark of Henry Holt and Company, Inc.
Copyright © 1999 by Eugene Ehrlich
All rights reserved.
Published in Canada by Fitzhenry & Whiteside Ltd.,
195 Allstate Parkway,
Markham, Ontario L3R 4T8.

Library of Congress Cataloging-in-Publication Data
Ehrlich, Eugene H.
What's in a name?: how proper names became everyday words /
Eugene Ehrlich.—1st ed.
p.   cm.
ISBN 0-8050-5942-3 (hb: alk. paper)
1. English language—Eponyms—Dictionaries.   2. Names—
Dictionaries.   I. Title.
PE1596.E38   1999   98-43166
423'.1—DC21   CIP

Henry Holt books are available for special
promotions and premiums. For details contact:
Director, Special Markets.

First Edition 1999

Designed by Paula Russell Szafranski

Printed in the United States of America
All first editions are printed on acid-free paper. ∞

1   3   5   7   9   10   8   6   4   2

This book is dedicated to Norma, my wife and gifted grandmother of our fine grandchildren. And to Anne, Emma, Tamara, and Rory—mothers of the Nonpareil Nine.

Acknowledgments

When I think of acknowledging the help I have been given in writing any of my books, the person I think of first is invariably my dear wife, Norma Solway Ehrlich. As I look back on our fifty years of marriage, I realize she has had to put up with much by way of accommodation with the special needs and annoyances brought on by the difficulty of living with a person who has spent so much time writing so many books.

There have been many ups and many downs in our half century together, but Norma has always given excellent editorial assistance without complaint, acting as first reader. And never has she said to me, Enough already, find a steady job.

But once I have acknowledged Norma's help, my mind goes on to others who pitched in on the present volume or taught me much over the years.

Most important of all is my colleague Bryan Bunch, science writer and editor extraordinary. Bryan gave mighty help in preparing the many entries that arise from physics, mathematics, chemistry, and medicine, in all of which subjects—as well as other scientific and technical subjects— he is so well informed.

Then there are the lexicographers from whom I have learned so much, particularly the late Stuart Berg Flexner, editor-in-chief of the *Random House Dictionary of the English Language, Second Edition*, and Joyce M. Hawkins, of the Oxford University Press Dictionary Department, editor of *The Oxford Reference Dictionary*.

Finally, I wish to acknowledge the assistance of my editors at Henry Holt and Company. *What's in a Name?* would have been less of a book without the expert ministrations of Alessandra Bocco and Elise Proulx.

To be fair it must be pointed out that when the idea for this book was first broached at Holt, it was the talented Darcy Tromanhauser who first received the idea with enthusiasm. In a short time, however, the excellent Alessandra came in from the bullpen, and worked carefully and well through the entire manuscript. Now my editor has become the lively and knowledgeable Elise, who has promised to stick with the book through thick and thin.

Introduction

The word stocks of British and American English were being readied for enrichment long before these languages even came into being. This enrichment, for which we can be grateful, has continued into the present.

What helped motivate expansion of our English vocabulary was, first, a series of invasions and occupations of Britain by foreign armies, bringing mixtures of foreign words that soon made their way into English.

A second factor was an increase in trade with other nations and, as the British Empire spread, the foreign travel of many British citizens playing vital roles in conducting this trade and administering governmental affairs. American and Canadian English originated at this time.

A third factor was the nineteenth-century flowering of science and technology in Britain, in the United States, and elsewhere, which continued and accelerated throughout the twentieth century and shows no sign of abating. Each time a step is taken beyond the frontier of what is known, it brings with it the need for new terminology.

Finally, the increasing cultural and social development of speakers of English has brought an ever-increasing need for new ways of expressing thoughts and tastes. The continuing enrichment of the language owes much to the growing number of students attending colleges and universities in

English-speaking countries and to the proliferation of journals published in English.

How rapidly is English growing? Consider, for example, the second edition of the *Random House Dictionary of the English Language*, published in 1987. It included more than 50,000 entry words and 75,000 definitions that had not appeared in the first edition, published just twenty-one years earlier.

The book you are now reading focuses on a highly specialized segment of the growing American and English vocabulary—words that originated in the names of persons who become celebrated because of their contributions to learning, history, science, technology, business, or entertainment. Among these words are those that originated in the names of mythological or literary figures, giving English the opportunity for especially vivid characterizations without which the language would be the poorer.

Think of it. Our children drink **Shirley Temples**. We wear **Mae Wests** when we go boating. We used to dance the **lindy hop** and get into a movie theater with **Annie Oakleys**. And we still enjoy **beef Stroganoff** and **beef Wellington**—whenever we can afford to dine in style.

All these phrases enrich our language. Some additional examples of this enrichment can be seen in the following:

- When Adam swallowed hard and discovered his **Adam's apple**.
- When **Achilles** died and worked his way into everyone's heels.
- When **Delilah** decided to become a hairdresser.
- When **Levi** Strauss headed west with a supply of tent canvas for gold prospectors and struck it rich in blue jeans.
- When the 4th Earl of **Sandwich** ate at the gaming table and gave his name to history.
- When General Henry **Shrapnel** found a way to increase human misery in wartime.
- When Count Ferdinand von **Zeppelin** conceived of and built his airship.
- And when the Norwegian Fifth Columnist **Vidkun Quisling** betrayed his country.

All these personages, imagined as well as real, and hundreds more are worth considering for their unwitting enrichment of our language. To all these men and women we are grateful.

And we welcome the romance of word origins, the entertaining and sometimes intricate stories behind many of the words.

At the same time, there are other words that have fascinating stories but are not included in this book because they derive from place names, not from the names of persons. Two examples of this are **serendipity**, meaning the faculty of making pleasing and unexpected discoveries, and **Shangri-La**, meaning a paradise on earth and a hideaway of idyllic beauty and tranquility.

Serendipity is a word coined by the English author Horace Walpole (1717–1794) from the title of a fairy tale, *The Three Princes of Serendip*, whose protagonists made happily unexpected discoveries. Serendip was an early name for a country called Ceylon and today is called Sri Lanka.

Shangri-La, which in Tibetan means *mountain pass*, is the mythical land of eternal youth and safety from war in the novel *The Lost Horizon* (1933), written by the English novelist James Hilton (1900–1954). Older Americans may also know Shangri-La as the code name given to the secret wartime hideaway of President Franklin Roosevelt. The area surrounding this hideaway, in Catoctin Mountain Park, Maryland, is still used as a presidential retreat and is today called Camp David, now named for David Eisenhower, who married one of President Richard Nixon's daughters.

However, sometimes the stories behind words—whether or not they have their basis in a person's name—are too good to be true.

Consider the word **condom**, which has been used in English since at least the beginning of the eighteenth century. It is popularly considered to have been named after a certain Doctor Condom, putative inventor of the device.

Hugh Rawson, author of a number of fine books on language, recently wrote of the origins of the word in his entertaining and scholarly book *Devious Derivations* (1994) and did as good a job as anyone can in dispelling the notion that the condom owes its role in life to this Doctor Condom. Rawson, in puncturing this myth, makes it clear there is no evidence that a person of this name and profession ever existed.

Be assured that lexicographers have long displayed admirable tenacity as they have gone about the task of finding Doctor Condom. The usual suspects have been rounded up: publications and diaries of the pertinent period in English history, medical registers from all over Britain, including all conceivable spelling variants of Condom. To no avail. And while there was mention in the mid-eighteenth century of a Colonel Condom as inventor of the condom, be advised that equally careful research has also failed to turn him up.

There is but one incontrovertible bit of information in the condom mystery: Condom is the actual and verifiable name of a town found to this day in southern France. Its name appears in maps as well on the labels of some of the best Armagnac money can buy. (Buy a bottle and try it. Or just peek at the label in a good liquor store.) No connection, however, has ever been shown between the name of this town and the sheath that is the topic of discussion.

Yet the name *must* have come from somewhere, so if the reader will grant me leave of my senses, I should like to offer two outrageous guesses—the emphasis is on guess—as to why we have failed to find a connection between Doctor Condom and the word *condom*.

Guess 1. The name *Condom* was made up, perhaps from the Latin infinitive *condere*, one of whose definitions is "to sheathe," in the sense to insert a sword or dagger into its sheath. Not a bad beginning. But where did Doctor come from?

Guess 2. The *Oxford English Dictionary* supplies a figurative use of the title Doctor: "Applied humorously to any agent that gives or preserves health." The first example of this figurative usage of Doctor is dated 1660 and speaks of "Doctor Diet and Doctor Quiet" as contributors to the improvement of health.

Then why not a figurative Doctor Condom, an anonymous person who may be said to give or preserve health and is at least as unreal as either Doctor Diet or Doctor Quiet?

In short, searching medical registers and the like for a physician named Condom is double futility.

But don't bet anything on the fanciful explanation of the source of condom.

But aside from the occasional fabricated historic figure, English abounds with words taken directly from the monikers of famous folk far and wide. And so, to take a cue from Odysseus, let us now commence our odyssey through the unusual origins of the words we use every day.

what's in a
Name?

A

* *

Aaron's rod   Any of various long-stemmed flowering plants, for example, goldenrod and mullein. In a biblical context, a miraculous rod that blossomed and bore almonds over a single night.

As one might expect, the **Aaron** of Aaron's miraculous rod was the brother of Moses and assisted him in leading the children of Israel through the wilderness toward the Promised Land. The Book of Numbers relates the role played by **Aaron's rod** in quenching hostility shown by dissident Israelites toward the leadership of Moses in the wilderness.

But on to the story related in Numbers. In the interest of unifying support for Moses, the Lord ordered that twelve rods be cut, one for each of the Israelite families, and that the name of each of the twelve assembled princes of the families be written on them. "And it shall come to pass that the man whom I shall choose, his rod shall bud: and I will make to cease from me the murmurings of the children of Israel, which they murmur against you."

Moses laid all twelve rods in a row "in the tent of the testimony" and on the next day he went into the tent. "Behold, the rod of

Aaron . . . was budded, and put forth buds, and bloomed blossoms, and bore ripe almonds. And Moses brought out all the rods . . . unto all the children of Israel." The demonstration of Aaron's rod had its desired effect on the dissidents, and the murmurings ceased.

In Exodus we encounter another **Aaron's rod**, also miraculous. The venue this time is Egypt, and the situation also calls for a display of the strength of the Lord. When Moses and Aaron have to respond to Pharaoh's demand for a miraculous demonstration, they are told that Aaron must take his rod and "cast it down before the Pharaoh and before his servants." And what happens next? The rod is transformed into a serpent.

Pharaoh thereupon called his wise men and sorcerers together and told them to match Aaron's feat. Sure enough, all the sorcerers "cast down every man his rod, and they became serpents." But then "Aaron's rod swallowed up their rods." The children of Israel were one step closer to gaining their freedom.

It is also worth mentioning that **Aaron's serpent** is sometimes used in English to denote something so powerful as to swallow up lesser competitors—for example, a predatory corporation always ready to gobble up weaker companies.

A lesson for gardeners: If you do not have a green thumb, discard your compost and your mulches, your fertilizers and your watering cans, and put your faith in the Lord.

Abbe condenser   In optics a combination of two or three lenses having a large aperture and used as a light gatherer for a compound microscope. Such an optical condenser collects and concentrates light in a specified direction.

The **Abbe condenser** is named for the German physicist and industrialist **Ernst Abbe** (1840–1905), who was research director and partner in the famous optical works of Carl Zeiss and became owner of the firm on the death of Zeiss in 1888.

Abelian   An adjective characterizing a mathematical structure for which operations are commutative—that is, able to be performed in any order. In an Abelian group, for example, $a + b = b + a$.

The term is named for the Norwegian mathematician **Niels Henrick Abel** (1802–1829), who is known best for proving—when he was twenty-one years old—that a fifth-degree equation cannot be solved algebraically. For about two centuries previously, mathematicians had searched in vain for general methods for solving such equations.

Abel was more than able.

abigail   A lady's maid.

The biblical **Abigail**, in 1 Samuel a woman "of good understanding, and of a beautiful countenance," was the wife of a wealthy man. When Abigail's husband died not long after she first met David, David took her as a wife. And from then on, Abigail repeatedly referred to herself as David's handmaid, "a servant to wash the feet of the servants of my lord." (This was before the emancipation of women.)

The word **abigail** came into English in the seventeenth century, when Francis Beaumont and John Fletcher in their play *The Scornful Lady* named one of the play's characters Abigail, characterizing her as a "waiting gentlewoman." The name was picked up by the novelists Jonathan Swift, Henry Fielding, Tobias Smollett, and others. It has also been suggested that the political notoriety of one Abigail Hill, a royal favorite and lady-in-waiting to Queen Anne, did much to popularize the name Abigail.

Soon enough, abigail came into use with the meaning of "lady's maid," even giving rise to the awkward word **abigailship** to denote the condition of an abigail. As might be expected, this infelicitous word has been lost from English.

English changes too rapidly to keep useless words in its active file.

Abraham's bosom   Heaven; the reward of the righteous.

Think of **Abraham's bosom** as the place where you, as one of the blessed dead, will eventually reside once your allotted time on earth has expired.

Abraham's bosom alludes to an ancient custom of permitting a dear friend to recline on one's bosom, as did John on the bosom of Jesus. And we read in Luke that when a beggar named Lazarus died, "he was carried away by the angels into Abraham's bosom."

It is a comforting thought to dwell on while tuning out the droning of a less-than-accomplished eulogist at the next less-than-inspiring funeral oration you sit through.

according to Cocker In Britain, a phrase meaning correctly or exactly; especially, according to established rules. See also **according to Gunter** and **according to Hoyle**.

Edward Cocker (1631–1675) was a London engraver who also taught mathematics and penmanship, and was said to have been the author of the popular *Cocker's Arithmetick*. The book, published posthumously in 1678, became known for its accuracy and went through 112 editions. So, invoking Cocker's name to support one's interpretation of the rules of arithmetic became the equivalent of citing Scripture for the rules of morality and the like. Ironically, the editor and publisher of *Cocker's Arithmetick* subsequently exposed the work as an inaccurate forgery.

Even pure science isn't without human corruption.

according to Gunter A phrase once popular in the United States, meaning carefully and correctly done, implying unquestionable correctness.

Edmund Gunter (1581–1626) was an English mathematician and astronomer who is remembered for his contributions to trigonometry and, especially, for his inventions of measuring instruments. His reputation for reliability made **according to Gunter** the equivalent of **according to Cocker** (which see).

according to Hoyle A phrase meaning according to accepted rules; according to the highest authority.

Edmond Hoyle (1672–1769) was an English authority on card games, whose first publication was a treatise on the rules of whist. He went on to compile rules of other games as well, including backgammon and chess, and these rules were gathered in his *Hoyle's Standard Games* (1748).

To this day his name is invoked as the last word on the rules of any card game, and also more broadly on the rules governing all human behavior. Thus we may hear, "I'm not sure the special prosecutor did everything according to Hoyle."

Does any public official?

Achates A bosom pal; more formally, a faithful companion.

Achates, the chosen companion of Aeneas in Virgil's *Aeneid*, is characterized in Latin as *fidus Achates*, faithful Achates, a man of unswerving fidelity. And if Achates was good enough for Aeneas—said to have been the founder of the Roman nation—any Achates you meet should be treasured if you value true friendship.

And who doesn't?

Achillean. See **Achilles heel**.

Achilles heel Also given as **Achilles' heel**, any vulnerable spot in the character of an otherwise estimable person, nation, or other institution.

For example, one might say, "Excessive fondness for rich desserts has surely been my Achilles heel" or "Inadequate financing proved the Achilles heel of the struggling corporation."

Achilles was the great Greek warrior of the Trojan War, celebrated in Homer's *Iliad*. His father was Peleus, king of the Myrmidons, in Thessaly. The singular form of Myrmidons was taken into English as **myrmidon** (which see).

Achilles' mother was Thetis, a sea nymph and one of fifty daughters of Nereus. Because Nereus was a very old man—how could the father of fifty daughters be anything else?—he was called The Old Man of the Sea.

Incidentally, a character called The Old Man of the Sea appears in "Sinbad the Sailor," a tale told in *The Arabian Nights' Entertainments* (see also **Aladdin's lamp**). That pesky old man clung uninvited to Sinbad's shoulders, much to Sinbad's discomfort, who finally managed to get the old man drunk and do away with him.

Old Man of the Sea in time became an English phrase and is used to this day to mean a burden, actual or imagined, of which it is impossible to free oneself without extraordinary efforts. We all know such burdens.

But back to Achilles and ancient Greece. A post-Homeric legend related that Thetis, the mother of Achilles, held her infant son by the heel and dipped him in the waters of the river Styx to render his body invulnerable to injury. Thetis's hand unfortunately covered Achilles' heel during the immersion, and his heel went unprotected.

As Achilles matured, it became clear that the Stygian waters had accomplished what Thetis knew they would. Achilles was found to be protected against all the inevitable injuries of childhood and, in his maturity, proved able to emerge unscathed from his many battles.

Until one fateful day during his leadership of Greek forces in the siege of Troy. It was then that a Trojan prince named Paris let fly an arrow that found its way to Achilles. And where did the arrow strike the Greek warrior? In his unprotected heel, of course, thus inflicting a mortal wound and giving English Achilles heel, **Achilles reflex** (which see), and **Achilles tendon** (which see), as well as the rarely used adjective **Achillean**, taken to mean invulnerable and invincible in addition to meaning resembling Achilles.

For those who may not remember, Paris had earlier eloped with Helen of Troy, the beautiful but married daughter of Zeus. This illicit romance has been taken as the proximate cause of the Trojan War, so to no one's surprise the vengeful gods did their thing—Paris was himself soon struck by a poisoned arrow and died. (Talk about tit for tat!)

So love does not always conquer all, and we are left with two lessons for overprotective parents: Guard your little darlings against injury, but be forewarned that you will not always succeed, and think twice before allowing your daughter to run off on her own—to or with Paris.

Achilles reflex   Also given as **Achilles' reflex** and sometimes known as ankle jerk, in humans a reflex extension of the foot, caused by contraction of the muscles of the calf following a sharp tap on the **Achilles tendon** (which see). (See also **Babinski's reflex**.)

Achilles tendon   Also given as **Achilles' tendon**, the strong band of tissue in humans attaching the fleshy part of the heel with the calf muscles. (See **Achilles heel** and **Babinski's reflex**.)

Adam's apple   Adam, everyone's ancestor, said by some to have lived in Paradise for only twelve hours before being cast out, gave his name to a prominent feature of the human male anatomy.

And why was he cast out of Paradise? He acted in defiance of an instruction not to eat a certain apple. But Adam did eat the apple, and you know the rest.

For our purposes, the most interesting part of the legend of Adam is that a piece of the apple stuck in his throat, giving us an apt name for the protuberance in the forefront of the throat that all men know to this day.

Breathes there a man or woman who knows a more succinct and technically correct name for what we all call **Adam's apple**, the projection of thyroid cartilage of the larynx? Write or call if you do.

Addisonian Since there have been two famous Addisons in English history, there are two separate meanings of the adjective **Addisonian**.

Writing is considered Addisonian if it is unusually clear and polished, with lengthy, well-balanced sentences. This characterization comes from the style of essays written by **Joseph Addison** (1672–1719) and Sir Richard Steele (1672–1729) for their gossipy and moral periodical the *Spectator*.

The other sense of Addisonian refers to the condition known as **Addison's disease**. Read on.

Addison's disease When the outer part of the adrenal glands—tiny caps on the kidneys—produces insufficient hormones, the condition known as **Addison's disease** may result. One possible reason for such insufficiency is underactivity of the pituitary.

The symptoms of Addison's disease include weakness, fatigue, brown spots on the skin, weight loss, low blood pressure, and gastrointestinal problems. Fortunately, if properly diagnosed, Addison's disease can be treated and its symptoms completely eliminated by a lifetime program of medications taken orally that restore hormone balance.

Named after **Dr. Thomas Addison** (1793–1860), an English physician. Basing his work primarily on observations made during autopsies, Addison recognized in 1849 that the symptoms he observed were connected to degeneration of the caps on the kidneys. The cause of the then fatal syndrome was unknown, since discovery of hormones was still more than half a century away.

Although Addison's disease is rare today, it is thought by some to have influenced events in American history, in that President John F. Kennedy suffered from the disease while he held office but kept his condition secret from the general public. Since his condition was diagnosed and treated, however, it should have had no effect on his energy or ability to make decisions.

But that doesn't stop conspiracy theorists from doing their thing.

Adlerian   As a noun, an **Adlerian** is a disciple of **Alfred Adler**, a pioneering Austrian psychologist (1870–1937) and prominent member of the psychoanalytical group that formed around Sigmund Freud (see **Freudian**). Adler moved to the United States in 1932 to teach, and is remembered today primarily for opening the first child guidance clinic in Vienna, in 1921, and for his introduction of the well-known term *inferiority complex*.

As an adjective, **Adlerian** characterizes Adler and his teachings, especially his belief that behavior is determined by compensation for feelings of inferiority.

Admirable Crichton   Any person distinguished by all-round talents, somewhat like a person we are apt to call—loosely, to be sure—a Renaissance man, but nothing at all like a down-market jack-of-all-trades. Also thought of today as signifying a perfect butler.

The original **Admirable Crichton** was **James Crichton** (1560–1585), a Scottish scholar, poet, linguist, and swordsman. Considered a prodigy and said to have been fluent in twelve languages, he was known as "the Admirable."

Crichton met an untimely death in a brawl with the son of the Mantuan duke whom he served. After Crichton's death, he was portrayed as the ideal man in a panegyric on the Scottish nation written by Thomas Urquhart (1611–1660) and entitled *The Exquisite Jewel*. We are indebted forever to Urquhart's fantastic account of the Admirable Crichton's exploits and the impetus it gave to Admirable Crichton as a splendid contribution to the English tongue.

But there is more to the literary history of Admirable Crichton. William Harrison Ainsworth (1805–1882), an English historical novelist, published his novel *The Admirable Crichton* in 1837, and J. M. Barrie (1860–1937), a Scottish novelist and playwright, staged his play *The Admirable Crichton* in 1902.

Barrie's play, still performed, is a social satire in which Crichton is a remarkably talented butler always ready with well-timed machinations that succeed in resolving all problems of the plot. (Not unlike the valet Jeeves, whom readers know in the novels of P. G. Wodehouse, 1881–1975.)

It is because of Barrie that modern readers think of an Admirable Crichton as a synonym for a jewel of a butler.

Adonis   Any strikingly handsome young man.

For example, "Our neighborhood **Adonis** struck fear in the hearts of all mothers of adolescent girls." But when a man of some years is sneeringly referred to as an Adonis, the word denotes an old codger who hasn't looked at a mirror in a long time and so thinks of himself as a lady-killer.

In classical mythology **Adonis** was a youth whose beauty earned him the love of Aphrodite, daughter of Zeus and goddess of beauty and love. The better-known Venus, identified with Aphrodite, is in Roman mythology the goddess of beauty and sensual love, as well as of gardens and spring. As everyone knows, the name **Venus** (which see), has come into English to mean a living doll, more conventionally an exceptionally beautiful woman.

But back to Adonis. While out hunting one day, Adonis was slain by a wild boar, but Zeus saw to it that the young man's career did not end there. Instead, by one account, Zeus permitted him from then on to spend four months each year with Persephone, who was the Greek goddess of the infernal regions and was called Proserpine or Proserpina by the Romans. Zeus also permitted Adonis to spend four months a year with Aphrodite, and the remaining four months with anyone he chose.

So, while Adonis may not have been an entirely successful hunter, when it came to good looks he didn't have to take a backseat to anyone. His name to this day gives us a reliable way of describing a young man of exceptionally good looks as well as enabling us to wax sardonic in referring to an older man whose conquests lie primarily in the past. Where they belong.

Aeaea.   See **Circe**.

Aeolian   An adjective with two definitions. As **aeolian** it means windblown, but as **Aeolian** it means pertaining to **Aeolus**—Greek god of the winds—or to winds in general.

An **Aeolian harp**, also called a wind harp, is a stringed instrument resembling a zither, with strings of equal length and tuned to the same note. When exposed to the wind, the strings vibrate, producing a series of chords. Which are always worth hearing.

Aesculapian   An adjective, also given as **Esculapian**, meaning pertaining to **Aesculapius**; now meaning pertaining to the healing art; medicinal. One might say, "Anne is master of the **Aesculapian** art."

Aesculapius was the Roman god of medicine and a son of Apollo. He was based on the ancient Greek Asclepius, or Asklepios, the Greek god of medicine and of healing.

The name Aesculapius has been used figuratively in English to mean physician. And since the customary offering to the god Apollo was sacrifice of a rooster, in England an old way of saying *pay a doctor's bill* was to say *sacrifice a cock to Aesculapius*.

All this, of course, before the introduction of those seemingly innumerable HMOs.

Airy disc　A bright circular region that is the center of a series of luminous rings produced by diffraction of a point of light, usually the light from a star.

The **Airy disc** was named for an English astronomer, **Sir George Biddell Airy** (1801–1892). Airy was famously unlucky, best known for ignoring the calculations presented to him by a fellow English astronomer, John Couch Adams (1819–1892).

Adams had deduced mathematically the existence and location of the planet Neptune. Soon enough the location was computed by a French astronomer, Urbain Jean Joseph Leverrier (1811–1877), employing what was essentially a French version of the same calculations Adams had offered Airy. And a few days later, in 1846, Neptune was actually discovered by a German astronomer, Johann Gottfried Galle (1812–1910).

The English finally forgave Airy for losing out in the competition to be first in finding Neptune, and he was knighted more than a quarter of a century after his famous error.

Not exactly noblesse oblige.

Aladdin's lamp　From the name of a lucky young man and a wondrous artifact central to a story in *The Arabian Nights' Entertainments*, a collection of ancient Persian-Indian-Arabian tales dating from about 1450, known also as *A Thousand and One Nights*. It was translated into many European languages beginning in 1704.

The phrase **Aladdin's lamp** has come to mean a source of wealth and good luck.

The tales of *The Arabian Nights' Entertainments* are told night after night by Scheherazade, the latest bride of a certain Sultan Schahriah, a man who believes all wives are unfaithful. His solution is simplicity itself: Take and enjoy a new bride each day and have her strangled at daybreak.

Knowing this, Scheherazade, a gifted storyteller, conceives of a way to stave off her execution. Each night she launches into a story that will intrigue the Sultan, but breaks off just before the climax of the story. What the Sultan does not realize is that Scheherazade also makes sure the Sultan can overhear her telling her sister the beginning of the next night's story.

As a result the Sultan is eager to let his bride live until the next day so he can learn the denouement of the interrupted story, as well as the entire story to be told on the following night. This goes on for 1,001 nights, when the Sultan finally disavows his intention to execute Scheherazade.

But what about **Aladdin**? In "Aladdin or the Wonderful Lamp," a Chinese lad named Aladdin obtains a magical lamp. He discovers its power when he happens to rub the lamp, whereupon two genies appear and promise to do his bidding. Through their good offices he becomes enormously wealthy and, after a complex series of ups and downs—grist for Scheherazade's story mill—settles down to enjoy life in his own palace.

So we learn from this that Aladdin profited from an occasional rub, and that even sultans love a good story.

Alberti bass In music, especially in eighteenth-century rococo compositions, a type of bass accompaniment consisting of arpeggios, also known as broken chords.

The **Alberti bass** is named for an Italian musician, **Domenico Alberti** (1710–1740), born in Venice and known for his harpsichord sonatas. His music today is virtually forgotten.

aldrin A white crystalline chlorinated hydrocarbon used as an insecticide.

The name is appropriate because **aldrin** is made using a process called the Diels-Alder reaction, an important method for synthesizing organic compounds by forming a ring of atoms.

The pesticide is named for **Kurt Alder** (1902–1958), a German organic chemist who was the junior partner of the Diels-Alder reaction.

He and his former boss, Otto Diels (1876–1954), shared the 1950 Nobel Prize in chemistry for their work on the reaction named for them.

alexandrite   A variety of the gemstone chrysoberyl, of interesting properties.

Alexandrite was discovered in 1833 and named for the future Russian czar **Alexander II** (1818–1881). Although green in sunlight, **alexandrite** has the odd property of appearing red in artificial light. Since green and red were the colors of the Russian Imperial Army, the gem became highly popular in nineteenth-century Russia.

Doesn't take much to please some people.

Alfvén wave   A type of oscillation of plasma particles.

A plasma is an electrified gas, generally considered by modern scientists to be a fourth state of matter. Although plasmas can exist only at very high temperatures—and therefore are rare on Earth—they are actually the most common state of matter in the universe as a whole.

In 1942 the Swedish theoretical physicist **Hannes Olof Gösta Alfvén** (born in 1908) predicted that characteristic waves, now called **Alfvén waves**, would develop in plasmas. The waves were later observed during work on development of fusion power.

Alfvén received a share of the 1970 Nobel Prize in physics for his work on the dynamics of plasmas in magnetic fields.

Algaroth powder   An emetic in the form of a white powder.

Named after **Vittorio Algarotto** (died 1604), a physician of Verona, Italy, who devised the **Algaroth powder**, based on antimony. It was a popular emetic in the seventeenth century but is no longer used for that purpose. Yet Algarotto is not forgotten because Algaroth powder reacts with cream of tartar to produce the compound tartar emetic, which is still used in medicine.

A word must be said about antimony, an element with properties similar to those of arsenic but not quite as poisonous. Antimony was known to the ancients as it sometimes occurs in nature, but about the time of Algarotto it was for the first time derived from ore.

When you consider how helpful an emetic can be, we must keep the lexicographic welcome mat out for Algaroth powder.

Alice blue   A pale greenish-blue color.

Named for **Alice Roosevelt Longworth** (1884–1960), daughter of President Theodore Roosevelt (1858–1919). Long a prominent Washington social figure and political hostess, she is recalled by people older than us in a song that made much of a pretty young woman who wore a sweet little **Alice blue** gown when she first wandered down into town.

Alice-in-Wonderland   Meaning unreal, totally impractical, totally absurd.

The term derives from events described in two highly regarded books written by Lewis Carroll, real name Charles Lutwidge Dodgson (1832–1898), an Oxford mathematician: *Alice's Adventures in Wonderland* (1865) and *Through the Looking Glass* (1871).

In the first of these books, **Alice** falls down a rabbit hole into a strange country where everything happens with a disturbing illogicality. In the second book, Alice climbs through a mirror and discovers that everything is reversed.

Lewis Carroll has given us a marvelous insight into the thinking of modern politicians struggling to balance national budgets: When they consider that expenditures are too high, their solution is to increase expenditures further.

Alzheimer's disease   Alzheimer's, as this serious disease is often called, causes loss of short-term memory and, over time, loss of so many other mental functions that persons with this condition become completely dependent on others for their care. They eventually die from loss of brain function.

As early as 1906, the German psychiatrist and neuropathologist **Alois Alzheimer** (1864–1915) observed the characteristic brain abnormalities of the disease that would be named for him. Not until recent years, however, have physicians learned to recognize behavior patterns characteristic of the disease in living patients.

Perhaps the best-known person whose **Alzheimer's disease** has been recognized in his lifetime is former president Ronald Wilson Reagan (born 1911).

Because Alzheimer's patients are often over sixty-five, many of us tend to think the disease is an inevitable and natural part of aging. It is not. Healthy persons can remain intellectually active and alert throughout their lives, experiencing little more than a slight drop in mental agility as they age. Just like the rest of us on Monday morning.

Amati   Any one of the premier violins extant that were made in the sixteenth and seventeenth centuries by members of the **Amati** family of Cremona, Italy.

Andrea Amati (c.1510–c.1578) is considered the founder of the Cremona school of violin making, setting the style for his family's instruments and, with modifications by Stradivari (see **Stradivarius**), for all modern violins.

Amati's sons Antonio (c.1540–c.1638) and Girolamo (1561–1630), known as the brothers Amati, made violas and violoncellos—cellos—in addition to violins. Nicolò (1596–1684), Girolamo's son, was a teacher of Stradivari and of Andreas **Guarneri** (which see) and improved the violin further. Nicolò's son Girolamo (1649–1740) was the last of the family to achieve distinction in the world of violin making.

By that time, perhaps the violin genes got tired.

America   People all over the world understand the nouns **America** and **American** and the adjective **American**; they also understand, albeit of several interpretations, the verb **Americanize**. A smaller group of people readily grasp the meanings of **Americana**, **Americanism**, and **Americanist**.

Whether we associate America with North, South, Central, Latin, Middle, or merely with the United States; or whether we attach American to African, Asian, Cuban, French, German, Irish, Jewish, Polish, and a host of other designations, one thing we do know: Everybody wants to get into the act.

And in the end all the many things and persons that get their names from America and American appear to owe a debt to **Amerigo Vespucci** (1451–1512), a man whose origins epitomize the American experience. He was born in Italy, became a naturalized Spaniard, and made several voyages to the New World while in the service of the king of Portugal.

Americus, the Latinized form of his given name, is believed to have first been attached to him by a German cartographer, Martin Waldseemüller (c.1480–c.1521), who used an account of Vespucci's travels to publish, in 1507, a map and globe showing the name *Americus*.

Two additional items of interest: The account of Vespucci's travels used by Waldseemüller was forged. And scholars do not agree that this account of the origin of America is entirely true.

Ames test A test for carcinogenic properties using a culture of micro-organisms.

Named for the American biologist **Bruce N. Ames** (born 1928), who developed the **Ames test** as a quick way to test a substance for carcinogenic properties. This test was especially welcome because it is difficult and expensive to test a newly synthesized chemical for possible cancer-causing potential in mammals, even in relatively short-lived, fast-breeding mice or rats.

Ironically, after gaining celebrity for his test, Ames became the leading exponent of the idea that most cancer-causing chemicals are natural substances found in food rather than synthetic chemicals of the type usually tested for cancer-causing potential.

Will All-Natural, No Chemicals lose out to All-Chemical, No Natural? It boggles the mind.

Amish The name given to a conservative sect of followers of **Jakob Ammann**, also spelled **Amann** and **Amen** (c.1645–c.1730), a Swiss Mennonite bishop, who separated from the Mennonites in Switzerland and Alsace in the late seventeenth century and went on to establish Amish communities in North America.

Early in the eighteenth century the **Amish**, also called **Amish Mennonites**, appeared in Pennsylvania first and soon established settlements elsewhere. Today, Amish communities are found primarily in various parts of Canada and the United States, where they are conspicuous for their men's and women's old-fashioned dress and rural, simple way of life. Amish men are bearded and they eschew automobiles for horse-drawn vehicles. Their lives are marked by industry, frugality, and colorful customs.

In Pennsylvania particularly, the Amish contribute to local economies by raising and marketing agricultural crops. They also attract large numbers of tourists who are happy to stare at them, dine on what they think are Amish foods, and buy locally made craft items.

ampere   The **ampere** is the basic unit of electric current in the International System of Units, used in most countries other than the United States and by scientists everywhere.

In the earlier metric system, the **ampere** was derived from the number of electrons passing through a wire. But the *current* definition—Yes, Virginia, there is a pun here—holds that it is the amount of current that would produce a specified tiny force between two wires a meter apart—No, Virginia, not an *electric meter*—when the current flows through them both in the same direction.

The old definition was, to say the least, more intuitive if perhaps harder to measure accurately. How would one actually count 6,250,000,000,000,000,000 electrons as they passed by?

When scientists found ways to measure electric current and energy, they thought to honor the founders of their subject. *Ampere, volt, coulomb,* and *ohm* started a trend that has continued with such units as *newton, joule,* and *kelvin*—all named for pioneering physicists.

It is interesting that it was Lord Kelvin (see **Kelvin scale**) who, in 1883, proposed naming the basic unit of electric current the ampere. This unit honors the French mathematical physicist **André-Marie Ampère** (1800–1864), who, between 1820 and 1827, discovered the basic laws of electromagnetism.

ampulla of Lorenzini   A sense organ found in the skin of sharks and rays.

Named for an Italian physician, **Stefano Lorenzini** (fl. 1678), who first described this interesting anatomical feature.

The Romans called a round flask with two handles an *ampulla.* Anatomists have taken up the term to describe any bulge in a bodily tube, and there are four or five such **ampullae** in the human body as well as similar bulges in the organs of other creatures. (See also **ampulla of Vater.**)

The **ampullae of Lorenzini** can detect even small changes in heat, pressure, or salinity, but their role in recognizing and quantifying electric currents in water appears to be their main function. It has been determined that sharks use small changes in electric current to find their prey, then use vision and smell to aim their attack.

And you thought it was safe to wear your waterproof watch while scuba-diving at Club Med.

ampulla of Vater The **ampulla of Vater**, named for German anatomist **Abraham Vater** (1684–1751), who described it in 1720, is the bulge in humans at the site where the tubes leading to the small intestine from the pancreas and from the liver merge to form the common bile duct. (See also **ampulla of Lorenzini**.)

anacreontic An adjective meaning convivial and amatory, taken from the name of **Anacreon** (c.570–c.475 B.C.), a Greek lyric poet famous for his satires and his elegant love poetry. The adjective **anacreontic** suggests the contents of Anacreon's poems in praise of love and wine.

Only fragments of Anacreon's work are extant, but his name is also recalled elsewhere in English. The capped adjective **Anacreontic** means in the style of Anacreon, and the noun **Anacreontic** means a poem in the style or subject matter of Anacreon. The phrase **Anacreontic poetry** is applied to verse written by or derived from that of Anacreon, and **anacreontic meter** is used to indicate the meter in which Anacreon and his Greek imitators wrote their poetry.

Ananias Any habitual liar.

We encounter the biblical **Ananias** in Acts. He was an early Christian who "gave up the ghost"—which usually means died, but in this case means struck dead. The act for which he received this divine retribution arose from a real estate transaction. He and his wife Sapphira sold their property and then withheld from the apostles part of the proceeds of the sale. The lie Ananias told was to claim falsely he had given the entire proceeds to the apostles.

And what happened to Sapphira, who had also profited from the sale? "About the space of three hours after . . . she gave up the ghost" and was soon carried out for burial alongside Ananias.

In those days, lying and greed were no small matters.

andradite A type of garnet, but not the kind generally used as a gem. Garnet is a crystalline mineral that often occurs as small regions in rock, and the rock also contains larger amounts of other minerals, such as limestone.

Andradite includes iron along with the calcium, silicon, and oxygen that characterize the mineral garnet. Thus, **andradites** may range in color from yellow to black.

Named after **José Bonifacio de Andrada e Silva** (1763–1838), a Brazilian who in addition to being a geologist and poet is considered to have been the architect of Brazilian independence.

andromeda   A shrub, especially the Japanese andromeda, *Pieris japonica*. This evergreen is popular among American landscape gardeners, who value its hardiness and drooping clusters of small, white blossoms. The word **andromeda** takes its name from a beautiful woman in classical mythology.

Andromeda was the daughter of Orpheus and Cassiopeia. When her mother boasted that Andromeda was more beautiful than the Nereids, the fifty daughters of Nereus (see **Achilles heel**), the Nereids were instrumental in having Andromeda punished. On orders of Neptune, she was delivered to a sea monster and soon found herself chained to a rock.

Talk about peremptory judgment! But just to set the record straight, it must be noted that she was delivered from her bondage by Perseus, who then married Andromeda. Perseus was the son of Zeus who slew **Medusa** (which see), a **Gorgon** (which also see).

After Andromeda died she was given a place among the stars and is recalled today by astronomy buffs who train their telescopes on the constellation Andromeda in the Northern Hemisphere. (See also **Andromeda galaxy**.)

Andromeda galaxy   A giant spiral collection of stars located in the constellation Andromeda.

Astronomers have designated this spiral as M31 (Messier catalog number 31) or NGC 224 (New Galactic Catalog number 224) and refer to it as the Great Nebula of Andromeda or the **Andromeda galaxy**.

The Andromeda galaxy is visible to the naked eye as a patch of light, resembling a cloudlet rather than a point, so it is called a nebula rather than a star. But with the help of a telescope it is revealed to be anything but a small cloud. Some 300 billion stars are arranged in the spiral that is the Andromeda galaxy.

When the structure of our own galaxy, the Milky Way, is analyzed, it too appears to be a spiral, so the Andromeda galaxy is taken to be a larger-than-life version of the Milky Way. Indeed, it is about twice the size of our galaxy.

Andromeda is the name of a girl more beautiful than the fifty daughters of Nereus and is surely worthy of a galaxy. As e. e. cummings wrote: "there's a hell of a good universe next door; let's go."

See **andromeda**.

angstrom An officially outmoded measure for small lengths, yet persisting in widespread use. More of this in a moment.

The **angstrom** was named for the Swedish physicist **Anders Jonas Ångström** (1814–1874), who was the first to recognize, in 1855, that a gas heated to glowing temperatures emits light of a characteristic wavelength, which then can be used to identify the gas. The formal birth of spectroscopy, based on this idea, came four years later and was the work of German physicists.

Ångström applied his idea to a study of the gases in the Sun, identifying hydrogen as the main component in 1862 and other elements subsequently. He measured wavelengths of light in ten-billionths of a meter, which came also to be used by others who based their work on his. In recognition of his work, in 1905 an international body of scientists formally designated the popular unit as the angstrom in his honor.

So back to the angstrom. One angstrom equals 10 nanometers, or 0.0000000001 meter; that is, 1 ten-billionth of a meter. We're talking small!

Aside from the tradition of using angstroms to measure the wavelengths of light and the sizes of microbes, the angstrom continues to be popular, despite official disapproval, because it is more convenient than the nanometer, which is the official length closest to the angstrom. For example, an average atom is 1 or 2 angstroms in diameter, which somehow is found easier to use than 10 or 20 nanometers.

Wouldn't you agree—if you were asked?

ankerite A mineral that often occurs in and around iron and coal mines, especially in England and central Europe.

It is named after an Austrian mineralogist, **M. J. Anker** (1772–1843), about whom little else is known.

Ankerite often forms large, dramatic crystals that are frequently brown, although they are sometimes creamy or even gray.

Annie Oakley A pass, or free ticket, to a theatrical performance, a baseball game, or the like.

Annie Oakley was an American sharpshooter who made her living in show biz. Annie, full name **Phoebe Anne Oakley Mozee** (1860–1926), learned to shoot as a child and went on to star in Buffalo Bill's Wild West Show. In one of her stunts she would shoot out cigarettes held between her husband's lips. His trust in Annie's ability was understandable: When Annie was twenty years old she had bested him in a shooting match.

In another favorite stunt she would shoot bullets through the pips of playing cards that had been tossed in the air. It was the resemblance of these bullet-perforated cards to punched tickets that is said to have given us the name **Annie Oakley** for any free ticket.

Apgar score   A scale for predicting the general health of a newborn, administered at delivery by the physician or midwife caring for the baby. In the regimen used for the **Apgar score**, the parameters judged are pulse, respiration, muscle tone, color, and reflexes.

This valuable scale was developed by **Virginia Apgar** (1909–1974), an American physician whose original field of specialization was anesthesiology. She created and led the Department of Anesthesiology at Columbia-Presbyterian Medical Center and developed safe methods for easing the pain of childbirth.

With her development of the Apgar score, Dr. Apgar achieved an enduring reputation as a woman who pioneered in a field dominated by men and advanced beyond the men of her day. Good to hear.

Apollo   Any exceptionally handsome young man.

In classical Greek mythology **Apollo**, sometimes identified with the sun god Helios, was the son of Zeus and Leto. In the world of gods he held many portfolios—he was the god of light, music, poetry, archery, prophecy, and the healing art. But it is the association of Apollo with manly beauty, made vivid by his most celebrated statue, the marble **Apollo Belvedere**, that gives us our use of his name as a term for a very handsome young man. (See also **Adonis**.)

Yet this does not explain why *Apollo* was selected as the name of the U.S. spacecraft that enabled astronauts to travel from Earth to the Moon and back. Maybe it stemmed from Apollo's identification with the sun god Helios.

Appian Way   Also called the queen of long-distance roads—it is about 350 miles long—this is the ancient Roman road leading from Rome to

Brundisium, now called Brindisi. Work on the **Appian Way** began about 312 B.C.

This road, in Latin *Via Appia*, takes its name from its builder, **Appius Claudius** (fourth–third century B.C.), a statesman and law-giver. In the Christian tradition the Appian Way is the road on which Peter and Christ meet when Peter is fleeing Rome to avoid persecution by the emperor Nero. Peter greets Christ with the famous question *Domine, quo vadis?*, Master, whither goest thou? When Christ replies, I am coming to Rome to be crucified again, Peter feels so shamed that he returns to face martyrdom in Rome.

The Polish novelist Henryk Sienkiewicz (1846–1916), winner of the Nobel Prize in literature in 1905, wrote the historical novel *Quo Vadis* (1896), dealing with the Rome of Nero's time and the early Christian martyrs. *Quo Vadis* has been translated into numerous languages.

aqueduct of Sylvius   Two men known as Dr. Sylvius have given their names to parts of the human body. **Jacobus Sylvius** was the Latin nom de plume of a French physician, **Jacques Dubois** (1478–1555). **Franciscus Sylvius** was the Latinized name of a German physician, **Franz de la Boë** (1614–1672).

Dubois, *de la Boë*, and *Sylvius* may all be translated as "of the woods," but the main effect of having two Dr. Sylviuses is that they are easily confused by historians.

To set the record straight, Jacobus is credited with describing a bone called the **Sylvian ossicle**. Franciscus catalogued the parts of the brain, including the cerebral tube called the **aqueduct of Sylvius**. Franciscus also described a crease in the brain, called the **Sylvian angle**, and a cavity in the brain called the **Sylvian ventricle**.

No wonder medical school is so tough.

Archimedean   An adjectival form derived from the name of **Archimedes**, one of the few great humans who have managed to excel in science, mathematics, and engineering. Any idea originated or explored by Archimedes is termed **Archimedean**.

Mathematicians rate the Greek Archimedes (c.287–212 B.C.) among the greatest mathematicians of all time. Although his contributions to physics are not quite in the same class as those in mathematics, they are elegant, original, and important.

Consider the **Archimedean property**, which postulates that one can always find a product of a number and a positive integer that is greater than any other specified number. Again, there is the **Archimedean spiral**, which is formed by a point moving at a constant rate and increasing or decreasing its distance from a particular point at a constant rate. Finally, there are the thirteen three-dimensional figures known as **Archimedean solids**, which are formed with more than one type of regular polygon for faces, but still with all the solid angles equal.

Archimedes is often said to have discovered the lever, but humans had been using levers for thousands, if not millions, of years before the time of Archimedes. What he did was work out the mathematics of simple machines and, in the process, may have discovered the compound pulley.

In a famous Archimedean story, he said, "Give me a place to stand on, and with a lever I will move the whole world." When challenged to support his claim, he obliged by using compound pulleys to launch single-handedly one of the largest ships made to that time, with full crew aboard.

Now consider his achievements when his native Syracuse was attacked by the Roman army and navy. Archimedes is said to have devised a number of improved catapults and crossbows that pushed back ordinary waves of attackers. When the Roman general Marcellus brought out his own secret weapon, Archimedes used levers to drop huge boulders on the attackers, sinking their ships.

There is much more to the story, but not enough room for it here. Read on.

Archimedes' principle During Archimedes' time, Syracuse was ruled by his cousin, King Hiero II, who felt that his crown did not have the amount of gold promised. Archimedes verified this suspicion by measuring the crown's density. He did this by submerging the crown in water and determining the volume of the water displaced. The pity is that, as with the story of the **Archimedean lever** (see **Archimedean**), the concept of density had been known before the time of Archimedes.

What Archimedes did discover was that a body immersed partly in a fluid displaces a weight of the fluid equal to the weight of the body. And that concept is what is known today as **Archimedes' principle**.

This principle extends beyond a method for detecting fraud in the manufacture of a king's crown. Anything that floats in a fluid owes much to Archimedes' principle. When the weight of the fluid displaced equals the weight of the part of the object that is submerged, the effective weight of the object becomes zero. No more of the object will be submerged unless some outside force presses on it. As a result, the object floats at a height in the fluid that depends on the total weight of the object and the volume that is submerged in the fluid. (See **Plimsoll line**.)

Now for a tricky thought: Air is a fluid, and we all are submerged in it. According to Archimedes' principle, everyone is buoyed a bit by the air that his or her body displaces. Thus, a person of great girth, who displaces more air than most persons, obtains the greatest benefit when standing on a scale.

Since air is not very heavy, however, the effect is imperceptible in this case. But read on.

Archimedes' screw   While Archimedes lived in Egypt, he invented the device known as **Archimedes' screw**—useful in irrigating land—the invention most closely associated with his name.

Think of Archimedes' screw as a helix—a screw—within a tube, the bottom of which rests in water or another fluid. When turned in the proper direction, the screw brings to the top of the tube the fluid at the bottom.

While we know that a vacuum pump can also be used to raise a fluid, we also know that a vacuum pump has limitations. Air pressure at sea level is only heavy enough to lift a column of mercury—in a barometer—up about 30 inches. This same air pressure can lift a column of water up to about 30 feet. At normal air pressure, therefore, these are the limitations on vacuum pumps. To paraphrase Galileo, nature may abhor a vacuum, but only for about 30 feet.

Since the Archimedes' screw is not dependent on air pressure, it can raise water higher than the 30-foot limit on vacuum pumps. As a result, Archimedes' screw is still used today for irrigation and other purposes.

Archimedes has certainly done more than his share to benefit agriculture and enrich the English language.

arfvedsonite   A black silicate mineral named after Swedish chemist **Johan August Arfvedson** (1792–1841).

Arfvedson is better known for his discovery of lithium in 1817, a soft silver-white element that is used in many commercial applications. Lithium carbonate is enormously useful in the treatment of manic depression.

Argand burner   The first really bright lamp was the **Argand burner**, also known as the **Argand lamp**, developed in 1784 by Swiss inventor **Aimé Argand** (1755–1803).

There is evidence that lamps based on burning fats or oils originated very early in human history, but these lamps were hardly better than candles at producing light. The Argand burner was much better than earlier types because it used a circular wick and an arrangement that enabled air to reach the flame from two sides at once. The greater the amount of oxygen available to produce combustion, the brighter the flame.

The contribution of the name Argand did not end with Aimé Argand. Read on.

Argand diagram   Three European mathematicians made substantial contributions to a method for understanding complex numbers. **Jean-Robert Argand** (1768–1825), whose name is recalled in the **Argand diagram**, was among them.

Complex numbers, which involve the imaginary square root of negative 1, are useful in pure mathematics. Prior to the work of Argand and the two earlier mathematicians, however, complex numbers were difficult to depict and, therefore, to understand. When a simple method for showing complex numbers was developed, near the beginning of the nineteenth century, these numbers lost some of their mystery and became one of the most useful creations of mathematics.

Let's make the discussion a bit clearer. Think of complex numbers as points on a plane, with negative numbers represented as below zero on the plane, and positive numbers as above zero. To this day, the Argand diagram remains the most common name for numbers on the complex plane.

But who are the other two mathematicians mentioned above? One is Karl Friedrich Gauss, whose name will be discussed later in this book; the other is a Norwegian surveyor named Caspar Wessel (1745–1818), whose name is not nearly as well-known as Gauss, or even as well-known as Jean-Robert Argand.

Argand lamp.   See **Argand burner**.

Argus   Any very vigilant person; a watchful guardian.

In Homer's *Odyssey* **Argus** was the faithful dog that immediately recognized its master Odysseus when he returned home after an absence of twenty years. No, he had not gone out for a pack of cigarettes. He had been playing an important role in the siege of Troy.

More important, in classical mythology **Argus** was a giant with one hundred eyes who was charged to guard Io. And who was this Io that she had to be watched so carefully?

At the time Io was guarded by Argus, she was a heifer—a young cow that has not yet produced a calf—but Io was an exceptional heifer. In her original configuration she was a young woman of exceptional beauty, and Zeus was sweet on her. Zeus had reconfigured Io to hide her from Hera.

And who was Hera? The sister and wife of Zeus! Thus, returning for a moment to the definition of Argus as an English word, we might also have the hyphenated **Argus-eyed**, taken to mean jealously watchful, and we can see why when we recall the jealousy of Hera.

But back to mythology. Soon enough Hermes, the messenger of the gods, caused the giant of one hundred eyes to fall asleep, whereupon Hermes slew Argus, and Hera transferred his eyes to the peacock's tail.

But what happened to Io? She wandered over the earth and finally settled in Egypt, where she resumed her human shape. And why Egypt?

Why not? Isis, the principal goddess of ancient Egypt, was worshipped throughout the ancient world and was identified with Io and Hera, among others. In addition, the cow was always sacred to Isis.

And what happened to the faithful dog Argus that waited patiently for its master to return home to Ithaca? Upon indicating its recognition of Odysseus and establishing Odysseus's identity for Penelope, his wife, who had not seen him in twenty years—and must have been terribly nearsighted after twenty years of weaving by day and unraveling her work by night—the poor dog dropped dead.

So, while we may be moved by the story of Argus as a faithful dog, we will always be grateful to Argus for giving the peacock its beautiful tail. The best example of organ transplant in classical mythology.

aristarch   A severe critic.

Taken from the name of the Greek philologist and critic **Aristarchus** (c.215–143 B.C.). The adjectival form of Aristarchus appears both as **Aristarchian** and **Aristarchean**.

Aristarchus is often referred to as **Aristarchus of Samothrace** to differentiate him from Aristarchus of Samos (c.310–c.230 B.C.), a Greek astronomer. Our Aristarchus, Aristarchus of Samothrace, who edited works of Homer, Pindar, Anacreon, and others, was a severe critic of Homeric poetry and rejected many of its lines as spurious.

Which explains why **aristarch** means a severe critic.

Aristotle's lantern   If you are not familiar with **Aristotle's lantern**, you will never guess what it is. A hint: The great Greek **Aristotle** (384–322 B.C.) is known today, inter alia, as the father of biology.

Not much of a hint? Well then, most persons think of Aristotle as a philosopher who had incorrect ideas about astronomy and physics. What's more, they know nothing of his careful work in embryology, marine biology, classification, and the like.

A further hint: Aristotle's lantern is a part of a kind of animal that is shaped like a lantern.

So think: What part of what kind of animal looks like the window in a fourth-century Greek lantern?

Give up? It is the feeding apparatus of a sea urchin, which, with its five so-called lips, each containing a tooth, looks like a window, so that the entire sea urchin looks like a lantern.

In his writing, Aristotle drew the comparison between urchin and lantern, and now Aristotle's lantern is the official name for the urchin's feeding apparatus.

And English is the richer.

Arminianism   The doctrines of **Jacobus Arminius** (1560–1609), original name Jakob Hermandszoon, also given as Hermansen.

Arminius was a Dutch anti-Calvinist theologian and the center of continuing controversy among his fellow theologians for his assertions that God bestows forgiveness and eternal life on all who repent of their sins and accept Christ, that God wills all people to be saved, and that God's predestination is founded on God's foreknowledge. All of this being a highly condensed presentation of **Arminianism**.

But detailed enough to indicate why Arminius was not popular with Calvinists.

artemisia The genus *Artemisia* includes such familiar and beautiful plants as dusty miller, southernwood, and silver king artemisia; the herbs tarragon and wormwood; and the sagebrush that epitomizes the American West of cowboy legend if not in fact.

All owe their generic name to the somewhat mysterious goddess **Artemis** who, in Greek myth, was the twin sister of **Apollo** (which see). Artemis was also the daughter of Zeus and Leto, who was one of Zeus's many girlfriends of little distinction—but Leto did bear the twins Apollo and Artemis.

The story does not end there. Artemis appears in various forms in the ancient world, including as a many-breasted goddess at the temple of Artemis at Ephesus, one of the seven wonders of the ancient world.

Artemis must have been something wondrous to behold, and the horticultural beauties called **artemisia** surely are well named.

Arthus' phenomenon An allergic reaction, also given as **Arthus' reaction**.

Allergic reactions in most cases manifest themselves as reddened and itchy skin, a stuffy or runny nose, or in somewhat more serious cases as hives or asthma. The most severe reactions, called *anaphylactic*, from the Greek for "a reversed defense," can be life threatening. Since the phenomenon we know as *anaphylactic shock* may involve rapid swelling, acute respiratory distress, and collapse of circulation, it is easy to understand why it may mean curtains for the victim.

Modern sufferers of allergic reactions—and their numbers appear to increase each day—owe much to the French physiologist **Nicolas-Maurice Arthus** (1862–1945), who observed in 1903 a form of anaphylactic reaction that includes fluid buildup in tissues, combined with inflammation. Building on the observations of Arthus, medical researchers have made much progress in helping allergy sufferers.

For which we all are grateful.

Aschheim-Zondek test In 1928 two gynecologists, **Selmar Aschheim** (1878–1965), a German, and **Bernhard Zondek** (1891–1966), an Israeli born in Germany, realized they had found a hormone that appears only in pregnancy. Its presence could, therefore, be used to determine whether a woman is pregnant.

You may think *rabbit* when considering a pregnancy test, but for the **Aschheim-Zondek test**, the animal involved is a young, female white mouse. Injection of human gonadotropic hormone into such a mouse will do the trick, enlarging its ovaries and causing its ovarian follicles to ripen.

In the good old days—before one watched anxiously for a color change in a home pregnancy test—a woman who had been tested would wait just as anxiously for a call from her doctor. If, indeed, the woman was pregnant, she might have been told: "The rabbit died." With the Aschheim-Zondek test, the message is: "The white mouse thinks she's pregnant."

Time to start eating for two.

Aschoff body Also given as **Aschoff nodule**, a tiny nodule that some-times develops in a heart muscle in response to an unchecked strepto-coccal infection. While strep is usually a localized infection, as in strep throat, blood poisoning, or tonsillitis, the bacterium can become widespread in the body.

When strep attacks the joints, the resulting disease is known as *rheumatic fever*. Some 60 percent of the time, rheumatic fever also affects the heart, causing damage to heart valves and the small bodies made from scar tissue in the heart muscle itself, which are known as **Aschoff bodies**, after German pathologist **Karl Albert Ludwig Aschoff** (1866–1942), who described them.

The Aschoff nodule should not be confused with **Aschoff's node**, which is not a disease symptom, but a small mass of muscle fibers that appears in the normal heart and is involved in conducting motion from one part of the muscle to another.

Athanasian An adjective meaning of or pertaining to **Athanasius**, properly St. Athanasius (c.298–373), a Greek Christian theologian and archbishop of Alexandria during the reign of the emperor Constan-tine. As a noun **Athanasian** means an adherent of the teachings of Athanasius.

His historic legacy is **The Athanasian Creed**, of unknown authorship, but embodying the teachings of Athanasius regarding the Trinity, stating in part: "And in this Trinity [God the Father, God the Son, and God the Holy Ghost] none is afore, or after other; none is greater, or less than another; but the whole three Persons are coeternal together: and coequal."

atlas A noun meaning a book of maps; also meaning a book of charts, tables, and the like intended to illustrate a subject.

The word came into use because the publisher of a book of maps prepared by the great Flemish cartographer Mercator (see **Mercator projection**) in the sixteenth century bore on its title page the figure of **Atlas** supporting the globe on his back.

In Greek mythology Atlas, one of the Titans, was condemned by Zeus to uphold the heavens on his shoulders. Quite a sentence for taking part in the war of the Titans (see **titan**).

This mythological incident also led to the use of Atlas to mean any person who supports a heavy burden, thus: "Franklin Delano Roosevelt is still seen as the Atlas whose burden was to carry his country out of the Great Depression and lead much of the world to victory over fascism."

On a lighter note, many people still recall a U.S. bodybuilder who took the name **Charles Atlas** (1894–1972), real name Angelo Siciliano. This modern Atlas got rich by showing off his outstanding physique in newspaper advertisements that promised to reveal—for a fee—the secret of *dynamic tension*, the cornerstone of his bodybuilding magic. Atlas promised that dynamic tension would turn what he called *97-pound weaklings* into real men.

The result: every small boy wanted to be Charles Atlas.

Atwood's machine English mathematician and physicist **George Atwood** (1746–1807) rigged up a simple pulley arrangement of two unequal masses connected by a lightweight thread with which he could demonstrate to students the truth of Newton's laws of motion.

This was **Atwood's machine**. It works because two masses of nearly equal weights connected in this way nearly balance each other on each side of a lightweight simple pulley. The name of his machine has been in the English language for about two centuries.

Augean An adjective meaning extremely difficult and unpleasant, a state resembling that of the filthy **Augean stables** of classical mythology.

Named after **Augeas**, a fabled king of Elis, in Greece, who had three thousand oxen in his stables, which had not been mucked out for thirty years. Don't even try to imagine the filth in those stables. Fortunately for Augeas, a means was at hand for accomplishing this insufferable task.

Hercules (see **Herculean**), a man of superhuman strength, had murdered his wife and children, and as punishment was ordered to perform twelve labors of great difficulty and danger. Talk about community service! One of these labors—you guessed it—was to clean, all by himself, the incredibly filthy Augean stables. And how did he do it? Easy! Hercules diverted the course of a nearby river, sending its waters right through the stables. Mission accomplished.

Thus, **clean the Augean stables** has to this day meant clear away any accumulated mass of garbage or corruption, whether political, moral, or doctrinal. Not a bad thing to do every so often.

Augean stables. See **Augean**.

August The eighth month of the year—in the Roman calendar the sixth month, called *Sextilis*—after March, when the year began. It was renamed *Augustus* in 8 B.C. in honor of **Caesar Augustus** (63–14 B.C.), the first Roman emperor.

The adjective **august**, meaning venerable, dignified, eminent, majestic—the list of laudatory synonyms goes on—does not derive from the name Caesar Augustus. Rather, august derives from the Latin adjective *augustus*, meaning consecrated or venerable, and this is why Caesar was so called. Think of *Caesar Augustus*, then, as meaning Venerable Emperor.

So our month of August is named for a Roman emperor who was considered august by his contemporaries. Tricky? Read on.

Augustan Age The golden age of Latin literature, when Horace, Ovid, Virgil, Livy, and others flourished. As you might suspect—correctly, in this case—this period (27 B.C.–A.D. 14) is associated with the reign of **Caesar Augustus** (see **August**).

Other nations, most notably England and France, have also used the term **Augustan Age** to characterize their own periods in which literature has flourished. So Caesar Augustus lives on.

Averroism The name given by philosophers to the tenets of **Ibn Rushd Averroës** (1126–1198), best known of the medieval Islamic philosophers.

His many commentaries, especially those on Aristotle and Plato, are still studied. These works, known mainly through their Latin or Hebrew translations, offer a partial reconciliation of Greek and Arabic philosophical traditions that greatly influenced later Jewish and Christian writers.

Avogadro's law The chemical principle that equal volumes of all gases at the same temperature and pressure contain the same number of molecules.

This odd rule was discovered in 1811 and named for its discoverer, the Italian scientist **Amedeo Avogadro** (1776–1856), born in Turin. Practically nobody believed Avogadro at first. One reason may have been that no one knew what a molecule was. According to some sources, Avogadro had himself recently coined the word *molecule*.

Even though other chemists remained skeptical about **Avogadro's law** until shortly after Avogadro died, he was able to make impressive advances on the basis of his principle. For example, he used his law and experimental evidence to show that water is a compound of hydrogen and oxygen, which had not been known previously. (See **Avogadro's number** to learn more.)

Avogadro's number In chemistry, a constant representing the number of molecules in a specific amount of any substance. (The constant will be revealed shortly.)

Named after the brilliant chemist and physicist (see **Avogadro's law**) who was the first to recognize that such a number exists.

Avogadro's law concerns volume, while **Avogadro's number** applies to mass, which on the surface of Earth can be taken to be equivalent to weight. Mass is measured in grams and kilograms, weight in ounces and pounds or, in the International System of Units, in newtons.

Now to explain how to determine the mass to which Avogadro's number applies. First, keep in mind that everything is made of molecules, which are made of atoms. A gas such as helium consists of molecules made of single atoms. Most substances, however, consist of molecules with more than a single atom. An ordinary oxygen molecule, for example, has two atoms, while ozone has three. Carbon dioxide has three atoms, one carbon and two oxygens.

To go on, each atom has an assigned number, called its atomic mass. An atomic mass is the sum of the protons and neutrons of an atom. For example, hydrogen is atomic mass 1, helium is atomic mass 4, carbon is atomic mass 12, oxygen 16, etc. The atomic masses supplied here are the atomic masses of common forms of these elements, although these elements are known to occur in forms with different atomic masses.

The molecular mass of something is the sum of the atomic masses of the atoms that make up the molecule. Thus, the molecular mass of water is 18 for two hydrogens of mass 1 and one oxygen of mass 16.

Having absorbed all this, you are ready to be given Avogadro's number. For the amount of substance whose mass measured in grams is equal to the molecular mass of the molecules of the substance, the total (constant) number of molecules is always:

$$602,600,000,000,000,000,000,000$$

B

· ·

babbitt A noun meaning a businessman of orthodox outlook and virtues; also meaning a Philistine with the faintest of aspirations to culture.

The word originated in the name and inclinations of the character **George Follansbee Babbitt**, a small-town, self-satisfied booster and joiner who is the central figure in the 1922 novel *Babbitt*, written by the American novelist Sinclair Lewis (1885–1951), winner of the Nobel Prize in literature in 1930. In Babbitt's sole deviation from a respectable personal and business life as a successful real estate agent—characterized by drive, hustle, and efficiency—Babbitt enters into a liaison with an attractive widow.

He soon abandons this flirtation when the fear of social ostracism quenches his ardor. Times were different then.

His life and personality have also given us **babbitry**, also spelled **babbittry**, a noun epitomizing the attitudes and behavior of a person whom any insufferable snob thinks of as a candidate for membership in a Chamber of Commerce, Rotary Club, or the like.

Babbitt metal Also given as **babbit metal**, **babbitt**, and **white metal**, any of a number of metal alloys that are very slick and therefore useful in housing bearings.

Babbitt metal was named for its inventor, **Isaac Babbitt** (1799–1862), a typical nineteenth-century Yankee inventor and entrepreneur from Taunton, Massachusetts.

Isaac Babbitt, who started out as a goldsmith, began to manufacture a tin alloy called Britannia metal, which was a harder substitute for pewter. In 1839, when Babbitt patented his design for a bearing, he suggested that the bearing box be lined with a similar tin alloy, now called Babbitt metal. In addition to being slippery—thus reducing friction—Babbitt metal is soft enough to shape itself into a close-fitting nest for a bearing.

Babinski's reflex   An indication of neurological health or impairment.

Tickle the sole of a foot, and you may or may not evoke giggling or signs of displeasure. Just make certain the sole you tickle belongs to someone you know well. But you can be certain that if the person whose sole you tickle is healthy, his or her toes will fan out, and the big toe will stick up and out.

This tickling is actually a diagnostic aid, called **Babinski's reflex** and sometimes **Babinski's sign** after its discoverer, the French neurologist **Joseph François Félix Babinski** (1857–1932). The response of toe-fanning and all the rest is the reflex of a healthy person; other responses or lack of response is a possible sign of upper motor neuron disease.

Incidentally, Babinski's reflex is a reaction that is not under control of the mind, so if a person appears to be paralyzed, a little discreet sole-tickling will establish whether the paralysis is mental or physical.

At any rate, Babinski appears to have been a man born to tap and tickle, since he also came upon ways to tap the human knee and the **Achilles tendon** (which see) to help in diagnosing sciatica and other disorders of the nervous system.

bacchanalia   Any drunken feast or orgy, sometimes capitalized, plural **bacchanalia** and **bacchanalias**.

In Roman times, **bacchanalia** were festivals in honor of **Bacchus**, the god of wine, but in time came to be characterized by drunkenness, debauchery, and licentiousness.

Today there is not even the slightest indication of paying honor to Bacchus in anything we characterize as **bacchanalian**, an adjective taken to mean nothing more nor less than unrestrained and drunken.

Baconian   An adjective meaning pertaining to the works or philosophy of **Francis Bacon** (1561–1626), English philosopher, statesman, and essayist. The noun **Baconian** means an adherent of Bacon's philosophy.

Bacon argued that the only knowledge important to mankind was empirically rooted in the natural world and that this knowledge should be gathered and studied judiciously and systematically. Bacon's advocacy of an inductive scientific method contravened the approach to science predominant since the Renaissance.

Another use for the noun Baconian concerns any serious student of literature who supports the claim that Francis Bacon wrote the plays generally attributed to William Shakespeare. This espousal is itself expressed by the noun **Baconianism**.

If Bacon actually wrote all those plays, he must have been one really busy philosopher, statesman, and essayist.

Baedeker   Any guidebook or pamphlet containing information helpful to travelers.

Originally, any of a famous series of guidebooks originated by the German publisher **Karl Baedeker** (1801–1859) and continued by his successors.

Baedeker's burgeoning enterprise did not go unnoticed by other publishers, and bookstores now offer travel books covering sites of interest all over the world. The **Baedekers** that travelers tuck under their arms also supply guidance in selecting restaurants, outstanding examples of architecture, and hotels.

Incidentally, Karl Baedeker introduced the system of using stars for each guidebook entry to indicate the quality of the sights and, especially, worthwhile hotels and restaurants. Contemporary restaurant and theater reviewers continue this practice as a shorthand way of indicating degrees of quality.

Bailey bridge   A bridge made of interlocking metal plates that can be assembled readily.

Named for its inventor, British engineer **Sir Donald Coleman Bailey** (1901–1985), who created this mobile, rapidly erected bridge during World War II. During that war, as in many wars that preceded it, troops also used pontoon bridges, an effectual design that goes back to the ancient Persians.

Sir Donald was knighted in 1946 for helping to win the war.

Baily's beads   The bright spots appearing along the edge of the Sun—a dark disk—during a solar eclipse.

These spots, described as bright jewels, are caused by the mountains of the Moon, or rather the valleys between them. Sunlight pouring through the valleys shines forth while the mountains shade the rest of the Sun.

If you are fortunate enough to observe an eclipse of the Sun—through a smoked glass, of course—watch closely just before and just after the Sun passes behind the Moon. You may see **Baily's beads**, the phenomenon that English astronomer **Francis Baily** (1774–1844) observed and noted for the first time on May 15, 1836.

How do we know the exact date? For two reasons: As an astronomer, Baily knew the importance of making accurate records of his observations. And because astronomers have kept track of solar eclipses for many years. Even if they have not recorded a particular eclipse that occurred before astronomy became a science, they can work back in time to find just when an observer in England—or anywhere else where astronomy is taken seriously—could have seen a solar eclipse.

Francis Baily had an interesting career. He worked first as a stockbroker and made a great deal of money. When he retired from business in 1825, he turned to astronomy and served for a time as president of the Royal Astronomical Society. During this second career, he brought prodigious energy to the task of cleaning up mistakes in astronomical publications while writing about his science and performing experiments.

But his memory is preserved not for his membership in the Royal Astronomical Society nor for putting the stars in their proper places, but for having seen those bright jewels on that day in May.

Bakelite   A hard, resilient black plastic.

Invented by **Leo Hendryk Baekeland** (1863–1944), a Belgian-born American chemist, and protected by trademark. After immigrating to the United States in 1889, he invented photographic printing paper that could be used with artificial light and, most important, in 1909 invented the first synthetic phenolic resin, which he named **Bakelite**—after himself.

Baekeland may also have had a pun in mind, since Bakelite was the first plastic that was hardened by baking in a mold. The first product made of Bakelite was the gearshift knob on the Rolls-Royce automobile, the height of quality and luxury then as it is now. In time Bakelite came to be used in many applications, the best known being the telephone handset, known to millions, and for many years available in any color desired, as long as it was black.

balaclava. See **raglan**.

Baltimore oriole More properly—but less interestingly—biologists and birders today call the **Baltimore oriole** the northern oriole. But, for our purposes here we will use the venerable term for this colorful bird and for the marvelous baseball team that long has used its name.

This bird, *Icterus galbula galbula*, of the starling family, is commonly found in eastern North America. It takes its name from the colors of the male, black and orange, which were the colors of the coat of arms of the **Lords Baltimore**. And who were these Lords?

The **Baltimore** family, as every Maryland schoolchild knows, played a prominent role in the early years of the colony of Maryland. In alphabetical order, moving from Charles to George to Leonard, we first encounter Lord Baltimore, full name Charles Calvert, 3rd Baron Baltimore (1637–1715), and for some years governor and proprietor of Maryland. His grandfather, Sir George, 1st Baron Baltimore (c.1580–1632), was founder of the colony of Maryland, and Charles's son, Leonard (1606–1647), was the first colonial governor of Maryland.

There also was Cecil, 2nd Baron Baltimore (c.1605–1675), who established the Maryland colony but didn't go into the family business there.

Bang's disease. See **brucellosis**.

bantingism A rarely used noun meaning a method of weight reduction. It is included here primarily to show that fad diets are not a twentieth-century American invention.

This method, also given as **Bantingism** or **Banting**, was introduced by **William Banting** (1797–1878), said in various sources to have been either a London undertaker or cabinetmaker or dietician, or maybe all three. The heart of his recommended diet was abstaining from beer and wine, and from sugar, starch, and fat. What was left? Protein.

Does this sound familiar?

At any rate, Mr. Banting in 1864 published a pamphlet entitled *Corpulence*, relating how in one year, by following the Banting high-protein diet, he had reduced his weight from 202 pounds to 156 pounds. (And does *this* sound familiar?)

But not all Bantings have been undertakers, etc. In 1922 a Canadian scientist, Frederick Grant Banting (1891–1941), discovered the hormone insulin, which has benefited millions of diabetics throughout the world. For this he, along with collaborators in the research, in 1923 was awarded the Nobel Prize in medicine or physiology.

And William Banting's prize? Royalties from his printers.

Barmecide   An adjective meaning imaginary or disappointing. Also, a noun meaning a giver of benefits that are imaginary or disappointing.

For the elegant word **Barmecide** we are indebted, once again, to *The Arabian Nights' Entertainments* (see also **Achilles heel** and **Aladdin's lamp**). One of the stories, "The Barber's Sixth Brother," tells of a dinner given by a **Barmecide** prince and practical joker—the fictional Barmecides were a wealthy family of Baghdad.

One of the guests at the feast is Schacabac, a poor starving man. As each dish is brought to his place at the table, it is found to be empty. Schacabac, eager not to offend the prince, pretends to get great pleasure from eating the imaginary food.

Finally, when imaginary wine is poured into Schacabac's wineglass, he sees his chance. Schacabac pretends to knock down the imaginary wine and soon enough pretends to be drunk, at which point he proceeds to knock down the prince. Seeing the humor of the incident, the prince forgives Schacabac and gives him real food, which he eats until he can eat no more.

The English language benefits by acquiring the phrase **Barmecide feast**, meaning any appealing illusion, especially one containing a great disappointment. And, of course, Barmecide feast also means an imaginary feast.

Baron Munchausen.   See **Munchausen, Baron**.

Baskerville   Any of various styles of type named after **John Baskerville** (1706–1775), an English printer. **Baskerville** type has passed the test of time and is still in use today.

Batesian mimicry   The protective resemblance, achieved through evolution, of an edible species to an unpalatable or dangerous species.

Named after **Henry Walter Bates** (1825–1892), an English biologist, who noticed examples of **Batesian mimicry**—this most sincere form of flattery—while he and naturalist Alfred Russel Wallace (1823–1913) were collecting some eight thousand species of previously unknown insects in the tropical rain forests of South America.

The most familiar example of Batesian mimicry in North America concerns the viceroy butterfly, a look-alike of the poisonous monarch butterfly. Experiments have shown that once a bird has tasted a monarch or two, the bird will not only pass up any future monarch meals but will also skip viceroy victuals. That same bird's sibling, if it has not been exposed to the monarch, is a vicious viceroy devourer.

Thus, reasoned Bates, a species that looks deadly can be safe without needing to go to the trouble of becoming deadly.

But what does this mean for you? Well, several flies practice Batesian mimicry, so the next bee you see may be nothing more than a harmless fly.

baud   A transmission rate for data that is about one bit per second, a bit being a unit of information.

From the name of the French inventor **Jean-Marie-Emile Baudot** (1845–1903), who devised a telegraph code that largely supplanted **Morse code** (which see) in the twentieth century.

Note that **baud**, like knot, includes the time interval—about one bit per second—and saying "56 bauds per second" is as incorrect as saying "6 knots per hour."

Bayard   Any man of unstained honor and exceptional courage.

Bayard has its origin in the name of **Pierre du Terrail, Chevalier de Bayard** (1476–1524), a celebrated French knight and national hero, known as *le chevalier sans peur et sans reproche*, the knight without fear and without reproach.

The Chevalier Bayard was born in the Château Bayard, near Grenoble, and after his heroic death in battle his body was sent home for burial.

Maybe there's something to be said for a little fear felt at the right time.

Beau Brummel   Also given as **Beau Brummell**, any man obsessive about his personal appearance; a fop, a dandy.

From the name of **George Bryan Brummell** (1778–1840), known as Beau Brummell, the English *arbiter elegantiae* who set the fashions for men's clothing in his time.

Brummell inherited a fortune in his early years and could afford to lead the good life, but when his money ran out, things went badly for him and he spent his final years in an asylum in France.

Maybe he should have learned a trade.

Beaufort scale   A scale of wind force no longer in strict technical use that enables the mariner to observe certain phenomena and thereby identify wind speeds at sea.

Named after British Royal Navy Admiral **Sir Francis Beaufort** (1774–1857), who devised the scale. By applying the **Beaufort scale**, the captain of a square-rigged ship would know how much sail to put up.

To use the scale, a captain or crew member would observe the effect of the wind on the water ahead of the ship and assign it a simple number, called a *force*. Force 0 indicates calm, no wind at all. At the other end of the scale is Force 12, a full-out hurricane, which requires taking down all the sails to save them and the ship as well. At Force 12, the high waves are streaked with dense white foam, and the ship rolls heavily. Head to port!

The Beaufort scale has been modified and improved over time, but old salts in English-speaking nations still use the old Beaufort names.

béchamel   In French cuisine a kind of fine white sauce thickened with cream.

Named after its inventor, **Louis, Marquis de Béchamel**, steward of French King Louis XIV (died 1703).

beef Stroganoff   A dish of beef sautéed with onion and cooked in a sauce of sour cream, seasonings, and, usually, mushrooms.

Named after **Count Paul Stroganov** or **Stroganoff**, a nineteenth-century Russian diplomat.

beef Wellington.   See **wellington**.

bel   A unit used in comparison of power levels in electrical communication or sound intensities, equal to 10 decibels.

Named after **Alexander Graham Bell** (1847–1922), the great American inventor, born in Scotland, who is remembered best for his work with deaf children and his invention of the telephone.

While **bel** and **decibel** both derive from Bell's name, it is decibel that receives the greater attention by far. Why? Because the rustle of leaves in the slightest of winds is about as loud as a bel, and the softest sound you can hear—that of the proverbial pin dropping—is about equal to a decibel.

Benedictine A member of the **Benedictine** order of monks, especially the members of the monastery founded at Monte Cassino, near Naples, Italy; also, a nun or a member of any congregation following the rules of piety laid down by St. Benedict.

The order was named for its founder, **St. Benedict of Nursia** (c.480–c.547). (Nursia is near Spoleto, and Spoleto is known for its music festivals.) The Benedictine monastery—one of twelve founded by St. Benedict—was renowned for the learning of its monks and later became one of the most famous in Italy. The Benedictines—but not the monks of the monastery at Nursia—are also noted for their manufacture of liqueurs.

This **Benedictine** is a French liqueur, still made on the site of the Benedictine abbey at Fécamp, on the English Channel northwest of Rouen, France, and still based on an early-sixteenth-century formula of one Brother Vincelli. (Of blessed memory!)

Benthamism The philosophical system of English philosopher, jurist, and social reformer **Jeremy Bentham** (1748–1832).

Bentham taught that the aim of life is the achievement of happiness—happiness being equated with pleasure. Thus, according to Bentham, the highest morality is the pursuit of the greatest happiness for the greatest number of people, a thumbnail characterization of **Benthamism**.

A philosophy I can live with.

Berkeleian An adjective pertaining to the philosophy of Irish Anglican bishop and philosopher **George Berkeley** (1685–1753). Also, a noun meaning a follower of Berkeley or his philosophy.

Berkeley was known for his dictum—evocative of Descartes' *Cogito ergo sum*—"To be is to be perceived."

According to Berkeley, matter does not exist. Only minds and mental events exist. The contents of the material world are ideas, which exist only when they are perceived by a mind.

For an antidote, turn quickly to **Benthamism** above. See also **Cartesian Philosophy**.

Bessemer process   A process for removing carbon and other impurities from molten iron by blasting air through it, thus converting the iron into a material suitable for making steel.

Named after **Henry Bessemer** (1813–1898), an English engineer and inventor who became interested in improving the quality of steel used in the manufacture of guns. And succeeded.

The evolution of steel is of some interest. Blacksmiths and other ironworkers knew that beating small amounts of carbon into iron produced wrought iron, which is stronger than iron and more resistant to corrosion. They soon learned that mixing in even more carbon by another method produced cast iron. But while cast iron is strong, it is somewhat brittle.

They observed that when carbon was beaten in, the outside part of the iron became much stronger than ordinary wrought iron. It was this hard part that came to be called steel. In time, ironworkers learned to increase the amount of steel they were making, enabling them to strip off the steel layers and combine them to make very strong and very sharp swords and other tools.

Bessemer's contribution to all of this was his economical **Bessemer process**, by which molten iron could be turned directly into steel by blowing air through the metal container called the **Bessemer converter** that held the iron during processing.

Bessemer's process was improved further by other engineers—indeed, he was not actually the first person to come up with the technique—but it is Bessemer's name that predominates when steel is being discussed. When English steelmakers proved reluctant to adopt the Bessemer process, an American named Andrew Carnegie embraced it and began to accumulate his large fortune.

For which U.S. public libraries are forever grateful.

Big Ben   The grand old bell in the clock tower of the British Houses of Parliament, in London.

Said to have been named after **Sir Benjamin Hall**, about whom little is known except that he served from 1855 to 1858 as First Commissioner of Works, when **Big Ben** was ordered. According to another account—less generally held—Big Ben took its name from the nickname of a famous prizefighter of the day.

bilharzia The former name—it is now called schistosomiasis—of a potentially life-threatening tropical disease caused by parasitic flatworms, called blood flukes.

Bilharzia was named after **Theodor Maximilian Bilharz** (1825–1862), a German parasitologist who discovered the blood flukes, which were assigned to the genus *Schistosoma*, a word in New Latin meaning "split body."

Following the general medical rule for naming parasitic diseases, bilharzia was then renamed schistosomiasis, using the medical suffix *-iasis* for "condition," which is most often used for diseases caused by parasites.

You may also be interested in knowing that the suffix *-osis* usually is employed for a condition that is caused by a fungus.

Binet-Simon scale A test, also known as the **Binet-Simon test**, for determining the relative development of intelligence, especially of children.

In the test, subjects are given questions and tasks graded with reference to the ability of the normal child to deal with them at successive age levels. The end product of these tests is a mysterious number, the intelligence quotient, or IQ.

The test, first published in 1905, was named for the two French psychologists who were its originators: **Alfred Binet** (1857–1911) and **Théodore Simon** (1873–1961).

And parents—encouraged by those who make their livings devising and coaching students for so-called achievement tests, a natural development from IQ tests—have paid inordinate attention ever since to the IQs achieved by their little darlings.

Bismarck herring A marinated herring eaten cold, more fully described as a salted fillet and roe of herring, pickled in vinegar, white wine, and spices, served especially as an hors d'oeuvre.

Named after **Prince Otto Edward Leopold von Bismarck** (1815–

1898), a German statesman instrumental in creating the German Empire, which he served as its first chancellor. Bismarck was sometimes called the Iron Chancellor, reflecting his steadfast leadership style.

Could that sobriquet also have had something to do with princely overexposure to the charms of **Bismarck herring**? Which has been known to stiffen the back, as well as add to the natural longing for spirituous liquors.

Blackwood convention   In bridge, a bidding convention in which a player bids four no-trump as an asking bid. The bidder's partner replies with a bid of five of a designated suit to indicate the number of aces he or she holds. As an extension of **Blackwood**, a subsequent bid of five no-trump is a request to indicate the number of kings held by the partner.

The convention is named for a twentieth-century American bridge expert, **E. F. Blackwood**, about whom little is known.

bloomers   An item of women's clothing, until recently knee-length underpants; originally a jacket, skirt, and trousers gathered closely at the ankles.

This item of apparel took its name from **Amelia Jenks Bloomer** (1818–1894), an American champion of women's rights and dress reform, who introduced the full costume in 1849 but met with little success in promoting it. **Bloomers** in a simpler form—as shortened trousers, or underpants—were eventually adopted by most women and were worn for many decades. In time, bloomers lost their popularity, and no truly modern woman is known to wear them—or admits to wearing them.

What was Amelia's modest assertiveness has today become Victoria's Secret. But Mrs. Bloomer remains everyone's favorite eponym.

Bluebeard   Any murderer, especially of one's wives or other women.

The word **Bluebeard** is taken from a tale written by the French writer Charles Perrault (1628–1703) in his 1697 book of fairy tales entitled *Contes du temps passé* (Stories of the Past). In one tale, Bluebeard, in French *Barbe-bleue*, goes off on a journey, leaving behind his wife and the keys of his castle. Bluebeard's instruction to his wife is that she is allowed to enter every room in the castle but one.

Curiosity inevitably overwhelms her. She opens the door to the forbidden room and there finds the bodies of all seven of Bluebeard's former wives, whom he had murdered. Talk about your serial killers!

But what happens to the wife when Bluebeard returns and finds that she has disobeyed him? He goes after her with an ax and is about to cut off her head when her two brothers rush in and kill him.

bobby   In Britain a colloquial term meaning policeman. **Bobby** does not carry the pejorative sense implicit in cop, copper, flatfoot, or fuzz.

Named after **Sir Robert Peel** (1788–1850), an English statesman. While serving as Home Secretary, Sir Robert ("Bobby") reorganized the London police force, in 1828 establishing the Metropolitan Police. The Criminal Investigation Department of the Metropolitan Police is Scotland Yard, well regarded by detective story aficionados everywhere.

When Peel was Chief Secretary for Ireland (1812–1819), he instituted the Irish constabulary, whose officers were nicknamed **peelers**, not half so attractive a term as bobbies, but one that soon caught on in England as well to mean policemen.

Bodoni   A style of type based on the original design of **Giambattista Bodoni** (1740–1813), an Italian printer. His press in Parma published elegant editions of the classics.

The **Bodoni** typeface is still widely used in newspapers and books. A particular New York journalist used to write amusing anecdotes of the antics of a Broadway character he named Boldface Bodoni.

Thus did people amuse themselves in the good old days.

boniface   Any innkeeper, especially a jovial innkeeper.

From **Boniface**, the name of a jovial innkeeper in the comedy *The Beaux' Stratagem*, written by George Farquhar (c.1677–1707), an Irish playwright. (See also **Lady Bountiful**.) Farquhar wrote this comedy, generally considered the best of his plays, while he was mortally ill. He died while his wit was still wowing audiences.

Send in the clowns.

Boolean algebra   An abstract system of rules for manipulating symbols applicable to solving logical problems.

Named after **George Boole** (1815–1864), a self-taught English mathematician. Though Boole lacked a university degree, he served as professor at the University of Cork in Ireland from 1849 until his death and is remembered chiefly for his development of **Boolean algebra**, an algebraic description of logical reasoning.

When set theory (the study of sets without regard to the nature of the items in the sets) was developed, about fifty years after Boole, the rules of combining sets emerged as an instance of Boolean algebra. Fifty more years after that, when computers were being invented, Boolean algebra was dusted off once again to handle the logic of switches and gates.

Pretty good for the son of an English cobbler who learned mathematics on his own.

boreal   An adjective meaning of or pertaining to the north or the Arctic; also, of or pertaining to the north wind.

From **Boreas**, in classical mythology the god of the north wind. And we all know the northern lights, more properly called **aurora borealis**.

boson   In nuclear physics, a particle that has a symmetrical wave function and therefore obeys Bose-Einstein statistics, with integral spin.

Since this definition sheds little light on the term **boson**, read on.

Named after **Satyendranath N. Bose** (1894–1974), an Indian physicist.

According to one version of modern physics, the forces that act on matter are produced by certain kinds of subatomic particles. This concept began with Albert Einstein in 1905, when he established that light sometimes acts as a particle, called a *photon*, instead of as a wave.

Later, a theory of how like electric charges repel each other, and unlike charges attract each other, was put into final form on the basis of the interchange of photons. Similar theories using other particles explain other forces in nature. For example, the nucleus of an atom is considered to be held together by interchanging particles, and one theory of gravity holds that its force is caused by interchanging particles.

In each case, the particles that are actually exchanged are collectively called bosons, and the behavior of bosons is different from that of particles of matter. Where two particles of matter cannot be in the same place at the same time, two similar bosons can be in the same place at the same time and will huddle together and merge.

Boswell   A biographer, especially the devoted biographer of a specific person. Thus, a biographer who has written a laudatory biography of Franklin Delano Roosevelt might be referred to as "Roosevelt's **Boswell**."

Named after **James Boswell** (1740–1795), Scottish man of letters and biographer of Samuel Johnson. Early in life, Boswell had become a careful and thorough diarist, a preoccupation that served him well during his lifetime—at least when he wasn't yielding to his hypochondria or actively engaged in woman-chasing.

His travels with Dr. Johnson included a trip to the Hebrides, and after Johnson's death Boswell published *The Journal of the Tour of the Hebrides with Samuel Johnson, L.L.D.* (1785). The success of this volume impelled him to write his masterpiece, the *Life of Samuel Johnson, L.L.D.* (1791).

The adjective **Boswellian** means resembling the devotion of James Boswell as a biographer, and the seldom-used verb **boswellize** means write in great detail in the manner of Boswell.

Ironically, in recent times almost every popular autobiography is written by a hired gun, that is, by an anonymous but well-paid Boswell.

bougainvillea Any of several tropical plants of genus *Bougainvillea*, having small flowers and large, showy leaves. Named after **Louis Antoine de Bougainville** (1729–1811), a French navigator, mathematician, and soldier.

The same **Bougainville** is also recalled in the name of the largest Solomon Island, well remembered by U.S. veterans of World War II who fought in the southwest Pacific theater.

bovarism An exaggerated, especially a romantic, conception of oneself. T. S. Eliot called **bovarism** "the human will to see things as they are not." And a **bovarist** is a person with this proclivity.

From the name of the protagonist of Gustave Flaubert's novel *Madame Bovary* (1856). **Emma Bovary**, unhappy in her marriage to a good-hearted but not very clever physician, finds her pathetic dreams of romantic love unfulfilled. She commits adultery, runs up enormous debts she cannot repay, and finally commits suicide.

Better to face things as they are.

bowdlerize A verb meaning expurgate (a book or other writing) by deleting material considered offensive or indelicate.

From the name of **Thomas Bowdler** (1754–1825), an English physician and man of letters. He published the *Family Shakespeare* (1818), a ten-volume edition of Shakespeare's plays in which "those words are omitted which cannot with propriety be read aloud in a family." As if **bowdlerize** were not enough to be remembered for, Dr. Bowdler has also given English the nouns **bowdlerism**, **bowdlerization**, and **bowdlerizer**.

The urge to clean things up is irresistible for some people.

bowie knife   A heavy sheath knife having a long, single-edged blade curved to the point.

Named after its inventor, **James Bowie** (1790–1836), an American pioneer who served as a colonel in the Texas army. Bowie died on March 6, 1836, at the fall of the Alamo, along with Davy Crockett and 185 other defenders of the fort.

Bowie fashioned the original knife from a blacksmith's rasp and soon arranged to have it manufactured by a Philadelphia firm, which marketed the copies as the **Bowie knife**.

Just another example of American marketing know-how.

bowler.   See **Derby**.

boycott   A verb meaning to act in concert to abstain from or prevent dealings with another as a means of intimidation or coercion: "Our town voted to boycott any company whose employees were striking." Also meaning abstain from buying or using goods: "A movement has begun to boycott products made in China."

The noun **boycott** means the practice of boycotting or an instance of boycotting: "National boycotts rarely succeed."

Named after **Charles Cunningham Boycott** (1832–1897), an English estate manager. While working in 1880 in County Mayo, Ireland, he became a victim—indeed, the first victim—of a policy of Charles Parnell's Irish National Land League, which advocated social excommunication—**boycott**, as it soon came to be called—for anyone who took over a farm from an evicted tenant.

Landlords and their lackeys have never been popular, have they?

Boyle's law   Physical laws describe how an ideal gas would behave if such an ideal ever existed, and these laws are named not for any intrinsic property but for the names of their discoverers.

Boyle's law was named for the Irish physicist and chemist **Robert Boyle** (1627–1691), who announced his discovery in 1662. There is also **Charles' law**, named after the French physicist **Jacques Alexandre César Charles** (1746–1823), who is also recognized as the first person to make a hydrogen balloon ascent. Then there is **Gay-Lussac's law**, named after French chemist and physicist **Joseph Louis Gay-Lussac** (1778–1850), also a balloonist and, more important, one of a pair of scientists who first recognized that hydrogen and oxygen combine in the ratio of two volumes to one to form water.

Thus far this discussion has been limited to the English names for these laws. As you might expect, the French called Boyle's law **Mariotte's law**, after **Edme Mariotte** (1620–1684), a physicist and priest. Mariotte reported a more precise version of Boyle's law when he rediscovered it independently some fifteen years after Boyle's announcement.

The plot thickens. The first version of Charles' law was a refinement of Mariotte's version of Boyle's law that was discovered by yet another French scientist, **Guillaume Amontons** (1663–1705). And Gay-Lussac's law was actually discovered by Jacques Alexandre Charles well before Gay-Lussac's work, although Charles failed to report it at the time.

Furthermore, since the Italian chemist **Amedeo Avogadro** (1776–1856) combined what are known as Charles' law and Gay-Lussac's law into one, the combined form is sometimes called Avogadro's law, although that term is usually saved for a further refinement. (See **Avogadro's law**.)

Do you have all this straight? Think of it this way: If a gas is ideal, according to Boyle's law, the product of its pressure and volume remains constant if temperature does not change.

But what is meant by an ideal gas? An ideal gas is one that obeys Boyle's law and, of course, the other laws mentioned above.

One can learn to hate science.

Braille   A system of embossed printing enabling the blind to read and write.

Sixty-two possible combinations of six raised points arranged in three oblongs represent punctuation and contractions as well as the entire English alphabet.

Named for its inventor, **Louis Braille** (1809–1852), a French educator, blind from the age of three. While serving as professor at the *Institution des Jeunes Aveugles* (School for Young Blind Persons), in Paris in 1829, he completed his work on Braille. His system is still in wide use in many parts of the world, enabling blind persons to read a great number of books printed in this manner.

Also in use for the blind is a system called **Moon type**, invented by **William Moon** (1818–1894), an English inventor, who was partially blind from an early age. He began teaching blind children to read with existing systems employing embossed type and in 1845 devised his own system based on Roman capitals. It is said that his type, while requiring more space, is easier to learn than Braille.

Bright's disease   A disease characterized by decline of the kidney function and heightened blood pressure.

Bright's disease is named for the English physician and researcher **Richard Bright** (1789–1858), who in 1827 was the first to recognize that kidney disease sometimes affects the eyes, a condition known for a time as **Bright's blindness**.

Persistent inflammation of the kidneys is known both as Bright's disease and as chronic nephritis. If the decline is not halted, the patient may have to use dialysis regularly, a procedure that mechanically handles some of the duties of the kidneys.

Not a pleasant way to spend your time.

brougham   Formerly a closed carriage for two to four passengers and drawn by one horse, with the driver's perch outside. Automobile manufacturers began to use the term **brougham** for sedans whose driver's seats were open to the weather.

Named, apparently for reasons of personal popularity, after **Henry Peter Brougham**, 1st Baron Brougham and Vaux (1778–1868). Lord Brougham had no hand in creating the brougham.

Nowadays, the term is applied willy-nilly to many automobile sedans.

Brownian movement   The irregular motion of microscopic particles suspended in a liquid, caused by the bombardment of the particles by molecules of the fluid.

Named after a Scottish botanist, **Robert Brown** (1773–1858), a pioneer expert in the use of a microscope, who first observed the phenomenon. While Brown was examining pollen suspended in water, he realized that the tiny grains moved as if they were alive. Being a careful investigator, he compared the pollen grains with similar-size dye particles in water and found that they also moved in the same way.

But no one in the nineteenth century could explain what caused this **Brownian motion** or **movement**. Then along came Albert Einstein (1879–1955), who was on a roll in 1905, the year in which he published his famous paper dealing with photoelectric emission and Planck's quantum theory (see **Planck's constant**) and his paper describing his special theory of relativity. Yet he had time to work out the equations demonstrating that Brownian movement is caused by the movement of molecules of the liquid slamming randomly into the particles.

There is more to Einstein's equations than meets the eye: It was the first proof that atoms or molecules actually exist.

A few years later, another scientist did some careful measurements and, using Einstein's equations, showed for the first time what the size of an atom is: "very small."

brucellosis A disease of cattle caused by bacteria of the genus *Brucella*, frequently resulting in spontaneous abortion. A similar disease in humans is called undulant fever.

Brucellosis is named after a Scottish physician, **David Bruce** (1855–1931). Bruce is much more famous for an achievement that is not commemorated with his name, however. He determined the cause of African sleeping sickness and its mode of transmission by the tsetse fly.

Bruce also discovered the bacterium that causes a human disease sometimes known as Malta fever. He mistakenly thought it was a spherical bacillus, but later investigators were able to show it is a rod-shaped bacillus. The bacillus had been identified separately by a Danish veterinary surgeon, **Bernhard L. F. Bang** (1848–1932), who recognized that it caused spontaneous abortion in cattle, so bovine brucellosis is called **Bang's disease**.

Alice Evans, a bacteriologist studying milk in the 1920s, more than thirty years after Bruce's work with Malta fever, demonstrated that the same or closely related bacteria cause Malta fever in Europe, which became known worldwide as **undulant fever** and proved to affect humans as well as cattle.

Despite all these contributions from others, when it was decided to rename the bacterium, it was not named for Evans or Bang, but for Bruce, by that time knighted as Sir David Bruce. So the disease most often called undulant fever, since its symptoms come and go, has as its more general name **brucellosis**.

It must be pointed out that were it not for Evans's work and follow-up by others, **pasteurization** of milk might still be as rare in the United States as it was in the late 1920s. Although pasteurization kills most bacteria in milk, it was epidemics of undulant fever caused by unpasteurized milk that led local governments to make pasteurization the general rule. (See **pasteurize**.)

Buchmanism   The theories or practices of a twentieth-century international movement variously called the Oxford Group, Moral Rearmament, and **Buchmanism**.

Named after **Frank Nathan Daniel Buchman** (1878–1961), an American evangelist. In the 1920s he was the founder, at Oxford University, in England, of the Oxford Group, which represented itself as an evangelical organization that promoted Christian principles.

After World War II the Oxford Group became openly political and concerned itself with social, industrial, and international problems.

Alcoholics Anonymous is an offshoot of the Oxford Group. AA meetings were first held under its auspices, but after a couple of years the two organizations split.

Bunbury   A noun meaning a fictitious excuse—a **Bunbury**—for paying a visit uninvited or for avoiding an obligation.

From **Bunbury**, the name of an imaginary character, described as "an invaluable permanent invalid," in Oscar Wilde's comedy *The Importance of Being Earnest* (1895). Wilde's Bunbury is conveniently blamed for anyone's socially inept behavior.

As one might expect, Bunbury has been put to use in various colorful applications: "He was known as our resident Bunbury." "He was past master at **Bunburying**." Even as "He **Bunburyed** his way through one overdue car payment after another."

Bunsen burner   A type of tubular gas burner that produces a very hot flame because additional air is allowed to enter at the base of the tube and mix with the gas.

As every student who has spent any time at all in a science laboratory knows. For the student of language, however, the interest in the **Bunsen burner** lies in determining why the burner was named after **Robert Wilhelm Bunsen** (1811–1899), a German chemist who had a distinguished career. He pioneered use of the spectroscope to analyze chemicals for their elements and is credited with many other inventions—but not of the Bunsen burner. At most, he developed it, in 1855, from the design of others.

The most popular account credits **Michael Faraday** (1791–1867) as its inventor (see **farad**). Bunsen's assistant, a man named Peter Desdega, recognizing a good thing when he saw it, copied the device and went into business manufacturing the burner. Bunsen then popularized the burner, using it in lectures on the spectrograms of various elements.

So this is why the Bunsen burner was named after Bunsen even though he did not invent it.

burke A verb meaning murder by suffocation or strangulation; also smother, or suppress; also shirk, avoid.

Named after **William Burke** (1792–1829), an Irish laborer. With an accomplice, William Hare (1790–1860), Burke committed a series of murders most foul in Edinburgh, Scotland. The two men suffocated their victims and sold the bodies to Dr. Robert Knox (1791–1862).

Knox, a well-known Edinburgh anatomist, used the bodies for dissection. According to the wives of both men, the trio worked its evil ways on fifteen women before being discovered.

Burke's associate turned King's evidence, Burke was convicted, and, in 1829, was hanged.

And what happened to Dr. Knox? His moral stature was said to have been impaired.

It seems that was the very *least* anyone could do.

burnsides A style of men's facial hair: full whiskers and a mustache worn with the chin clean-shaven.

Named after the whiskers worn by **Ambrose Everett Burnside** (1824–1881), a Union general in the American Civil War (1861–1864) whose record of success in battle was offset by a list of defeats. Nevertheless, he succeeded in holding Knoxville in 1863 and, under

Ulysses S. Grant (1822–1885), in 1864 led a corps through the several battles of the Wilderness and the battle of Cold Harbor, both in Virginia.

For those interested primarily in language, his lasting contribution was the style of his beard, affectionately called **burnsides**, but by the latter part of the nineteenth century called **sideburns**, which has been the term used ever since.

Byronic   An adjective meaning of or pertaining to the poet Byron; characteristic of, or after the manner of, Byron or his poetry.

George Gordon Byron, 6th Baron Byron of Rochdale (1788–1824), is usually referred to as **Lord Byron**. He is considered the embodiment of romanticism and, with Shelley and Keats, one of England's trio of great romantic poets. Byron left behind a great body of work, and his masterpiece, the 16,000-line *Don Juan* in sixteen cantos begun in 1819, was left unfinished at his death.

Byron dramatized himself as a man of mystery, a gloomy romantic figure—his youth spent in shabby surroundings, the son of a profligate father and violent-tempered mother. Before long he entered into a short-lived marriage, and gossip cast him as the incestuous lover of his half sister, Augusta Leigh. Byron, who had many affairs, was even for a time the lover of a Venetian countess.

What more could be asked of a romantic figure? You guessed it. In 1823 he joined Greek insurgents in their uprising against Turkish rule and died in the next year after contracting malaria, then called marsh fever, at Missolonghi, in Greece. He was all of thirty-six years old.

It is no surprise, then, that English also has the term **Byronic hero**, meaning any defiant, melancholy young man, brooding on some unforgivable sin in his past.

C

Cadmean victory A victory with disastrous results for the victor.

This term alludes to the actions of **Cadmus**, in Greek mythology the founder of Thebes, in Boeotia. Legend has it that Cadmus, once he had slain the dragon that guarded the fountain of Dirce, in Boeotia, scattered the dragon's teeth on the soil. Up sprang warriors who intended to kill Cadmus. He thereupon threw a precious stone among them, and when the men fought to recover the stone, they set about killing one another in the struggle. Only five of the men survived.

A costly victory indeed. (See also **Pyrrhic victory**.)

Caesarean section When delivery of a baby cannot be accomplished in the normal way, the cut made through the wall of the mother's abdomen and into the womb to facilitate delivery.

From the name of **Gaius Julius Caesar** (c.100–44 B.C.), who, according to tradition, was born that way. Shakespeare, by the way, wrote in *Macbeth* the line "Macduff was from his mother's womb untimely ripped." He was, of course, not speaking of Caesar.

In fact, **Caesarean section**, also given as **Caesarian**, dates at least since the eighth century B.C., and in all early cases the operation was performed only after the death of the mother during labor.

Until recent times, attempts to perform a **Caesarean** on a living woman resulted invariably in her death. Even in the 1950s the operation was considered risky, and most physicians avoided it unless circumstances indicated that birth could not possibly be accomplished naturally. Due to advances in surgical technology, it is performed more often today and considered far less risky.

Caesar's wife   A wife in the public eye who must be above suspicion of marital infidelity.

The Caesar of this phrase is, of course, the famous Roman **Gaius Julius Caesar** (c.100–44 B.C.). But Caesar was married three times, so who is the wife?

In order of their marriages, the first Caesarean wife was Cornelia, divorced in 67 B.C. The second was Pompeia, divorced in 62 B.C. The third was Calpurnia, widowed in 44 B.C.

You're right. Pompeia was the wife Caesar said had to be above suspicion. No matter that Caesar said he did not suspect her of infidelity. It was enough that she was the subject of gossip.

The standard had been set—and has often been violated throughout human history. A public official and the wife of a public official must not only be free of crime but free of any suspicion of crime.

calliope   A musical instrument, also called a steam organ, that makes crude-sounding music on a set of steam whistles activated by a keyboard. Known to all devotees of circuses and circus parades.

Named after **Calliope**, who was the muse of epic poetry and poetic inspiration. In Greek **calliope** literally means "beautiful-voiced."

Quite a stretch for anyone who's heard the sounds made by a calliope.

Cardan joint   In machinery, a coupling that can transmit power by shafts meeting at any selected angle. Also called a universal joint.

The basic idea of a **Cardan joint** is that two two-pronged forks are interlocked, transmitting rotary motion from one shaft to another in virtually any positions of the shafts.

Traditionally, the invention of the Cardan joint is ascribed to an Italian mathematician, **Girolamo Cardano** (1501–1576), sometimes called in English **Jerome Cardan**, though little evidence supports this idea.

Cardan did describe, in 1550, the arrangement known as the **Cardan suspension** for keeping an instrument or other object level while on a bumpy ride. But the suspension was an invention of the Chinese, and even Cardan—a notorious thief of intellectual property—did not claim it as his own.

Invention of the Cardan joint is attributed to Philon of Byzantium in about 250 B.C. In any case, slight variations of the joint were reinvented by others about a hundred years after Cardan.

cardigan A knitted woolen sweater or jacket with sleeves, usually collarless and buttoned down the front.

Named after **James Thomas Brudenell, 7th Earl of Cardigan** (1797–1868), an English cavalry officer, whose troops wore a knitted woolen jacket that was given his name when his cavalry fought in the bitterly cold Crimean winter. (See also **raglan**.)

The Earl of Cardigan is remembered especially for his role as commander in Crimea of the Light Cavalry brigade. This was the ill-fated unit known as the Six Hundred that he sent to be slaughtered under the superior Russian guns at Balaclava in 1854.

Do you recall your Tennyson?

> *Theirs not to make reply,*
> *Theirs not to reason why,*
> *Theirs but to do and die.*
> *Into the valley of death*
> *Rode the Six Hundred.*

So if you wear a distinctive sweater in winter, it does not matter that troops under your command take a terrible shellacking.

As long as you are the Earl of something, that is.

Cartesian Philosophy The philosophical system of **René Descartes** (1596–1650), emphasizing that thought must proceed from soul, and therefore mankind is not wholly material. Soul must be from some Being not material, and that Being is God.

Descartes gave us the best-remembered Latin phrase in philosophy: *Cogito, ergo sum*, I think, therefore I am.

And the adjective **Cartesian**, formed from his name.

But there is more to the story. The ordinary perpendicular *x* and *y* axes form the **Cartesian Coordinate System**, which is the foundation of analytic geometry, invented by Descartes in 1637.

Casanova   A rake; a man with a reputation for having many amorous adventures.

From the name of **Giacomo Girolamo Casanova de Seingalt** (1725–1798), an Italian adventurer who kissed and told. His expulsion at age sixteen from a Venetian seminary presaged a lively career as charlatan, gambler, and inamorato. He appears to have traveled in the best circles all over Europe, bedding one woman after another and repeatedly finding it necessary to skip town.

From these amorous exploits was born Casanova's widely known racy memoir, written in French, giving us a plethora of passages for the titillation of adolescent readers, but also of scholarly interest as a vivid depiction of eighteenth-century European society. The first full English edition of *Mémoires écrits par lui-même*, was published, in six volumes, from 1966 to 1971. This was many years after its first publication, in Leipzig (1828–1838).

Which tells us there's nothing new in the scheduling practices of the publishing industry.

Caslon   A graceful old-style typeface named for its designer, **William Caslon** (1692–1766), an English type founder and designer.

Caslon was used extensively in Europe and the United States until it went out of fashion toward the end of the eighteenth century. Popularity of the typeface revived in the mid-nineteenth century and has continued until the present.

Cassandra   Any person who prophesies doom but is fated never to be believed.

Cassandra in Greek legend was a daughter of Priam, king of Troy. She was loved by Apollo, who gave her the gift of prophecy as a token of his affections but turned on her when she put off his advances. In retribution, Apollo arranged things so that no one would believe Cassandra's dire prophesies, even though they were accurate.

If you want to know about frustration resulting from inability to be taken seriously by persons you are trying to help, get in touch with Cassandra. If her line is busy, try Chicken Little.

We, of course, have our modern **Cassandras**; for example, publishers of stock market tip sheets, whose prophecies are far from accurate but foretell a dark future.

Yes, Virginia, you don't have to invest your money in the stock market to get rich. With only a modest investment in paper, printing, and stamps, you can make a darned good living by practicing direct-mail prophetic flimflam.

Catherine wheel   A type of firework that revolves on a pin, making a wheel of fire or sparks; also called a pinwheel.

Named for **St. Catherine of Alexandria** (died 307), a Christian virgin of royal descent and a martyr who is the patron saint of wheelwrights.

Catherine defended the Christian faith at a public disputation with heathen philosophers, which drew the wrath of Roman emperor Maximinus. For her defense of Christianity she was strapped to a wheel. No garden variety wheel but, as portrayed in so many medieval paintings, a spiked wheel known now as a **Catherine wheel** or **catherine wheel**, a fiendish contraption intended to cause death by bleeding from multiple wounds. Yet, each time the wheel was turned, Catherine's bonds were miraculously broken.

So what happened next? She was beheaded. End of story.

On a lighter note, the Catherine wheel has given its name as well to the so-called **Catherine wheel window**, sometimes called a rose window, with radiating divisions.

Catilinarian   Any conspirator, especially a person who participated in Catiline's conspiracy of 63 B.C. to bring down the Roman government.

The term **Catilinarian** was named for **Catiline**, full name **Lucius Sergius Catilina** (c.108–62 B.C.), a Roman politician and conspirator. In 63 B.C. he plotted with other young Roman nobles to assassinate the great orator and statesman Cicero (see **Ciceronian**) as part of a revolution against the Roman government.

The plot was uncovered, and when the assassins came to Cicero's door, they were repulsed. Two days later, Cicero delivered the first of four speeches against Catiline in the Senate. Catiline's response was drowned out by catcalls, and a death sentence was decreed against him after the fourth speech.

Catiline fled Rome, but some of his fellow conspirators were arrested and executed. In the following year, along with some of the remaining conspirators, Catiline died in battle.

Students remember Catiline—not without malice—when they have to memorize chunks of Cicero's "First Oration Against Catiline."

Celsius scale A temperature scale, with 0 degrees for freezing water and 100 degrees for boiling water.

Named after **Anders Celsius** (1701–1744), the Swedish astronomer who devised the scale.

Several persons invented versions of the thermometer, beginning with Galileo, although the first version that was anything like the modern one was invented in 1654 by Ferdinand II, Grand Duke of Tuscany.

The scale on early thermometers was somewhat arbitrary, but by 1730 the French physicist René Antoine Ferchault de Réaumur (1683–1757) had the idea of using the interval from freezing water to boiling water for a scale. He thought 80 divisions would make suitable degrees.

Twelve years later, in 1742, Celsius had the better idea of using the same interval from boiling to freezing, but separating it into a comfortable 100 degrees. But Celsius almost made a fatal error, for his version of this centigrade scale had 0° for boiling and 100° for freezing. In the next year he came to his senses and turned the scale right side up.

Scientists everywhere began to use the system and, after the French Revolution, when everything else was being regularized, Celsius's centigrade system became part of the metric system.

Of course, people being what they are, the measurement gurus decreed that it would be more appropriate to call the scale the **Celsius scale** instead of the centigrade scale. Today, the size of the degree is the same as in the Celsius scale, but the official temperature measurement scale used by scientists, a part of the International System of Units, is the **Kelvin scale** (which see).

Everybody wants to get into the act.

Chagas' disease An infectious disease characterized by fever and palpable lymph nodes, often causing damage to the heart.

The source of the problem is the so-called kissing bug, which transmits the parasite *Trypanosoma cruzi*, named for the Brazilian bacteriologist Osvaldo Conçalves Cruz (1872–1917), who identified it.

But the entire pattern of disease transmission was uncovered by a Brazilian physician, **Carlos Chagas** (1879–1934), giving us the most common name for the disease today, **Chagas' disease**, although it is sometimes called *Cruz's disease* as well as by its official name, *American trypanosomiasis*, which almost no one ever uses. You can see why.

Lest you think Chagas' disease is rare, consider that in Central and South America, the parasitic infestation caused by the kissing bug has long been a serious problem and remains so today.

About 18 million persons are infected, making Chagas' disease third on the list of global health problems, according to the World Health Organization. The first and second are malaria and schistosomiasis. Persons who live in thatched huts are particularly vulnerable, as the kissing bug—a relative of the assassin bug, also known as the cone-nose bug and as the Chagas bug—tends to live in thatch during the day and invades bedding at night. A kiss from the bug leaves a characteristic swelling, called a ramona, found most often near the eye of the victim.

Many persons believe the mysterious disease that afflicted Charles Darwin and kept him virtually housebound after his return from the voyage of the *Beagle* was Chagas' disease. In his journal for March 25, 1835, Darwin recorded that he was bitten by an inch-long, black kissing bug. But it was not until nearly a century later that Chagas unearthed the connection between bug bites and the disease, and English doctors treating Darwin were mystified by his malady.

Charles' law. See **Boyle's law**.

Charybdis. See **Scylla and Charybdis**.

Cherenkov radiation Also given as **Cerenkov radiation**, a form of light produced when subatomic particles, such as electrons, travel faster through a medium than the speed of light in the same medium.

Named after Soviet physicist **Pavel Alekseevich Cherenkov**

(1904–1990), who first observed the phenomenon, which he described as a blue light.

Now, if you read the definition of Cherenkov radiation with care, you noticed that it spoke of subatomic particles traveling faster than the speed of light. And every educated person has been taught that nothing can travel faster than the speed of light.

However, as just stated, that fact is untrue. The correct wisdom is nothing can travel faster than light *in a vacuum*. When passing through a medium other than a vacuum, it is possible for a material body to exceed the speed of light. But a price must be paid, and that price is Cherenkov radiation.

The radiation is like a visible shock wave produced by a motorboat on a quiet lake, or like the boom produced by a jet airplane exceeding the speed of sound in flight.

Cherenkov radiation has become one of the most important ways of detecting speedy subatomic particles. As a bonus, the precise speed of the particle is revealed by the angle that the light makes with the path of the particle.

Thank you, Dr. Cherenkov.

chesterfield A type of overcoat, single-breasted or double-breasted, worn by men and having a fly front and a narrow velvet collar. Also, especially in Britain, a large, overstuffed divan or sofa with upholstered back and arms. In Canada, any large sofa or couch.

Named after an eighteenth-century **Earl of Chesterfield**, perhaps Philip Dormer Stanhope, the 4th Earl (1694–1773), who is remembered in literary circles as the author of a remarkable series of *Letters to His Son*, written between 1737 and 1768 and first published in 1774.

Yet none of this explains why a once-popular brand of American cigarettes was called **Chesterfields**, a name that bears no relationship either to overcoats or sofas. Could it have been that the manufacturers of these cigarettes thought they could cash in on the cachet of all things English? Come to think of it, they might have been better off making overcoats or sofas, which are not suspected of causing cancer.

At least not so far.

Cheyne-Stokes breathing   A spell of breathing for short periods—through both the nose and the mouth at the same time—while gasping for air, and with 5- to 50-second intervals of no breathing.

This form of respiration, called **Cheyne-Stokes breathing**, was first observed by a Scottish physician, **John Cheyne** (1777–1836), who was practicing in Ireland. An Irish physician, **William Stokes** (1804–1878), who wrote the nineteenth-century classic textbook on diseases of the chest and heart, independently made the same observation.

Cheyne-Stokes breathing is seen particularly in patients who suffer from a debilitating brain condition, such as the last stages of **Alzheimer's disease** (which see), or from some forms of heart failure.

Chippendale   A light and elegant style of furniture.

From the name of **Thomas Chippendale** (1718–1779), an English furniture designer. His graceful Neoclassical furniture, especially his chairs, were made mostly of mahogany. His son Thomas (1749–1822) carried on his work. (See also **Hepplewhite** and **Sheraton**.)

Churchillian   As an adjective, meaning of, pertaining to, or characteristic of Winston Churchill, his life, works, etc. As a noun, meaning a specialist in the life and works of Winston Churchill.

The Winston Churchill of **Churchillian** is, of course, the English statesman **Sir Winston Leonard Spencer Churchill** (1874–1965), leader of his country during the dark days of World War II. When he took office as prime minister in May 1940, he offered his people nothing but "blood, toil, tears and sweat" and, after his electoral defeat in 1945, gave up leadership secure in his enduring reputation as "the greatest living Englishman."

But in what ways do we consider **Churchillian** worthy of its meaning and place in the English language? Think first of his reputation as the last of the classic orators, with an unfailing command of the English language. Then think of his writings—to mention but two works, *The Second World War* (6 volumes, 1948–1954) and *A History of the English-Speaking Peoples* (4 volumes, 1956–1958)—which can be described accurately as Augustan in style (see **Augustan Age**) and fortified by great breadth of mind and a profound sense of the sweep of history. In 1953 he was awarded the Nobel Prize in literature.

Above all, think of him as a great statesman and an intensely human, rich, and vivid personality—courageous, imaginative, magnanimous, and patriotic to the core.

But there was another **Winston Churchill** (1871–1947), a successful American historical novelist. Born in St. Louis, Missouri, the American Churchill is remembered particularly for two of his novels: *Richard Carvel* (1899) and *The Crisis* (1901). Although the adjective-noun **Churchillian** is not applied to Missouri's Churchill, one cannot help but wonder whether his life and career would have been different if he had not shared his name with the English Churchill.

What's in a name? Plenty.

cicerone Any person who acts as a guide for sightseers, pointing out and discussing objects of interest, especially antiquities.

The person whose name is reflected in **cicerone** is **Cicero** (106–43 B.C.), none other than **Marcus Tullius** himself, the great Roman orator, philosopher, and statesman. The application of Cicero to **cicerone** implicitly endows guides with the knowledge and eloquence of the great Roman. See also **Ciceronian**.

Ciceronian An adjective meaning of or pertaining to Cicero or his writings; also meaning in the style of Cicero, characterized by melodious language, clarity, and forcefulness of presentation.

A noun meaning a person who is an expert on or specializes in the study of the works of Cicero; also a person who admires or imitates the style of Cicero.

As every suffering secondary school scholar once knew—back in the days when the study of Latin was de rigueur—**Marcus Tullius Cicero** (106–43 B.C.) was the Roman writer and orator known by young students especially for attacking the conspiracy of Catiline and his associates (see **Catilinarian**) before the members of the Roman Senate. Well, Cicero's speeches against Catiline were not all there was to Cicero's output. His surviving works include many speeches, treatises on rhetoric, philosophical works, and letters recording his political and personal interests and activities.

Cimmerian Dark and gloomy. Also, in classical mythology, of, pertaining to, or suggestive of the **Cimmerians**, a people believed to dwell in perpetual darkness.

Homer, perhaps because he had heard stories of the dark Arctic night, supposed that the Cimmerians dwelled in a land where the sun never shone, giving us the phrase **Cimmerian darkness**.

After Homer's time, the Cimmerians were known as a people who lived on the shores of the Black Sea.

cinchona The tree of the genus *Cinchona* from which quinine is derived.

Its name was assigned by Linnaeus, the great taxonomist, who believed a thoroughly debunked story that continues to be told.

The story begins in 1638, when the beloved young wife of the Spanish viceroy of Peru falls desperately ill with malaria, from which she is cured by ingesting powdered bark known to indigenous Peruvians as *quinaquina*.

Upon recovery, the lady, **Francisca Enriques de Ribera, Contessa of Chinchón**, returns to Spain and brings with her quantities of the miraculous bark, which becomes known as the **Contessa's powder**. Thus, when Linnaeus comes to assign a name to the quinine-producing tree in 1742, he knows the story of the contessa and gives the tree the generic name *Cinchona*, which soon becomes the common name for the tree as well.

But what happens when a certain Dr. W. A. Haggis decides in 1941 to track down the facts? He finds that there had been two contessas of Chinchón married to the Peruvian viceroy. One died before the trip to Peru, and the other kept a diary that shows she never had malaria and had not returned to Spain.

Ruining an intriguing story. And Dr. Haggis never found out how this legend got started in the first place.

Cinderella A worthy person or meritorious thing persistently neglected in favor of others. Also, a person thus treated who achieves unexpected or sudden success or recognition.

Named for, of course, the heroine of the fairy tale "**Cinderella**," who is mistreated by a wicked stepmother but hits the jackpot when her fairy godmother enables her to meet—and promptly love and be loved by—a rich and handsome prince.

Cinderella's story appeared in the sixteenth century in various languages and was popularized beginning in 1697, when it appeared in

Charles Perrault's *Contes de ma mère l'oye* (Tales of Mother Goose), also known as *Contes du temps passé* (Tales of Days Gone By). Perrault (1628–1703) was a French writer whose reputation rests solely on his recounting of fairy tales. (See **Bluebeard**.)

Circe   Also called **Aeaea**, a dangerously, irresistibly fascinating woman, the kind one doesn't want to mess with.

In Greek mythology **Circe** was a sorceress who lived on the island of Aeaea. When Ulysses came ashore on the island, Circe gave him and his companions a magic potion, which turned all of them except Ulysses into swine. Ulysses managed to thwart Circe by taking moly, an herb given him by Mercury (also called Hermes).

Perhaps suggesting that all men need not be pigs. And that there may be more to herbal remedies than some of us believe.

clerihew   The name given to a four-line humorous verse form, with rhymed lines of uneven length and irregular meter.

Often biographical and satirical, the **clerihew** is usually distinguished by the appearance of the name of a well-known person in its first line. The clerihew was named for **Edmund Clerihew Bentley** (1875–1956), an English journalist and novelist known today for creating this verse form.

One of Bentley's favorite clerihews is reproduced here from the excellent *Brewer's Dictionary of Phrase and Fable*, 14th edition:

> *It was a weakness of Voltaire's*
> *To forget to say his prayers,*
> *And one which, to his shame,*
> *He never overcame.*

To show that clerihews are not as easy to write as the uninitiated may think, here is an example written by an untalented lexicographer who tried his best and failed:

> *Industrious Richard Milhous Nixon*
> *Hired aides to play dirty tricks on*
> *Those who might thwart a Republican victory*
> *And hurt Dick's place in history.*

Incidentally, those who read detective novels may recognize Edmund Clerihew Bentley as the author of the classic *Trent's Last Case* (1913).

Cocker. See **according to Cocker**.

Collins. See **Tom Collins**.

Colt A brand of revolver, protected by trademark.

Named for its inventor, **Colonel Samuel Colt** (1814–1862), born in Hartford, Connecticut, who also was interested in submarine mines and a submarine telegraph. The best-known **Colt** weapon is the Colt .45.

Incidentally, this weapon is so well known that its name has also been taken for a brand of bottled beer, suggesting that the drink packs a punch.

Cook's tour Today a once-over-lightly vacation trip made by a tourist or group of tourists in which too many sites of interest are covered in too brief a time. Thus the sardonic tag—with many variants—"If today is Thursday, we must be in Brussels."

Named after **Thomas Cook** (1808–1892), by the British affectionately called Tommy Cook, who was a British travel agent and pioneer promoter of tourism. The firm he founded bears his name and is still in operation.

By the way, the first **Cook's tour**, in 1841, was conducted by rail in England and covered a distance of approximately fifty miles, from Leicester to Loughborough. Of some interest is the fact that the tour was organized for supporters of the temperance movement.

Surely, a good time was had by all.

Copernican system The theory that Earth and the other planets revolve around the Sun.

From the Latinized name of the Polish astronomer **Nicolaus Copernicus**, original name **Koppernigk** (1473–1543), who promulgated this theory.

Copernicus considered his idea so radical that he did not authorize publication of his book on the subject until he was on his deathbed. He was not the first to propose that Earth goes around the Sun instead of vice versa, but the person who was had not fared too well. Aristarchus of Samos (c.310–c.230 B.C.) is known today only because Aristotle and Plutarch derided his views (see **aristarch**).

It would be a mistake to think that the ideas expressed by Copernicus are exactly what we believe today. For one thing, Copernicus used circles instead of ellipses to describe the orbits of the planetary bodies, so eventually his system was just as complex and messy as the **Ptolemaic system** (which see) it was intended to replace.

Even with the complexity, however, it was clear to some fellow astronomers that the **Copernican system** offered many advantages. Early in the seventeenth century, Kepler replaced the complex system of circles with a relatively simple system of ellipses, and Galileo found indisputable evidence for the Copernican system with his telescope.

Nothing like taking a good long look.

Coriolis effect   Also given as **Coriolis force**, a fictitious force—actually attributable to the rotation of Earth—that causes objects moving in any direction except along a parallel of latitude to swerve somewhat to the right in the Northern Hemisphere and somewhat to the left in the Southern Hemisphere.

Named after the French physicist **Gaspard Gustave de Coriolis** (1792–1843), who demonstrated the effect experimentally in 1835 and worked out a proof showing that it must be true of any rotating body.

Although the Coriolis force is often characterized as apparent or even hypothetical, it is just as real as gravity or centrifugal force, both of which are also in the class known technically as fictitious despite their profound effects.

What so-called fictitious forces have in common is that they affect every object equally. The best-known example is that heavy objects fall at the same rate as light ones—answering the old question: Which falls faster, ten pounds of lead or a ten-pound box of feathers?

At any rate the pattern of currents in air and water around the world results from a combination of geography with the Coriolis effect. Hurricanes in the North Atlantic, for example, originate near the west coast of Africa and begin to move south. But they are propelled across the Atlantic by the Coriolis effect to strike the east coast of North America. That is, they turn to the right. Similarly, the

Gulf Stream gradually turns to the right as it moves north, ultimately warming England and enabling palm trees to thrive in Cornwall and Ireland.

To the surprise of newcomers to those areas.

Couéism A world-famous form of self-help popular especially in the United States in the 1920s. It was dependent on autosuggestion and featured the slogan "Every day in every way I am becoming better and better."

Talk about alternative therapies!

The term **Couéism** took its name from the pioneer of autosuggestion, **Emile Coué** (1857–1926), a French pharmacist and hypnotist who studied psychotherapy for a few years and opened a free clinic in Nancy in 1910.

Beats counting pills all day long.

coulomb A unit of electricity, specifically the amount of a one-ampere electric current that flows during a single second—the *ampere second.*

Like most units of measure in the International System of Units, it was named in honor of a pioneer in the field, in this case the French physicist **Charles Augustin de Coulomb** (1736–1806). Coulomb was the first to establish and publish the discovery that an electric charge obeys the same inverse-square law that gravitation obeys.

An English scientist had guessed and published the correct rule earlier, but had not shown that it was correct. Another English scientist had determined the correct rule by experiment, but failed to publish. Had either man carried through, we might today speak not of a **coulomb** of electricity but of a priestley or a cavendish of electricity. But they didn't, and we don't.

Croesus A very wealthy man.

Historically, the name of the rich and powerful last king of Lydia (560–546 B.C.), **Croesus**, who subjugated the Greeks of Asia Minor and extended his kingdom eastward across the river Halys. The conquests of Croesus brought in so much tribute, and the income from his mines was so vast, that his name became synonymous with wealth. Who has not heard the expression **rich as Croesus**?

But, alas, one day his kingdom fell to Cyrus of Persia—and now the river Halys comes back into the story.

Croesus had consulted the Delphic oracle before launching the war he was contemplating against Persia, and the oracle answered: "When Croesus crosses over the river Halys, he will overthrow the strength of an empire." Consistent with oracular pronouncements, this wisdom was ambiguous. It did not specify which empire would be overthrown.

Croesus, being so taken with himself, saw the river crossing as portending the overthrow of the Persian empire. A fatal misinterpretation. When things turned out wrong for Croesus, it became clear—an awkward word to use in discussing oracular wisdom—that it was Lydia that would be destroyed.

Money, it seems, cannot always buy happiness.

Crookes tube   A form of cathode-ray tube.

Named after the distinguished English scientist **Sir William Crookes** (1832–1919), who played an important role in developing the cathode-ray tube.

These tubes are omnipresent today, indispensable in television sets and in computer monitors. But once the tube was invented, its name was changed almost every time someone improved its manufacture.

It all began in 1855, when a German glassblower named Heinrich Geissler (1814–1879) developed a way to make closed glass vessels that contained almost nothing—a vacuum tube, as we still call such a vessel. And what did scientists using this tube in their experiments call it? The Geissler tube, of course.

Twenty years later, Crookes started making his version of the vacuum tube, and it had a much better vacuum than Geissler's, so scientists switched to calling it the **Crookes tube**. One scientist who used the Crookes tube was the English physicist Sir Joseph John Thomson (1856–1940), who discovered the electron.

It must be pointed out that the stream of electrons produced in a Crookes tube had been called cathode rays since the 1870s, and the name of the tube was gradually changed to cathode-ray tube after Crookes departed this life, in 1919.

And that's the way it goes.

curie   One of several basic units connected with the measurement of radioactivity.

The *rad* measures the amount of energy absorbed per gram of material. The *rem* measures the biological damage caused by radiation. But the **curie** is indifferent to the specific type of radioactivity and is not a measure of energy, like the **joule** (which see), but rather a somewhat variable amount of a substance. That is, the amount varies inversely with how radioactive the substance is. Technically, it is the amount of an isotope that undergoes 37 billion radioactive decays in a second.

The curie was named in honor of the Polish-born French physicist and chemist **Marie Skłodowska Curie** (1867–1934), who, with her husband **Pierre** (1859–1906), a physicist, discovered the element radium.

Their method of obtaining radium is worth mentioning. Beginning with tons of uranium ore, the Curies over and over again separated it chemically into fractions of greater and lesser radioactivity, then similarly separated the fractions with the greater radiation. Finally, they obtained one gram of highly radioactive radium—from *eight tons* of ore.

Marie died at age sixty-seven of leukemia, surely induced by prolonged exposure to radioactive materials. But how did it happen that Pierre died at age forty-seven?—he was struck down in a traffic accident in Paris.

curium Element 96, an artificial radioactive element with properties similar to those of uranium and plutonium.

Named after French physicist **Pierre Curie** and his wife, **Marie Curie** (see **curie**). Although the Curies did not discover **curium**, they did discover the elements polonium and radium. And while comets are normally named after the first person or persons to sight them, elements are often named to recognize a person or even an institution that discovered another element, at another time. At the least, the tradition has been that the discoverer gets to pick the name of the element.

For example, when Glenn T. Seaborg and associates discovered a pair of elements in 1944, they had the privilege of choosing names for them. For element 95, they chose the name Americium, after their country, and for element 96, they chose curium, after the Curies.

When this same group, working at the University of California at Berkeley, discovered two more elements, they chose berkelium and californium for those elements.

Just for the record, five elements recently discovered are named einsteinium, rutherfordium, bohrium, meitnerium, and seaborgium. Within these names you surely perceive the names of five distinguished scientists: Einstein, Rutherford, Bohr, Meitner, and Seaborg.

D

· ·

daguerreotype   An obsolete type of photograph taken on a silver-coated copperplate sensitized by exposure to iodine. Pictures made on this surface were developed by exposure to mercury vapor.

The **daguerreotype** was named for its inventor, **Louis Jacques Mandé Daguerre** (1789–1851), a French painter and photographic pioneer. Until his photographic process succeeded, he supported himself by painting scenery for the Paris opera.

Beats waiting on tables.

daltonism   Also given as **Daltonism**, a type of color blindness, especially the inability to differentiate red from green.

Named after the English physicist and chemist **John Dalton** (1766–1844), who gave the first detailed description of color blindness, a condition he and his brother experienced.

While Dalton is known among scientists for his resurrection of the ancient Greek idea of the atom, establishing the atom as the basis of chemistry, his name is recognized by word lovers as the core of the word **daltonism**.

Besides, color blindness is something that even nonscientists can understand.

Whether they do or not.

Damocles. See **sword of Damocles**.

Damon and Pythias A pair of faithful friends.

In Greek legend **Damon**, a fourth-century B.C. Pythagorean philosopher, was a close friend of **Pythias**, also given as **Phintias**, who was himself a Pythagorean philosopher. When Pythias was sentenced to death for plotting against Dionysius the Elder, the tyrant of Syracuse (see also **sword of Damocles**), Pythias pleaded for permission to go home in order to settle his affairs.

Damon offered his own life as pledge that Pythias would return, an astonishing act of friendship. The offer was accepted by Dionysius, and Pythias went home. Pythias duly returned—albeit not until the last moment—to save Damon's life.

How did it all turn out? Dionysius was so impressed by the mutual devotion of the friends that he pardoned Pythias.

Giving the world, especially the English language, a time-tested phrase for any pair of faithful friends. At the same time teaching us the value of a last-minute rescue.

Dantean One of a pair of adjectives—the other is **Dantesque**—derived from the name of Dante, the celebrated Italian poet. While we are accustomed to adjectival forms of people's names, having two such adjectives from one name is something special.

The adjective **Dantean** is taken to mean of or pertaining to Dante or to his writings. A secondary meaning of Dantean is Dantesque, in the style of Dante, meaning characterized by impressive elevation of style with deep solemnity or somberness of feeling.

It is said that **Dante Alighieri** (1265–1321) in his greatest work, *Divina Commedia* (The Divine Comedy), established the Italian language. That is, before Dante wrote his account of a journey through Hell and Purgatory, guided by Virgil, and finally to Paradise, guided by Beatrice, his lifelong pure and Platonic love, no Italian would have written serious literature in any language but Latin.

Darwinian As an adjective, referring to ideas similar to those of Charles Darwin. As a noun, a person who professes Darwin's ideas.

Named after the English naturalist **Charles Robert Darwin** (1809–1882), whose writings on natural selection caused such a stir, particularly among those who misunderstood Darwin.

The basic **Darwinian** idea can be summarized quickly, beginning with a statement of what the idea is not: Darwin's theory does not say that evolution occurs.

It is closer to correct to say that Darwin's theory attempts to describe the mechanism by which evolution occurs. This is the mechanism he called *natural selection* and which is often characterized as *survival of the fittest*.

If some slight change makes an individual better adapted to a particular environment, that individual is likely to leave more offspring, who will tend to share the same slight change. Which is the basic Darwinian idea.

Davy lamp   A lamp that burns a small flame inside a metal cage, once used in coal mines to prevent methane explosions.

Named after its inventor, the English chemist **Sir Humphry Davy** (1778–1829), who was knighted for his invention, which saved the lives of many coal miners.

The invention was somewhat tainted by the almost simultaneous and very similar invention of George Stephenson (1781–1848), an English railway engineer who was not knighted but was paid a thousand pounds for his invention. Many of us recall Stephenson as the inventor of one of the first locomotives.

But back to the **Davy lamp**. Its secret lies in its metal cage, which dissipates enough heat to keep the flame from igniting the dread gas methane, which miners call *damp*. In use, miners soon learned that the flame burned brighter in the presence of gas, so the lamp could also be used to detect gas buildup.

Thus, the lamp not only prevented explosions, but also helped miners avoid suffocation. Two for the price of one.

decibel.   See **bel**.

degauss   A verb meaning neutralize any residual magnetism in a piece of iron or other ferromagnetic material.

And where did the residual magnetism come from in the first place? From electric currents, Earth's magnetic field, or some other source.

The word **degauss** probably started as engineer's slang, since the **gauss** is one of the basic units of measure for magnetism. Reducing the magnetic flux to zero on a ship could be called **degaussing** it.

The gauss is named after a German mathematician and astronomer, **Karl Friedrich Gauss** (1777–1855), who was better known as a mathematician than as an investigator of magnetism. For example, he was the first to propose that virtually all units of measure can be derived from a very few fundamental units—and the gauss is such a derived unit.

Sometimes we may tend to think that scientists spend most of their time playing intellectual games, so it is worthwhile to point out that degaussing is more than idle exercise. During World War II, for example, Allied steel-hulled ships were degaussed to protect them against Axis mines that used magnetic fields to trigger detonation.

Practical enough for you?

Delilah   A wily temptress, seductive and treacherous. Watch out for such persons.

Although the biblical **Delilah** is not described in Scripture, she must really have been something to see. Samson, a mighty Israelite, loved her madly. Accounts of famous love affairs surely are the stuff of best-selling fiction, and when such affairs involve secrets of state and come to a tragic end, so much the better.

Our story begins in Judges with an account of Samson's conception and birth. His previously barren mother is told by "the angel of the Lord" that she will bear a son. She is instructed to "drink no wine or strong drink, and eat nothing unclean," sound advice to this day. When she bears her son, she is told further, "No razor shall come upon his head . . . and he shall begin to deliver Israel from the hand of the Philistines."

His mother obeys, of course, and to her is born a son she names Samson. Soon, Samson is helping his fellow Israelites by causing all manner of trouble for the Philistines, enemies of the Israelites, and is cutting up with one woman after another, among them some he actually marries.

There comes a time when Samson lays eyes on a Philistine woman named Delilah and immediately falls for her. Hard. When the Philistine leaders find out their archenemy is in the capable hands of Delilah, they tell her: "Entice him, and see wherein his great strength lies, and by what means we may overpower him." For this act of betrayal each leader promises her "eleven hundred pieces of silver."

Samson is no fool. He knows Delilah is trying to find the secret of his strength. So, in response to her continuing inquiries, he offers one fictitious explanation after another. Finally, the self-confident Samson decides to spill the beans: "A razor has never come upon my head . . . if I be shaved, then I shall become weak, and be like any other man." Frankness was to prove his undoing. As any experienced lover knows.

Delilah tells the story to the conspirators and accepts the promised money. When Samson falls asleep—in Delilah's arms, where else?—one of the men shaves off his hair. Sure enough, when Samson awakes, he is unable to stop the conspirators, who are occupied with gouging out his eyes.

The blind Samson has lost Delilah as well as his great strength. For the surprising denouement of the story of Samson and for details of his feats of strength, see **Samson**. Sorry about that.

Moral: Don't trust a woman who wants to know all your secrets, especially one who has razor-wielding friends who specialize in eye-gouging.

Derby   A word with several meanings. The first is that of a race, usually for three-year-old horses, that is run annually. For example, the **Kentucky Derby** at Churchill Downs; and the **Derby**, a much older race run at Epsom Downs in England, dating from 1780.

The term **derby** is loosely applied as well to any horse race and occasionally to any venture that is regarded as a competition, for example, a mayoral derby.

Another **derby** is a man's stiff felt hat with rounded crown and narrow brim, sometimes also worn by women. This derby was once part of the accepted dress of Wall Streeters, along with the **chesterfield** (which see). (The derby hat is known in England as a **bowler** and is said to have taken its name from a certain **J. Bowler**, a London hatter who designed it in 1850.)

Derby in the horse racing definitions took its name from **Edward Stanley, the 12th Earl of Derby**, who died in 1834. Little is known of him beyond the fact that he instituted the Derby at Epsom Downs, the most famous of horse races, run on the last Wednesday in May or the first Wednesday in June.

derringer   Also given as **deringer**. An early short-barreled pocket pistol. Named after **Henry Deringer**, born in Philadelphia, a nineteenth-century gunsmith who supplied rifles to the U.S. Army and invented the **derringer** in 1852.

Dewey decimal classification Also given as the **Dewey decimal system**. A method of classifying books and other works into ten main classes of knowledge, with further subdivisions by use of the numbers of a decimal system. Protected by trademark.

This system takes its name from its founder, **Melvil Dewey** (1851–1931), an American librarian, who published it in 1876. His system was used for generations in many libraries in the United States and elsewhere, but has been replaced in most major United States libraries by the Library of Congress classification.

Dickensian An adjective meaning of Dickens or his works, also meaning resembling situations described in his works.

From the name of the great English novelist **Charles Dickens** (1812–1870), who wrote convincingly of the mistreatment and abuse of poor children by adults; exposed political corruption and court inequities; and satirized selfishness, hypocrisy, and financial speculation. At the same time, in his social criticism he created memorable characters, such as Oliver Twist and David Copperfield.

diesel An internal combustion engine that ignites its fuel as a result of compression, so no spark plug is required—although some modern **diesels** improve their efficiency with the addition of a simple electrically heated filament.

A further advantage of the diesel is that it does not require explosive fuel, such as gasoline.

Named for its inventor, **Rudolf Diesel** (1858–1913), a German automotive engineer. His engine was first built in St. Louis, Missouri, because Diesel's work was sponsored by a beer company there. The early diesels were too large and heavy for automobiles, but they were replacing steam engines on trains by 1912.

Most large ships and trains are still powered by diesels, and smaller versions of the diesel have made inroads into the automotive market.

Dionysian Sensual, unrestrained, recklessly uninhibited, orgiastic. Also of, pertaining to, or honoring Dionysus or Bacchus.

And who was **Dionysus** that his name engenders such rich evocations in English? A Greek god, also called Bacchus (see **bacchanalia**), and a son of Zeus. Dionysus was a god of the fertility of nature and came to be a god of wine who loosened care and inspired followers to music, poetry, and orgiastic rites.

Sounds like the kind of god you want to invite to a party.

diophantine equation   An equation written so that all the numbers that appear are whole numbers and are intended to be solved only for whole-number solutions. In some formulations of **diophantine equations**, rational numbers (fractions) are also allowed.

Named after **Diophantus of Alexandria**, a Greek mathematician about whom little is known, although it is thought he flourished about A.D. 250. Diophantus is called the father of algebra despite the fact that his only surviving work, *Arithmetica*, is not what we call algebra today. It is a collection of problems solved by using equations, some of them similar to the equations we might encounter in first-year algebra, and some of them **diophantine** in nature.

It will be of interest to anyone who follows developments in mathematics to know that the French mathematician **Pierre de Fermat** (1601–1665) was reading an edition of *Arithmetica* with large margins when he was inspired to think of what has become known as **Fermat's Last Theorem**, until 1997 the most famous unsolved problem in mathematics. The margins of *Arithmetica*, he said, were too small to accommodate his proof.

In 1900 the influential German mathematician David Hilbert (1862–1943) suggested a now-famous list of twenty-three important problems he hoped mathematicians could solve during the twentieth century. Problem 10 was to determine whether a general method existed that could determine whether any given diophantine equation has a solution. With great difficulty, and the combined efforts of several mathematicians, it was finally concluded late in the twentieth century that no such general method exists.

Too bad Fermat is not around to hear this.

Disneyesque   In the style of the animated cartoons produced by Walt Disney and his associates.

The world has not been the same since **Walter Elias Disney** (1901–1966), the American animator and movie producer, achieved prominence, leading inevitably to creation of the adjective **Disneyesque**.

And then there are **Disneyland** and **Disney World**, both meaning a fantasyland; a theme park; and, most broadly, a land or place of make-believe. A cynic might say, for example, that the U.S. House of Representatives is a Disneyland in which our worst dreams are played out.

Dixon. See **Mason-Dixon line**.

Dolly Varden A woman's large hat with one side drooping and with flowered trimming.

From the name of a character in Dickens's *Barnaby Rudge* (1841), one of the author's least successful novels.

Dolly Varden is also remembered by fishermen who go after the **Dolly Varden trout** and may do so with the assistance of the popular **Dolly Varden trout fly**, and Newfoundlanders out on the water are known to drink their coffee from **Dolly Vardens**, which are large decorated drinking cups.

All this from the name of one Dickens character.

dolomite A common mineral as well as a rock formed when limestone is invaded by magnesium.

Chemically, the mineral **dolomite** is calcium magnesium carbonate, and limestone is mostly calcium carbonate—known to mineralogists as calcite and to unfortunates suffering from indigestion as Tums.

Dolomite usually looks similar to limestone, but it has somewhat different chemical properties. The **Dolomites**, often called the **Dolomite Alps**, are a range of mountains in northern Italy that got their name from being composed largely of dolomite. When subjected to great heat and pressure, dolomite—like limestone—turns to marble, which in the case of dolomite is known as **dolomite marble**.

All this started in 1791, when French geologist **Déodat Guy Gratet de Dolomieu** (1750–1801) discovered that what appeared to be calcite was sometimes a different mineral. The mineral he later discovered came to be called dolomite after its discoverer.

Doppler effect The apparent change in frequency of a wave caused by relative motion toward or away from an observer.

Named after the Austrian mathematician and physicist **Christian Johann Doppler** (1803–1853), who enunciated the Doppler principle in 1842.

The Doppler effect is most familiar as a phenomenon affecting sound waves—as a siren approaches on a speeding vehicle, its pitch is perceived as becoming higher, but after the vehicle passes, the pitch reduces. This effect has been used with considerable success by astronomers who can, by measuring quite precisely the frequency of light, determine even small motions of distant stars and galaxies.

doubting Thomas   Any incredulous or skeptical person.

A phrase alluding to **St. Thomas**, the Apostle who doubted, in the Book of John.

The New Testament's man from Missouri was not present when the other Apostles met Jesus after his Resurrection and reported: "We have seen the Lord." That testimony was not enough for Thomas, who wanted to see for himself, and he replied: "Except I shall see in his hands the print of the nails, and put my finger into the print of the nails, and put my hand into his side, I will not believe."

Eight days later, the Apostles once again met Jesus, this time with Thomas present. Thomas had all the proof he needed and gave up his doubts.

Nevertheless, reputations once established being difficult to erase, to this day we refer to any skeptic as a **doubting Thomas**.

Douglas fir   A giant evergreen tree, slightly smaller than the redwood and sequoia, native to the American and Canadian West. Because the **Douglas fir** is not a true fir, it is also called the **Douglas spruce** and **Douglas hemlock**.

Named after **David Douglas** (1798–1834), a Scottish botanist who traveled to North America several times in search of New World plants. In 1825 he described the *Pseudotsuga menziesii*, calling it the Oregon Pine. A few years later, it was renamed the Douglas fir.

If you are old enough to take note of how long celebrated people have lived, you may be wondering why Douglas was only about thirty-six when he died. The explanation is that during a trip to Hawaii, he was gored to death by a wild bull.

He was probably looking at the trees instead of watching his step.

Dow Jones Average   The name of a stock index, protected by trademark, showing the relative prices of securities on the New York Stock Exchange at the end of every trading day, based on the average closing prices of groups of representative industrial and other stocks.

Named for two Americans who devised the **Dow Jones Average** in 1897: **Charles H. Dow** (1851–1902), a financial statistician; and **Edward D. Jones** (1856–1920). Incidentally, these two men also founded *The Wall Street Journal*, in 1882.

Down syndrome Also given as **Down's syndrome**, a genetic defect caused by the presence of an extra, or third, copy of the chromosome to which geneticists have assigned the number 21. As a result, physicians often refer to this condition as *trisomy*, since it is caused by three bodies—three chromosomes, that is—where there should be two.

Named after a British physician, **John L. H. Down** (1828–1896), who was the first to describe the condition formally, in 1866.

Individuals with **Down syndrome** usually have a distinctive appearance from birth and throughout their lives, with some of the following characteristics: small head, flattened in back; broad, flat face, with low brow ridges, cheekbones, and nose; relatively small eyes, turned up at the outer corners, often with a crescent-shaped fold of skin at the inner corner; oversize tongue in a small mouth; a deep, single horizontal line across the palm of the hand, instead of the usual head and heart lines; and short stature, with short limbs and stubby fingers.

The condition used to be called *mongolism* because the uplifted eyes seemed to resemble those of Asian people from Mongolia. The term has been discarded not only because it is considered offensive but because it is inaccurate.

Despite a tendency toward developmental disability and possible congenital malformations of the heart and gastrointestinal system, many Down syndrome persons can live a nearly normal life provided that their developmental disability is not so great as to prevent functioning outside an institution.

Draconian Often given as **draconian**, meaning harsh, unusually severe or cruel. As **Draconian**, meaning of, pertaining to, or characteristic of **Draco** or his code of laws.

Draco, also given as **Drakon** (seventh century B.C.), was an Athenian statesman who revised the code of laws of Athens with estimable impartiality. Unfortunately, the severity of the sentences he prescribed—death for almost every offense—made the imposition of his code unpopular. Fortunately, it was superseded about thirty years later by the more reasonable code devised by another Athenian, **Solon** (c.640–559 B.C.), known as a lawgiver, whose name gave us the word **solon**, meaning a wise lawgiver.

It took the United States only thirteen years to repeal the draconian Eighteenth Amendment to the Constitution, which outlawed production of alcoholic beverages. Quaffing a good stiff drink apparently meant more to lawmakers than prescribing reasonable punishment.

dry-as-dust   Also given as **dryasdust**, meaning dull and boring, especially applied to a heavy, plodding author.

From **Dr. Dryasdust**, the name given by the Scottish novelist and poet Sir Walter Scott (c.1771–1832) to a fictitious "reverend doctor," very dull and very learned, to whom he addressed some of his prefaces.

Today we are inclined to label such persons pedants or mere academics.

dry martini.   See **martini**.

dulcinea   One's ladylove.

Is there no better way to define **dulcinea**? Light of one's life? Dream girl? Sweetheart? Maybe. After all, the name **Dulcinea** is derived from the Latin *dulce*, meaning sweet, and the English dulcinea derives from a well-known Dulcinea in literature.

In Cervantes's *Don Quixote* (1605), Dulcinea is the lady to whom the gaunt, hapless knight Quixote pays homage. Because of the knight's inability to see things as they really are (see **quixotic**), we are not surprised when his squire, Sancho Panza, describes her as a sturdy wench, well-muscled.

Surely one more proof of the adage "Beauty is in the eyes of the beholder."

dunce   This cruel word means a stupid person, an ignorant person. If you doubt the cruelty of **dunce**, consider a few of its synonyms: blockhead, ignoramus, nincompoop, numbskull, and simpleton.

How it came to have these meanings is intriguing. Dunce derives from the name **[John] Duns Scotus** (c.1260–1308), a highly respected Franciscan philosopher born in Dunse, Scotland. His reasoning ability earned him the title of the "Subtle Doctor," and he exerted a

profound influence on theology in the Middle Ages with his arguments in opposition to the teachings of Thomas Aquinas. He held that
faith was a matter of will, not dependent on logical proofs.

By the time of the Renaissance, however, just two centuries later,
the theories of Duns Scotus had fallen out of favor, and his followers
were ridiculed by humanists and reformers for the subtleties of their
arguments.

When the opponents of Duns hurled abuse at his followers, the
term *Duns* or dunce began to acquire its present negative meanings
and first appeared in written form early in the sixteenth century.

This, of course, was not the first time a person had fallen far in
public esteem, and it was not to be the last. But to have one's name
become a synonym for blockhead and the rest is almost more than a
body can bear.

dundrearies Also given as **dundreary whiskers**, meaning men's long
side whiskers, or muttonchops.

Named after the side whiskers worn as theatrical makeup by
Edward Askew Sothern (1826–1881), an English comic actor, in his
portrayal of **Lord Dundreary**, the chief character in *Our American
Cousin* (1858). Dundreary was the personification of the good-
natured, lazy, blundering, empty-headed swell. The play was written
by a Scottish dramatist, Tom Taylor (1817–1880).

While Sothern's performance in the play made his reputation as an
actor, it was the whiskers he sported that achieved lasting reputation
as part of the English language. (See also **burnsides**.)

Taylor's play, *Our American Cousin*, in its time was a great success in
the United States, but it is most often mentioned today as the play that
drew Abraham Lincoln and his wife to the theater on the fateful Good
Friday night of April 14, 1865, when the president was assassinated.

E

E. coli   The informal name for a bacterium whose full name is *Escherichia coli*, commonly found in the intestines and feces of almost all animals.

Named after a German physician, **Theodor Escherich** (1857–1911), about whom little is known.

It is customary for biologists to abbreviate a scientific name after a first mention or when the name is frequently used. And these days, **E. coli** appears to be on everyone's lips—not literally, of course.

Scientists use E. coli in studies because it is so easy to obtain. Much has been learned from these studies, including the knowledge needed to genetically engineer various human proteins and create a test for water purity.

But it is the most recent information about E. coli that has attracted the greatest notice. A strain of E. coli has been found to have infected meat and fruit juice, causing many serious illnesses across the United States and killing several children who had eaten undercooked hamburger or drunk unpasteurized apple juice.

Edwardian   As a noun an **Edwardian** is a person who lived during the reign of Great Britain's **Edward VII** (1901–1910).

As an adjective **Edwardian** means of or pertaining to the reign of Edward VII, son of Queen Victoria, and this period became forever known as the **Edwardian era**. Edwardian also means reflecting the opulence or self-satisfaction characteristic of this era.

In Great Britain, **Edwardian** as an adjective characterizes the style of dress of the Edwardian era as adopted by many young men and youths in the 1950s and 1960s, who came to be known as Teddy boys, Teddy being an affectionate diminutive of Edward. Unfortunately, the Teddy boys became known as much for their antisocial behavior as for their distinctive dress.

Before succeeding to the throne, Edward VII served as Prince of Wales for sixty years and cut a prominent figure in European café society, becoming known as a devotee of horse racing, the theater, and the sport of yachting. It was widely known as well that the Prince of Wales, although married, had several mistresses and was even named as a witness—a euphemism—in a divorce suit. Showing that later adventures of British royalty, in the twentieth century, were not unknown in earlier times.

Nevertheless, Edward VII brought a certain vitality to the monarchy and actually played a useful role in international diplomacy.

einsteinium A radioactive metal, atomic number 99, in the same family as uranium and plutonium.

Named in honor of **Albert Einstein** (1879–1955), the leading scientist of the twentieth century, who had recently died.

The element **einsteinium** was first discovered by a team led by Albert Ghiorso in the United States in 1952, in the debris of an H-bomb detonation. For a few years the discovery was withheld from the press as classified information. (See also **fermium**.)

Electra complex In psychiatry, the theory that a daughter may have an unresolved, unconscious libidinous attraction to her father, at the same time feeling hostile toward her mother.

The phrase **Electra complex** has its basis in classical mythology. **Electra** was the daughter of Agamemnon and Clytemnestra, who incited her brother Orestes to kill their mother in revenge for Clytemnestra's murder of Agamemnon.

With these details in mind, you can see why Electra—lacking the benefits of modern psychotherapy—might have wanted her mother done in. And why Aeschylus wrote his tragic drama *Oresteia*, in which Electra has a great role. And why both Sophocles and Euripides wrote plays entitled *Electra*.

To even things out for women in the psychiatry game, see **Oedipus complex**.

Elzevir   An edition of the work of a classic author published by the house of **Elzevir**. Also a style of typeface recognizable by its firm hairlines and stubby serifs.

Elzevir was a Dutch firm of printers, publishers, and booksellers that was founded in Leyden in 1580 by **Louis Elzevir** (1540–1617) and continued operating until 1712 without ever being taken over by a merger-happy publishing giant or broadcasting company.

Elzevir was known for its production of inexpensive quality editions marked by sound scholarship and, in its time, published works written by Bacon, Comenius, Descartes, Hobbes, Milton, Molière, and Pascal.

Talk about a backlist!

eonism   In psychiatry, the adoption of feminine mannerisms, clothing, etc., by a male; transvestism.

Named after **Charles Geneviève Timothé d'Eon de Beaumont** (1728–1810), usually known as the **Chevalier d'Eon**, a French diplomat with this proclivity, who often wore feminine dress as a disguise.

In 1774, while serving in London as minister plenipotentiary of the French government, the chevalier was recalled because there was fear that masquerading as either sex he might betray state secrets to the British. As part of his settlement of the unpleasant charges, the French government stipulated that he would wear women's clothing from then on.

It must be observed that after the chevalier's death, an autopsy established finally that he was indeed a man. Apparently, even his parents had some difficulty in ascertaining his sexual status at the time of his baptism.

Charles Geneviève—one vote for each sex!

epicure   A person devoted to the pleasures of the table who cultivates a refined taste, especially in food and wine; a connoisseur.

Named after **Epicurus** (341–271 B.C.), a Greek philosopher and founder of the Epicurean school, which taught that pleasure was the highest good. But Epicurus construed pleasure as something more than good living, which is the sense intended today.

For Epicurus, pleasure was right living, which leads to tranquility of mind and body. A consummation—and a safe level of cholesterol—devoutly to be wished.

The noun **epicurean**, also derived from Epicurus, is used interchangeably with **epicure**, but the adjective **epicurean** is more complex. It means: (1) pertaining to good eating and drinking; (2) having luxurious tastes or habits, especially in food and drink; (3) fit for an epicure; and (4) pertaining to or characteristic of Epicurus or his teachings. The teachings of Epicurus are called **Epicureanism** or **Epicurism**.

An early Greek philosopher who occupies a prominent and happy place in the English language.

erbium   A metallic element in the rare-earth group. The name derives not from the name of a person but from the name of a place.

First, a word about the science part of the story. Metals in the rare-earth group are not especially rare. Nor are they earths in the chemist's language. The earths were metal oxides that were difficult to break down and, therefore, were believed at one time to be elements.

Rare-earth metals are much alike in all their properties and so are difficult to separate from each other. Finally, none of them are commonly known, although some have important commercial uses.

As for the history of the word **erbium**, early in the nineteenth century, when the oxides of erbium and similar metals had not been separated, chemists began investigating an earth found near the village of **Ytterby**, in Sweden. Treatment with chemicals eventually showed this earth was not an element, but contained a metal that was an element. The metal, discovered in 1843 by Carl Gustav Mosander (1797–1858), was named **yttrium** after the village of Ytterby.

Soon after, Mosander found a second element, which he named erbium, a re-spelling of Ytterby in bastard Latin. Mosander then found a third element in the same earth, so he named that one **terbium**, as the third in the series. Mosander also thought he had found a fourth element, although it was later shown that the fourth metal was really two different but almost identical twin metals.

The story is not quite over. More than fifty years later, a French chemist, **Georges Urbain** (1872–1938), went back to the earths quarried just outside Ytterby and found two more metals, one of which was ultimately named **ytterbium**, bringing to four the number of elements named after just one small Swedish village.

Not too bad for a little village.

Eros Preoccupied with matters sensuous, as modern society undoubtedly is, it comes as no surprise that the name **Eros**, the Greek god of love, has spawned a cottage industry of English coinages.

First there is Eros itself, meaning: (1) the Greek god of love; (2) a representation of this god; (3) a winged figure of a child—à la Cupid, the Roman counterpart of Eros—representing love or the power of love; and (4) sometimes given as **eros**, sexual desire, physical love.

But this is merely the beginning. Consider the adjective **erotic**; the nouns **erotica, eroticism, erotism, eroticist,** and **eroticization**; the adverb **erotically**; and the verb **eroticize**.

If this listing is not sufficiently satisfying, consider the nouns **erotogenesis, erotology, erotomania,** and **erotomaniac,** as well as the adjectives **erotogenic, erotogenous,** and **erotomanic**.

All this from an innocent four-letter Greek name. But if you wish to see this boy of great beauty, check out his statue—complete with wings and golden bow and arrow—in Picadilly Circus, London, if it still is there.

Escherichia coli. See **E. coli.**

Esculapian. See **Aesculapian.**

Euclidean geometry Geometry based on the postulates of **Euclid,** especially the postulate stating that through a given point there can be drawn only one line parallel to a line not on that point.

Named after the Greek mathematician **Euclid of Alexandria** (c.325–c.270 B.C.), whose geometry textbook is still in use—albeit with modifications—in modern times. To this day, students spend a good deal of time absorbing geometry according to Euclid's axioms, postulates, and proofs.

Everything was proceeding happily for **Euclidean geometry** until several nineteenth-century mathematicians recognized the existence of non-Euclidean geometries, which replace the postulate stated above with such alternatives as *more than one line* or *no line* instead of *one line*.

Still, most people believed these non-Euclidean geometries were flights of mathematicians' fancies, although it was possible to see how one particular non-Euclidean geometry could describe geometry on a sphere if one changed the meaning of *line*. Einstein upset the entire geometric apple cart when he demonstrated that space is not Euclidean after all. Instead, it is more like, but not exactly like, the three-dimensional analog of the geometry of the surface of a saddle.

Kilroy was here.

euphuism   An ornate, high-flown style of writing or speaking. Also an ornate style in imitation of the work of John Lyly (1554?–1606), an English dramatist and novelist, especially in his two-part romance *Euphues: the Anatomy* (or *Anatomie*) *of Wit* (1578) and *Euphues and his England* (1580).

The noun **euphuism** is taken from **Euphues**, which is based on a Greek word suggesting "a man well endowed by nature," and the name of the hero of Lyly's romances, which are characterized by overly generous servings of alliteration and by long series of antitheses and similes relating to mythological natural history.

While euphuism was well received by readers in the sixteenth century, the style is highly inappropriate in modern writing. But that does not mean it is unwelcome in English. In fact, the word itself has a special charm by virtue of its interesting origin in the name of a fictional character. (See also **Gongorism**.)

Eustachian tube   Also given as auditory canal, in humans a short tube connecting the back of the throat or base of the nose to the middle ear—as anyone with postnasal drip will tell you.

Named after the Italian anatomist **Bartolommeo Eustachio** (1520–1574), in Latin **Eustachius**, who was the first person to describe several body parts. Although there were also a **Eustachian vale** and a **Eustachian catheter**, the only designation that achieved immortality was the **Eustachian tube**.

It appears that the role of the Eustachian tube is to keep the air pressure in the middle ear the same as air pressure outside the body.

When this fails to work, as when you are transported abruptly to a different air pressure in an airplane and the Eustachian tube lags behind, a strong yawn can usually solve the problem.

If the Eustachian tube is clogged as the result of a disease, however, more heroic measures may be needed, even minor surgery.

So chew gum during takeoff and landing—and keep your seat belt buckled.

Everyman   John Q. Public; the typical or average person; everybody; everyone.

From the name **Everyman** of the central character of a fifteenth-century morality play, *Everyman* (c.1529), author unknown. The play is thought to have been translated from a fifteenth-century Dutch play—author also unknown—but whatever its provenance, *Everyman* became the most famous of the English morality plays.

Everyman is summoned by Death and invites all his acquaintances—Kindred, Good Deeds, Worldly Goods, Knowledge, Beauty, and Confession, among others—to accompany him, but only Good Deeds agrees to do so. Not much of a turnout for Everyman.

Just when a feller needs a friend.

F

Fabian A member of the **Fabian Society**, an English organization founded in 1884 to propagate socialism by gradual means through increasing state intervention in the economy.

From the name of **Quintus Fabius Maximus Verrucosus** (died 203 B.C.), a Roman soldier who went on to serve in high positions in the Roman Republic. His nickname was *Cunctator*, or Delayer, reflecting his defensive military tactics and giving us the English word *cunctator*, meaning procrastinator. He would avoid direct encounters, instead carrying on guerilla warfare. His armies, for example, without risking a pitched battle, were able to outlast Hannibal's invading Carthaginian forces because Hannibal, being far from home, could not replace fallen soldiers.

Thus, the Latin *Fabianus* and its English form, **Fabian**, came to be synonymous with gradualism and was selected as a name by the distinguished founders of the Fabian Society. The persons most closely associated with the Fabian Society were Sidney and Beatrice Webb, economists and social reformers who were husband and wife; and the Irish playwright and essayist George Bernard Shaw.

But did the Fabian Society ever achieve its objective of bringing socialism to England? Well, there were some brushes with success, but nothing permanent.

Going slow sometimes may work wonders in military enterprises, but not necessarily in politics.

Fagin Also given as **fagin**, meaning a person who teaches crime to others. Also meaning a dealer in stolen goods, a fence.

From the novel *Oliver Twist* (1838), by Charles Dickens, whose character **Fagin** is a villainous old man—not surprisingly for nineteenth-century England identified as a Jew—who receives and sells stolen goods, and trains boys as pickpockets and thieves.

Such was life for youths trying to make their way in the world of poverty and prejudice that was nineteenth-century London.

Fahrenheit The most common temperature scale used in the United States, with 32° for water freezing and 212° for the boiling point of water.

Named after its inventor, **Gabriel Daniel Fahrenheit** (1686–1736), a German physicist who lived and worked in Holland. He devised a thermometer that used alcohol in 1709 and a thermometer that used mercury about 1714. But how did he settle on the numbers 32 and 212 for the bottom and top temperatures in his scale?

He set about producing the lowest temperature of water he could, even adding salt to lower its freezing point (if you have ever tried to make ice cream, you know that salt can lower the freezing point of water). He called his lowest temperature 0°.

He then chose 100° for the temperature of a human body but, it has been said, wanted to be able to separate the interval between lowest and highest into more than 10 equal, large, and integral divisions. So he changed body temperature to 96°. But since that gave a fractional value for boiling, he made another adjustment to make boiling a whole number, or 212°. This juggling made body temperature 98.6°.

Between you and me, I don't buy this story. Human body temperature is never 98.6° precisely, but varies up and down with the individual person and the time of day. So I think Fahrenheit used his own body temperature as 100°, and that was that.

Consider, therefore, that the distance from 32 to 212 is 180. And 180 is a number divisible by 2, 3, 4, 5, 6, 9, 10, 12, 15, 30, 36, 45, and 90. Which leads me to believe that if Gabriel Fahrenheit were searching for divisors, he knew a good number when he saw one: 180°—can't beat it. But see also **Celsius scale** and **Kelvin scale**.

fallopian tube   Also given as **Fallopian tube**, one of a pair of passages in females that link the uterus to the ovaries so that eggs can travel from an ovary to the uterus.

Named after an Italian anatomist, **Gabriele Falloppia**, in English given as **Gabriele Falloppio** (1523–1562), who described this anatomical feature.

The end of each **fallopian tube** near the ovary widens and faces the ovary with a fringed opening. The fringes wave continuously toward the ovary, so when an egg is released by an ovary, it becomes caught in the fringe and directed into the fallopian tube, which carries the egg toward the uterus with sweeping motions of the hairlike projections that line the tube. In reproduction, sperm deposited in the vagina also move through the tubes, where they encounter an egg if one is present.

Sometimes, unfortunately, a fertilized egg lingers in the tube, causing a serious condition known as an ectopic pregnancy.

Falstaffian   Like or characteristic of **Falstaff**, especially in regard to his robust, bawdy humor, good-natured rascality, and self-indulgent braggadocio.

From the name of the character **Sir John Falstaff** in Shakespeare's *Henry IV*, parts I and II, who also appears in *The Merry Wives of Windsor*. Falstaff revels in his lechery and chicanery, sometimes shows cowardice, and lies without scruple, but his knavery is engaging and his lust for life keen.

Just the kind of fellow you might invite to a bachelor party, but not to the wedding.

farad   A unit of measure of capacitance (the ability to store a charge of electricity) that can be defined in several ways, including: (1) 1 ampere-second per volt; and (2) the amount of capacitance of a capacitor set up so there is a potential difference of 1 volt when the capacitor is charged with 1 coulomb of electricity.

Named in honor of the English chemist and physicist **Michael Faraday** (1791–1867), who is considered the greatest of experimental physicists.

In an attempt to make the **farad** a bit more understandable, let us begin by defining a capacitor as two conductors separated by a thin insulator, as in a Leyden jar, which is a device for storing electric charge. Thus, a Leyden jar that has 1 farad of capacitance will deliver a shock of 1 volt when discharged into one's body.

This is less than the shock that comes from walking across a hotel carpet in winter and then touching a doorknob. Still, physicists find the farad too large for their purposes, so they use **microfarad** as their common unit of measurement, a microfarad being 1 millionth of a farad.

faraday   Also known as the **faraday constant**, the charge produced by the number of molecules that is **Avogadro's number** (which see) when each of the molecules is singly ionized.

Another example of a scientific term named in honor of a great scientist of the past, in this case that person being **Michael Faraday**. (See **farad**.)

To clarify the definition, a **faraday** is the charge of 602,600,000, 000,000,000,000,000 electrons.

Does that help any?

Fata Morgana   A type of mirage, specifically one frequently seen in the Straits of Messina, between Italy and Sicily. It is described as comprising multiple images, as of distorted and magnified cliffs and buildings that resemble castles.

From the Italian **Fata Morgana**, literally *fairy Morgan*, and in English usually given as **Morgan le Fay**, meaning Morgan the Fairy. Morgan le Fay in Arthurian legend was a magician and fairy sister of King Arthur, and associated with magical castles.

Let us stop and consider what we know about King Arthur. He was a king of England who (a) insisted on seating his knights at a round table so no one of them would think he was superior to any other; (b) is generally thought to have been not a king at all, but at most a fifth- or sixth-century chieftain or general; and (c) appears to have had a fairy sister who could perform magic. Not a bad start.

But how did the story of Morgan le Fay pop up in Italian? Easy. The legend of Morgan (**Morgana**) is believed to have been carried to Sicily by Norman settlers, and Morgan's reputation as an enchantress survived so that, by the nineteenth century, the mirages we call **Fata Morganas** were attributed to her.

Thus, English has been enriched by an Italian name for a particular mirage, said to be the work of a fairy who could perform magic, and whose brother's kingly status was highly questionable.

Fermat's Last Theorem. See **diophantine equation** for identification of Fermat.

fermion In modern physics, any of a category of subatomic particles that make up matter. The **fermions** include the electron, proton, neutron, and all the quarks as well as several obscure particles.

Fermions were named after the Italian-American nuclear physicist **Enrico Fermi** (1901–1954), who worked out the mathematics of their interactions. Each **fermion** occupies a definite space, so two fermions cannot be in the same place at the same time. It is this characteristic that makes fermions so different from photons and the other bosons (see **boson**).

Fermi was revered by most physicists, not only for his insight and wit, but also because he was one of the few admired both as a theoretician and experimentalist. In the latter role, he directed construction of the first atomic reactor ever, in Chicago. It was this secret project that led to construction of the first nuclear bomb.

When Fermi's reactor began operating successfully on December 2, 1942, a famous coded message was sent to President Franklin D. Roosevelt to alert him of the achievement: "The Italian navigator [has] reached shore safely and found the natives friendly." In other words, Fermi had created a nuclear chain reaction, and it had not blown up Chicago.

You might wonder how it was that Fermi, at age twenty-seven appointed professor of theoretical physics at the University of Rome, and awarded the Nobel Prize in physics in 1938, came to live in the United States. The explanation is that Fermi's wife was Jewish, and he feared for her safety once Italy began to promulgate anti-Semitic laws. So he went straight from the Nobel Prize presentation in Stockholm to the United States, where he became professor of physics at Columbia University in 1939.

fermium   Element number 100, a synthetic radioactive metal of the same general type as uranium and plutonium.

Like element 99, **einsteinium** (which see), **fermium** was first discovered, by an American team led by Albert Ghiorso in 1952, in the debris from an H-bomb detonation. For several years the discovery was classified information, and when it came time to name elements 99 and 100, both Albert Einstein and Enrico Fermi had recently died, so Ghiorso's team chose to honor them both.

Ferris wheel   An enormous upright wheel erected in amusement parks, fairs, and carnivals to rotate slowly on a fixed stand. Cars or seats around its rim are suspended freely so occupants remain right-side up as the wheel turns.

Named after its American inventor, **George W. G. Ferris** (1859–1896), who designed and built the first such wheel for the World's Columbian Exposition of 1892, held in Chicago, Illinois. The wheel was 250 feet in diameter and had 36 cars, each with a seating capacity of 40 passengers.

As a **Ferris wheel** rotates, stopping frequently to take on and discharge passengers, loving couples have the opportunity to cuddle while paying scant attention to the panorama unfolding beneath them.

A first-class American institution, soon to take its place (in the form of what's said to be the largest Ferris wheel in the world) alongside the River Thames in London to commemorate the start of the third millennium. Thank you, Mr. Ferris.

Fibonacci numbers   Any of the counting numbers found in a sequence formed by adding the two preceding numbers of the sequence to find the next number—assuming the initial numbers are 0 and 1.

Thus, the first ten **Fibonacci numbers** are 1 (repeated in the sequence), 2, 3, 5, 8, 13, 21, 34, 55, and 89. Try it yourself: $0 + 1 = 1$; $1 + 1 = 2$; $1 + 2 = 3$; $2 + 3 = 5$; and so on.

Named after **Leonardo Fibonacci**, an Italian mathematician.

Be aware that the Fibonacci numbers are not merely mathematical fun and games. For example, they help botanists understand growth patterns in plants. The whole idea originated in the following problem:

How many pairs of rabbits will be produced, beginning with a single pair, if every month each pair bears a new pair that becomes productive from the second month on?

As you may have guessed, the answers for each month are 1 pair, 1 pair, 2 pairs, 3 pairs, 5 pairs, 8 pairs, and so forth.

The rabbit problem was among many proposed and solved by the most influential mathematician of the Middle Ages, **Leonardo of Pisa**, also known as **Fibonacci** (c.1170–c.1240). And there is today a Fibonacci Society, devoted to studying the properties of the Fibonacci numbers and the **Fibonacci sequence**.

If the spirit moves you when you're next in a scholarly library, you might inquire as to whether the library subscribes to *The Fibonacci Journal*.

fidus Achates.   See **Achates**.

filbert   Also called hazelnut; an edible, thick-shelled nut of the hazel shrub or tree, especially of a cultivated European variety, *Corylus avellana*.

Named after **St. Philbert** (called **Philibert** in Britain), his saint's day being August 22 (20 August in Britain), because **filberts** generally ripen on or about August 22.

FitzGerald-Lorentz contraction   Also given as **FitzGerald contraction**, the hypothesis that a moving body exhibits a contraction in the direction of motion when its velocity is close to the speed of light.

Thus, while we do not see a passing automobile as shorter than a parked automobile, if we could speed the car up to 161,000 miles a second, it would appear to be half its length.

This effect was first postulated by the Irish physicist **George Francis FitzGerald** (1851–1901) as a possible explanation of the failure of a famous 1887 experiment that was conducted to determine the precise speed of Earth through space. The idea was to measure the change in the speed of light from two directions perpendicular to each other.

When no change was observed, FitzGerald suggested that the distance light traveled through the measurement apparatus might be shortened just enough in the direction of motion to compensate for Earth's motion. But that would mean that the apparatus was shortened in that direction, and when FitzGerald made this radical suggestion, few gave it much credence.

The same explanation of the behavior of objects in motion was reached shortly afterward by a Dutch physicist, **Hendrick Antoon Lorentz** (1853–1928), who was much more influential than FitzGerald. Although Lorentz was not exactly gaga over the hypothesis, he was driven to it by other evidence as well.

Then, in 1905, Einstein proposed the theory of special relativity, which included the **FitzGerald-Lorentz contraction** as one of its main conclusions. And that was that.

By the way, Lorentz shared the 1902 Nobel Prize in physics with the Dutch physicist **Pieter Zeeman** (1865–1943), who discovered that when a light ray from a source placed in a magnetic field is examined under a spectroscope, the spectral line is widened, sometimes doubled. This is the **Zeeman effect**.

FitzGerald died in 1901, the first year the Nobel prizes were awarded—awarded, that is, to the living.

flack   As a noun, meaning a press agent; also meaning publicity. As a verb, meaning promote, publicize; also meaning serve as a press agent.

Said to be named after a man called **Gene Flack**, reputed to have worked in Hollywood as a movie press agent. When one sees *said to* and *reputed to* in the same sentence, beware.

Foucault's pendulum   A swinging pendulum so long that its force, which maintains the pendulum's swing in the same plane, is great enough to keep the pendulum oriented while Earth rotates underneath it.

Thus, over a 24-hour period, the plane of the pendulum at the North or South Pole would appear to swing around in a circle once. It would circle a bit slower at lower altitudes and would not circle at all at the equator.

Named after the French physicist **Jean Bernard Léon Foucault** (1819–1868), remembered best as the person who, in 1851, employing a freely suspended pendulum, proved that Earth rotates. Of course he had trouble making a pendulum long enough to observe the effect, so Emperor Napoléon III got into the act by offering a church in Paris for the test. A pendulum over 200 feet long was very gently set in motion in such a way that it would make a mark in a bed of sand with each pass. As the marks gradually turned the proper amount for the latitude of Paris, nearly 32 hours, the rotation of Earth was demonstrated experimentally for the first time.

Since then **Foucault's pendulums** have been set up in several science museums around the world, and Foucault's Paris pendulum, now in the church of St. Martin du Champs, is a central object in the 1988 novel *Il pendolo de Foucault* (Foucault's Pendulum) by Umberto Eco. Its motion is maintained by a small motorized magnet.

Foucault, in the year after his pendulum experiments, realized that a rapidly moving sphere would show the same effect on a smaller scale. He experimented to demonstrate that this was true and, in the process, invented the first form of gyroscope—to the delight of many children as well as grown-up navigators.

Fourdrinier machine   Also given as **Fourdrinier**, a mechanized system for making continuous rolls of paper.

Named after **Henry** (1766–1854) and **Sealy** (died 1847) **Fourdrinier**, inventors and papermakers. Their **Fourdrinier machine**, which the brothers patented in England in 1807, was an improved design of a papermaking machine that could produce a continuous sheet of paper.

The same type of machine is used to this day.

Fourier analysis   The expression of any periodic function as a sum of sine and cosine functions.

Named after **Jean Baptiste Joseph, Baron de Fourier** (1768–1830), the French mathematician who devised **Fourier analysis**, still an essential tool in mathematical physics and considered the most important mathematical tool of the twentieth century, especially in various improved versions developed during the past half century.

The success of Fourier analysis depends on the simplicity of handling sine curves with calculus and related mathematical disciplines. Virtually any complicated mathematical relationship can be replaced by the sum of an infinite number of sine curves in a straightforward way, called a **Fourier transform**. Then, as many of these sine curves as are required for the accuracy needed in a given problem can be chosen and the problems solved using the sine curves.

Reversing the original process gives the solution using the original intractable relationship. Variations on this idea are also used for tomography, which is the basis of the CT and PET scans used in diagnostic medicine. The data collected with X rays or positron emission are turned by a reverse transform into a computer image of the object being scanned.

This gives doctors a way to see what's going on inside our bodies—without having to open us up.

Fourierism A social system under which society is radically reorganized into self-sufficient units that are scientifically planned to offer the greatest possible cooperation and self-fulfillment to its members. Living arrangements, property ownership, and the institution of marriage would be redesigned.

Fourierism is a translation of the French word *fouriérisme* with the same meaning; named after the French social theorist **François Marie Charles Fourier** (1772–1837), whose ideas attracted many adherents in France and in the United States.

Then faded from sight.

Franciscan As a noun, meaning a monk or nun of the mendicant order founded by St. Francis in the thirteenth century. As an adjective, meaning of or pertaining to St. Francis or to this order.

The order took its name from **St. Francis of Assisi** (1181–1226) of Italy, whose original name was **Giovanni Bernadone**. He acquired the name *Il Francesco*, the little Frenchman, from his youthful familiarity with the language of the troubadours.

St. Francis founded his order of mendicant monks, or friars, in 1210. They are also known as the Gray Friars, so called from the color of their habits. Two years later he founded his order of nuns, the Poor Ladies of San Damiano, also called Poor Clares, named for Clare Scifi, later **St. Clare of Assisi**, who with her sister Agnes, later **St. Agnes of Assisi**, became followers of St. Francis.

The Franciscan system is founded on poverty, chastity, and obedience, with the emphasis on poverty. Accordingly, Bernadone repudiated all idea of property, even in things required for personal use.

frangipani   A perfume imitating or prepared from the aroma given off by the flower of *Plumeria*, a fragrant shrub or tree of the dogbane family. **Frangipani** is also the shrub or tree itself.

Named after a sixteenth-century Italian, the **Marquis Muzio Frangipani**, who is said to have invented the perfume. Whether he did or not, he was a descendant of a noble Roman family that gave English a mellifluous word for a beautiful aroma.

Beats naming a perfume after a number.

Frankenstein   A person who creates a thing that goes out of control or that brings about its creator's ruin.

Also given as **Frankenstein monster**, erroneously intended to mean the destructive thing itself; correctly given as **Frankenstein's monster**, since Frankenstein created it.

From the name of the title character **Frankenstein** in a novel by Mary (Wollstonecraft) Shelley (1797–1851), wife of the poet Percy Bysshe Shelley.

In Mary Shelley's novel of 1818, *Frankenstein, or the Modern Prometheus*, Frankenstein is a young German student who animates a monster made of corpses taken from graveyards and dissecting rooms. The soulless creature, unnamed in the novel—and this is of some importance in the context of the subject of this book—turns to evil and takes deadly vengeance on Frankenstein, the young student, for creating life, thus usurping the Creator's prerogative.

But recall *The Modern Prometheus* subtitle of Mary Shelley's novel, and that Shelley's monster—we could just as well call it Frankenstein's monster—came to an unpleasant end. Recall further that the demigod Prometheus of classical mythology, who is credited with creating mankind, made men of clay and water, and that Athene, the Greek goddess of wisdom, breathed a soul into them.

Recall finally that Prometheus eventually suffered big-time punishment—he was chained to a rock where an eagle tore at his liver every day. The liver grew back every night, only to be torn at again the next day. Not to worry. Hercules came along after a while and freed Prometheus.

Now for the matter of the name Frankenstein. Its second, incorrect meaning—the destructive thing itself—became common when the movie of the novel was made and soon was followed by a great number of *Frankenstein* movie clones, a fit fate for Frankenstein films. In a short time, moviegoers transferred the name Frankenstein from the creator of the thing to the thing itself. It did not take long for the mistaken usage to overtake the correct one.

As usually happens. And what can we do about it? Nothing.

Franklin stove   A free-standing cast-iron stove or a fireplace with cast-iron top, sides, and back for heating a room.

Named for its American inventor, **Benjamin Franklin** (1706–1790), statesman, scientist, printer, inventor, author of an autobiography that has been translated into many languages, and publisher of the highly successful *Poor Richard's Almanack*, published from 1732 to 1757.

Offering such invaluable advice as "Early to bed and early to rise / Makes a man healthy, wealthy, and wise" and "God helps those who help themselves."

Those of us who have reached a certain age value Franklin's borrowed wisdom—usually from classical sources—and, particularly, Franklin's invention of bifocal eyeglasses.

Freudian   As an adjective, concerning **Freud** or his theories and methods of psychoanalysis, especially with respect to the causes and treatment of neurotic and psychopathic states and the interpretation of dreams. As a noun, **Freudian** means a person, especially a psychoanalyst, who adheres to Freudian practices.

From the name of **Sigmund Freud** (1856–1939), Austrian neurologist and psychotherapist, whose influential writings and teachings established him as the central figure of his profession—even though, by the close of the twentieth century, he no longer is considered the last word on questions of cause and treatment of mental illness.

One locution that has invaded and conquered ordinary social conversation—and is in no danger of being supplanted—is **Freudian slip**—an unintentional error that seems to reveal unconscious wishes, motives, or attitudes.

Friday   The day preceding Saturday and, therefore, beloved by those who have managed somehow to show up at work all week long.

Taken either from **Freya's day** or **Frigga's day**. Who are **Freya** and **Frigga**? In Scandinavian mythology, **Freya** is the goddess of love and of the night. A sort of northern Venus. **Frigga** is the wife of Odin and the goddess of the hearth and of married love—a steadier creature with family values.

Whatever the correct origin of **Friday**, we also know the word in another context. Robert Louis Stevenson, in his *Robinson Crusoe* (1719), gave us the memorable **man Friday**, which has itself spawned **girl Friday**.

Stevenson's man Friday was a devoted servant, but man Friday has entered English with the meaning of right-hand man, a male assistant to a business executive. Girl Friday, often given as **gal Friday**, is a woman who acts as general assistant to a business executive, capable of performing secretarial duties, managing the executive's schedule, and maintaining confidential files.

But don't ask her to make coffee.

G

....

Galahad   A man of flawless character, showing devotion to the highest ideals.

From the name of **Sir Galahad**, in Arthurian legend the noblest knight of the Round Table, and the son of Sir Lancelot and Elaine. It was Galahad who eventually retrieved the Holy Grail.

And gave all men and boys a model to emulate.

gal Friday.   See **Friday**.

Galilean satellites   The four largest moons of Jupiter: Ganymede, Io, Europa, and Callisto.

From the name of their discoverer, the Italian scientist **Galileo Galilei** (1564–1642), usually called **Galileo**. The satellites are named for four of the god Jupiter's favorite consorts—in the classical Greek style, **Ganymede** (which see) was a male lover, while the other three were female.

The moons were the first heavenly bodies to be discovered, in 1610, with the assistance of the astronomical telescope developed by Galileo the year before. The discovery of the moons of Jupiter was one of several achievements Galileo made about that time that convinced him Copernicus had been correct about Earth and the other planets traveling about the Sun, for Galileo could observe the four satellites moving about Jupiter in just the sort of paths Copernicus had described.

After Galileo published his *Dialogo dei due massimi sistemi* (Dialogue on the Great World Systems) in 1632, he found himself in deep trouble with the Church. In the next year, he was tried before the Inquisition, charged with proclaiming and defending the Copernican system, which the Church had called heretical.

And did the great scientist Galileo recant? Of course. He was not inclined to sacrifice his remaining years to a fruitless heroism.

gallium   Element 31, a metal that, like mercury, is liquid at room temperature.

Not the temperature of an air-conditioned room, you understand, but about 86.6°F, the same as a warm summer day in most of the United States.

The most interesting part of the **gallium** story is the origin of its name. The element's discoverer, **Paul-Emile Lecoq de Boisbaudran** (1838–1912), a French physical chemist, chose the name gallium. Besides gallium, he discovered samarium and dysprosium.

Like all scientists, Boisbaudran was aware of the unspoken rule against naming a discovery after oneself. So, in naming the element gallium, all he was doing was choosing a name based on the ancient Latin name *Galle*, meaning France.

But people began to talk. "Isn't part of the discoverer's name **Lecoq**? In French *le coq* means rooster, and in Latin *gallus* also means rooster."

Could the gossipers have been on to something? Was this a clever way to break the unspoken rule? Fortunately, when Boisbaudran went on to discover two other elements, he played the naming game as straight as anyone could desire.

At least as far as scientists know.

Gallup poll   An assessment of public opinion on a subject of interest, ranging from the acceptability of a new commercial product to preferences among candidates for public office. Such a poll is made by eliciting and recording the responses of a representative sample of persons to a series of questions and then processing the responses by statistical techniques.

From the name of **George Horace Gallup** (1901–1984), an American statistician, who introduced the modern concept of polling.

Which has robbed us of the excitement of election nights by enabling television networks to name winners before many of us have had a chance to vote.

galvanic   An adjective, in physics meaning producing or caused by an electric current; in common use meaning startling, shocking; stimulating, energizing.

To bring the physical meaning and common meaning together, we can correctly characterize a White House news bulletin or a declaration of war as **galvanic**, with the meaning of *electrifying*.

Galvanic comes from the noun **galvanism**, an old name for direct current, named after an Italian physiologist, **Luigi Galvani** (1738–1798), whose accidental discovery in 1771 of a way to produce an electric current startled Europe and eventually the world.

Happening to have some frogs' legs in his dissecting room, perhaps to study them, perhaps to ready them for his dinner, he noticed that a spark from his nearby Leyden jar—a device for storing electric charge—made the legs twitch. So he set about confirming Benjamin Franklin's finding that electricity and lightning are the same phenomenon.

He attached the frogs' legs to brass hooks outside his dissecting room, against an iron railing. The idea was to wait for a thunderstorm to see if the legs twitched. But he found that they twitched immediately, without an electric storm.

Galvani believed he had discovered animal electricity, although very soon **Alessandro Giuseppe Anastasio, Count Volta** (see **volt**) improved on the current generated by using two different metals in a chemical bath. Nevertheless, despite the fact that Volta had it right and Galvani was way off, people began calling current electricity *galvanism* to distinguish it from static electricity, which was the only type of electricity known before the discoveries of Galvani and Volta.

Don't worry about this example of Volta's lack of recognition. He did very well. But do marvel at how many examples of **galvanic** are in use today: **galvanic battery, galvanic cell, galvanic couple, galvanic** pile, **galvanic skin response**, and too many words beginning with the prefix **galvano-** for the amount of space left in this book.

And then there's the verb **galvanize** . . .

galvanize   Galvanize is named after **Luigi Galvani**, as is **galvanic**.

Originally, persons became **galvanized** by the application of direct current to their skin, in the hope that a jolt of electricity would cure them of various ills.

Since a person who is shocked—that is, galvanized—would immediately leap to the action of avoidance, **galvanize** came to mean stimulate into sudden activity, even by means other than electricity. And there its sense remains to this day, along with its electrical meanings.

So we have such thoughts as "The House Committee resisted action on recommending impeachment until a spate of verified, unsavory reports revealed the depths of the vice president's character and **galvanized** the committee into taking action."

Returning to electricity, we know that a direct current can be used to cause atoms of one metal to move to and coat another metal. While this process is used to make silver plate and to gild other metals, its product most commonly encountered is iron coated with zinc to keep the iron from rusting. The iron then is known as **galvanized iron**, and it is used in nails, roofing, and many other common applications.

gamp   An informal British word with two meanings. A **gamp** is an umbrella, and a **Gamp** is a less than fully qualified maternity nurse given to excessive drinking.

Both derive from Charles Dickens's novel *Martin Chuzzlewit* (1844). The first, **gamp**, is from the bulky umbrella carried by nurse **Mrs. Sarah Gamp**. The second, **Gamp**, is from the behavior of this bibulous and disreputable nurse.

Dickens has made his mark again on the English lexicon. (See also **Dickensian, Dolly Varden, Fagin,** and **pecksniff**.)

Ganymede   A boy or youth who is in a sexual relationship with a man.

In Greek mythology, **Ganymede** is a Trojan youth so beautiful that he was abducted—sometimes said to have been carried by an eagle—by Zeus to Olympus, where he was made cupbearer to the gods. This was an appointment of some importance, since a cupbearer is entrusted with filling his master's cup with wine. At any rate, Ganymede became immortal.

Not just another pretty face.

gargantuan An adjective meaning enormous, gigantic.

From the name of **Gargantua**, the giant-hero of *Gargantua and Pantagruel*, published in five volumes, 1532–1552, posthumously, by François Rabelais (c.1490–1553), the great French satirist and humorist.

Gargantua, while entering this world through his mother's left ear, shouted "Drink, drink, drink!" A great way to make your first public appearance. Gargantua was a man of great appetites, at one point in his life swallowing whole a salad of five pilgrims complete with staffs. Gargantua also rode to Paris on a mare whose tail switched so violently that it felled a forest. He had to protect himself against a lawsuit accusing him of having stolen the bells of the Cathedral of Notre Dame. And so on.

All this was a way of satirizing the practices and social institutions of the sixteenth century, including the immorality of the clergy, poets, self-professed ascetics, judges, fortune-tellers, the legalistic pedantry of Sorbonne theologians, prigs, despotism, and monasticism.

The name Rabelais has also given English the adjective **Rabelaisian** (which see). Two English adjectives from one French source, **gargantuan** and **Rabelaisian**. Not bad.

Gatling gun An early type of machine gun, with a revolving cluster of ten parallel barrels around a central axis, firing 1,200 shots a minute.

Named after **Richard Jordan Gatling** (1818–1903), its American inventor. An ingenious feature of the **Gatling gun** was its automatic loading and firing of each barrel. Picture the speed of the operation.

The American slang word **gat** for a pistol or revolver, once favored by script writers for Hollywood gangster movies and now appropriated by some rap artists, is an abbreviation of **Gatling**.

Gaullist A supporter of the programs and principles of **Charles de Gaulle** (1890–1970), the French general who became the first president of the Fifth Republic; especially, a person who supported the French Resistance against the Nazi occupation of France during World War II.

The number of those who claimed to have been supporters of the French Resistance appears to be greater than the total population of French men, women, and children alive at the time.

gauss.   See **degauss**.

Gay-Lussac's law.   See **Boyle's law**.

Geiger counter   Also given as **Geiger-Müller counter**, a device for detection and rough measurement of radioactivity.

Named after its inventor, **Hans Wilhelm Geiger** (1882–1945), a German physicist who worked under the British physicist Ernest Rutherford from 1906 to 1912. It was during this period that Geiger developed his prototype counter for detecting alpha particles. Later, with an associate named Walther Müller, he improved the sensitivity of his device, making it useful for measuring all types of radiation. (See **roentgen**.)

Geissler tube   A sealed glass tube containing a small amount of gas for production of a luminous electrical discharge.

Named after **Heinrich Geissler** (1814–1879), a German inventor who was expert in blowing glass. Intent on capturing a vacuum, Geissler had the idea in 1855 of using a column of the heavy liquid-metal mercury to empty a glass tube of most of its air and then sealing the tube. He achieved the best vacuum attained to his time, and physicists quickly began to use **Geissler tubes** for experiments with the passage of electricity through a near vacuum. The small amount of gas in such a tube was ionized by the current and proceeded to glow.

One line of experimentation based on this phenomenon led to discovery of X rays and the electron. But the glow itself was eventually used as the basis of the fluorescent light, such a light being nothing more than a Geissler tube that glows with a high energy but produces invisible ultraviolet light. The ultraviolet light, in turn, makes phosphors inside the Geissler tube glow at visible wavelengths.

gentian   Any of the plants of the genera *Gentiana*, *Gentianella*, and *Gentianopsis*, having flowers of various colors. The blue-colored flowers of the mountain **gentians** are considered especially beautiful.

Named after **Gentius**, a king of Illyria, an ancient country along the east coast of the Adriatic, dating from the third century B.C.

Those of us with knowledge of World War II jungle combat recall

gentian violet, a dye used especially in medical treatment of jungle rot. Ugh. (See also **Gram positive and negative**.)

gerrymander As a noun, the artful manipulation of electoral district boundaries to give one party disproportionate influence in elections. As a verb, to manipulate to achieve this advantage.

Named after **Elbridge Gerry** (1744–1814), governor of Massachusetts, who rearranged the electoral districts in his state in 1812 to secure an advantage for the Republican party.

It is said that the American artist Gilbert Stuart (1755–1828), who painted George Washington several times, once looked at a map of a district in Essex County post-rearranging and noticed that district's outline resembled a *salamander*. He modified the outline to emphasize the resemblance and showed the result to a newspaper editor, who responded, "Better call it a **gerrymander**."

So *gerry* + *mander* gave English an enduring word to describe an enduring political practice. But what happened to Gerry? He went on to serve two years as vice president of the United States—a political black hole—and died in office. He is now largely forgotten, but the practice of **gerrymandering** will live on as long as we continue to suffer politicians.

Gilbertian Said of a moral dilemma, a situation, or the like: ludicrous or paradoxical, as in the topsy-turvy intricacies of a Gilbert and Sullivan light opera.

From the name of **Sir William Schwenck Gilbert** (1836–1911), a parodist and librettist, best remembered for his fourteen incomparable collaborations with the composer Sir Arthur Sullivan (1842–1900), filled with pokes at English institutions and social classes.

While most of the nuances of Gilbert's underlying meanings are no longer understood by modern audiences, generation after generation in Britain and in the provinces still enjoy the legacy of music, plots, and lyrics of Gilbert and Sullivan.

girl Friday. See **Friday**.

Gioconda smile An enigmatic smile resembling that of the woman in the *Mona Lisa*.

From the Italian title *La Gioconda*, in English given as the Mona Lisa, of the most celebrated portrait by Leonardo da Vinci (1452–1519). The

Italian word *gioconda*, masculine form *giocondo*, can be translated as *jocund*, which means cheerful, merry, etc., and even when we examine the *Mona Lisa* closely we can hardly see signs that its beautiful subject was jocund.

So we have to look further to find the source of the Italian name of the portrait. Soon enough we find that the lady whose portrait Leonardo painted was the wife of one **Francisco del Giocondo**, a Florentine merchant. So, if people live up to their names, maybe business was good and Francisco's family had reason to be *jocund*. Or maybe the family took its name from a district near Florence named *Giocondo*.

Nevertheless, the real question persists: Why did *La Gioconda*, the *Mona Lisa*, smile so enigmatically, so mysteriously? The question, alas, is doomed to go unanswered.

Unless the secret diaries of Leonardo turn up.

Gladstone bag   A kind of suitcase made in various sizes, hinged to open in two compartments of equal size.

Named after the English Liberal statesman **William Ewart Gladstone** (1809–1898), who served as prime minister four times between 1868 and 1894, the days when Liberals and Tories operated a revolving door for leadership of the House of Commons. It was only advanced age that led to his final resignation as prime minister, in 1894.

A warning: **Gladstone bags** have gone out of style, so don't approach a young salesclerk to ask where the Gladstone bags are displayed.

Gongorism   Also given as **gongorism**, a Spanish literary style imitative of the ornate and intricate style of poet **Don Luis de Góngora y Argote** (1561–1627) and marked by inversion, antithesis, and classical allusion, corresponding to **euphuism** (which see) in English style.

From this term, named after Góngora, came the noun **gongorist**, designating someone who writes in imitation of **Gongorism**, along with the inevitable adjectives **gongoristic** and **gongoresque**.

Modern writing style being what is, anyone today whose writing is described as gongoristic probably has reason to sue for slander or libel.

good Samaritan.   See **Samaritan**.

Gordian knot   We encounter Gordian knot mainly in the expression **cut the Gordian knot**, which is interpreted in two ways: to get out of a difficult situation by a single decisive action; and to solve a problem by acting with force or taking evasive action.

Named after **Gordius**, a peasant who was chosen king of Phrygia, an ancient kingdom in Asia Minor. Gordius attached the yoke of his wagon to the beam with a bark rope knotted so cleverly that no one could untie it. This was the original **Gordian knot**.

Alexander the Great was told that whoever undid the knot would rule over the entire East, whereupon he announced he would accomplish the task. What did he do? He cut the knot in two with his sword.

Alexander had **cut the Gordian knot**, solving a difficult problem by taking evasive action.

Why solve a knotty problem by conventional means? Cut through it. And we clever moderns think we invented lateral thinking! (See also **Midas**.)

Gorgon   Also given as **gorgon**, meaning an unusually hideous person, especially a repulsive woman.

In classical mythology, any of the three **Gorgons**, snake-haired sisters who had wings and brass claws. The number one sister was **Medusa** (which see) and the other, less celebrated sisters were called Stheno and Euryale. It must be noted, however, that Stheno and Euryale had the advantage of being immortal, and if you know your Medusa story, you know she was not. You also know that Medusa's mortality did not serve her well.

The Gorgons shared one attribute of special interest: Anyone who looked at a Gorgon, especially anyone who looked a Gorgon in the eye, was immediately turned to stone. Now, you might ask why anyone would want to look at such ugly creatures, much less look them in the eye.

Mythology answers this question. A certain king was trying to make time with Danaë, the mother of Perseus, whose father was Zeus, and felt he had to get Perseus out of the way. So he sent the fine young fellow off on a hunting trip to bring back the head of Medusa. The gods helped him succeed in his quest, and he returned—unpetrified—with the head. He soon enough used the head to turn the dastardly king to stone. An example of poetic justice?

Even though Medusa met her match, her sister **Gorgons** are still around, menacing all oglers. Might be a good thing to have them walk down the avenue where construction workers hoot at women walking by.

Graafian follicle   Also given as **graafian follicle**, one of the small sacs in a mammal's ovary containing a developing ovum.

Named after the Dutch physician and anatomist **Regnier de Graaf** (1641–1673), who studied the workings of the reproductive organs.

A woman's ovaries normally contain hundreds of thousands of follicles, each containing an undeveloped ovum. At a specific time in a mature woman's menstrual cycle, the follicle-stimulating hormone shows up in the blood. This appearance causes one of these many follicles and its ovum to begin to change into mature form.

After some growth, an ovum—by then the follicle is considered a **Graafian follicle**—is set free, to be captured by the **fallopian tube** (which see), and the follicle turns to another concern. It manufactures a yellow body that releases a hormone telling the body an ovum has left its follicle—like reporting that Batman has left the Bat Cave—and is on its way to its destiny. The follicle then recedes into anonymity.

Having already done more than you might expect.

Gradgrind   Any cold person, interested only in facts.

A marvelous noun, thus far used primarily in Britain. It is included in this book in hope that **Gradgrind** will find greater use in American speech and writing.

From the character **Thomas Gradgrind** in the novel *Hard Times* (1854) by Charles Dickens, master of the art of assigning memorable names to fictional characters.

Gradgrind is fanatically occupied with demonstrable fact. This inclination permeates the everyday life of his family, and his son and daughter grow up steeped in the efficacy of grim practicality and, as a result, are emotionally atrophied.

A warning to all moms and dads.

graham cracker   The familiar rectangular cracker made of whole wheat, and accompanied—in the Norman Rockwell tradition—by a cold glass of milk. For more years than imaginable, every schoolchild's favorite after-school snack.

Named for **Sylvester Graham** (1794–1851), an American dietary reformer, whose love affair with the benefits of whole wheat was legendary. Thus, in addition to the familiar cracker, there were **graham bread**, **graham flour**, **Grahamism**, and **Grahamite**, the latter two denoting respectively Graham's vegetarian principles and a supporter of these principles.

Nowadays, we hear little about the bread, flour, or the rest, but the **graham cracker** continues to be delicious and popular, despite the depredations of marketing experts who insist on coating these crackers with chocolate.

Gram positive and negative   A means of classification of bacteria by observing their reaction to staining by **Gram's method**.

Named after **Hans Christian Gram** (1852–1938), a Danish bacteriologist, who developed Gram's method.

Simply stated, in this procedure a smear containing bacteria is stained with both the synthetic dye gentian violet (see **gentian**) and an iodine solution known as **Gram's solution**. Excess stain is then washed out with alcohol. The bacteria are then seen to be either violet or quite dark (**Gram-positive**) or faintly pink (**Gram-negative**).

Gram-positive bacteria differ from Gram-negative in many ways, of which perhaps the most important lies in their different reactions to antibiotics. For example, Gram-positive bacteria are stopped in their tracks by penicillin and related antibiotics, while Gram-negative bacteria respond to antibiotics that are similar to streptomycin.

If you're lucky, your physician knows which antibiotic to use. If your HMO agrees.

grangerize   Illustrate (a book) by inserting illustrations cut from published books. Also, mutilate (a book) by cutting pages in order to get illustrations for this purpose.

Named for **James Granger** (1723–1776), an English biographer, who published editions of his work with blank pages for the convenience of readers interested in collecting illustrations to paste into them. It has been said that many fine editions have been ruined by people taken with this impulse, and Granger himself is said to have **grangerized** thousands of engraved portraits from other persons' books.

Granny Smith   An Australian variety of apple, crisp and green-skinned, with excellent keeping qualities.

Named after **Maria Ann "Granny" Smith** (c.1801–1870), an Australian orchardist, who developed the variety in Eastwood, near Sydney. At the time, she was experimenting with a hardy French crab apple from Tasmania, which has a cool climate conducive to apple-growing.

Graves' disease   The disease known as **goiter** and as **exophthalmic goiter**, because the eyeballs typically protrude.

Goiter is the abnormal swelling in the neck that is characteristic of hyperthyroidism, abnormal thyroid growth caused by iodine deficiency. It was described for the first time in detail by an Irish physician, **Robert James Graves** (1796–1853), and so is most often referred to as **Graves' disease**.

But Graves' disease, or goiter, is also called **Basedow's disease** after **Karl Adolph von Basedow** (1799–1854), a physician who described the disease in Germany; **Glajani's disease** after **Giuseppe Glajani** (1741–1808), a physician who described the disease in Italy; and **Parry's disease** after **Caleb Hillier Parry** (1755–1822), a physician who described the disease in England.

So, as far as the name that goes with the disease is concerned, it looks like dealer's choice.

It is indisputable, however, that iodized salt has wiped out goiter almost everywhere, so most people today have never seen anyone with goiter. But those who are of a certain age remember vividly seeing people so afflicted.

Gregorian calendar   The correction of the calendar proclaimed in 1582 by **Pope Gregory XIII** (1502–1585).

Although the Egyptians recognized that the year to the nearest day is 365 days long, after a few years the seasons gradually changed, beginning at different times in the Egyptian calendar. Julius Caesar recognized this problem and legislated a new calendar, called the **Julian calendar**, based on 365.25 days. It added a leap day every fourth year, beginning after 46 B.C. In the first year of the new calendar, however, 80 days had to be added to bring the system into line. And after 1,500 years it became apparent that the seasons had continued to slip, albeit at a slower pace.

Thus, the seasons were 10 days off when Gregory proclaimed his new system. After correcting for the extra 10 days produced by the

Julian calendar, the Gregorian calendar of 1582 retained the leap year every four years, *except* when the year ends in two zeros, *unless* it is also divisible by 400.

For this reason the leap day was omitted in 1900 but will be on its regular 4-year schedule again in the year 2000. As you surely know.

Meanwhile, modern astronomers keep careful track of the length of the year and add a leap second every few years as needed to maintain the Gregorian calendar.

Gregorian chant   The plainsong used in the Roman Catholic ritual, plainsong being traditional church music in medieval modes and in free rhythm, sung in unison.

Named after **Pope Gregory I** (c.540–604), known as **Pope Gregory the Great** and especially esteemed for his systemization of the church's sacred chants.

Gresham's law   According to **Gresham's law**, as every student of Introduction to Economics knows, when two currencies of equal legal exchange value are in circulation, that of the lower intrinsic value will tend to drive the other out of use.

It appears that this is so because money people will hoard the currency of higher intrinsic value, presumably because it will be safer than the currency of lower intrinsic value.

This observation was named after **Sir Thomas Gresham** (1519–1579), an English financier active in currency affairs domestic and international, who amassed tremendous wealth. It was he who convinced Elizabeth I that her government should borrow from London merchants instead of from foreigners.

Nothing like making money at home, among people you know and trust. Especially when interest rates are lower there.

grog   Any strong liquor, especially a mixture of rum and water with various sweeteners and flavors.

Said to have been named after the coat worn by **Edward Vernon** (1684–1757), an English naval commander known affectionately as **Old Grog**, grog being short for *grogram*, a coarse fabric formerly in use.

But there is more to the story, as there almost always is. In 1740, Vernon ordered navy rum to be diluted with water, and the mixture was known from then on as **grog**.

It had been the English navy practice to issue spirits to all hands twice a day. This meant a total daily ration of eight ounces of rum with a quart of water. Over the years this ration was cut and eventually eliminated entirely.

It's enough to ruin a man's fighting spirit. And, in today's navy, a woman's fighting spirit as well.

Grundy, Mrs.   A narrow-minded, straitlaced person who is extremely critical of any action judged to be a breach of propriety.

From the name of the character **Mrs. Grundy**, frequently mentioned but never appearing in *Speed the Plough* (1798), written by the English playwright Thomas Morton (1764–1838), who was successful in his career but is today remembered solely for Mrs. Grundy. She has no lines, yet she has survived in the line "What will Mrs. Grundy say?" as a substitute for the more mundane "What will the neighbors say?"

So the next time you have need of censuring somebody careless enough to commit an impropriety in your presence, remember to say, **What will Mrs. Grundy say?** or **What will Mrs. Grundy think?** After all, if you are foolish enough to judge the behavior of others, you may as well be quoting a line from an eighteenth-century play.

Guarneri   Any of the fine violins made by any of several members of the famous **Guarneri**—or **Guarnieri** or **Guarnerius**—family of Cremona, Italy, who flourished in the seventeenth and eighteenth centuries.

The Guarneris followed in the footsteps of the Amatis, the famous violin makers of Cremona who preceded them. Indeed, Nicolò **Amati** (1596–1684, see) was a teacher of Andreas **Guarneri** (c.1626–1698). But he was also a teacher of Antonio **Stradivari** (c.1644–1737), better known as **Stradivarius** (which see).

And where do Strads come from? Cremona, of course. What was there about Cremona that made this town in Lombardy produce so many talented violin makers? Did they have the best wood in Italy for making violins? Was the water especially good? Was special DNA floating around?

At any rate, thank you, Cremona.

And if you happen to own a **Guarneri**, remember not to leave it behind in a cab when you head for Carnegie Hall.

guillotine A machine for beheading a person that saw its first use in Paris in 1792. Sure enough, there's the verb **guillotine**, which means execute (a person) with a guillotine.

The heart of the devilishly efficient machine is a sharp knife blade held aloft in grooved wood until the order is given to let it down—rapidly and decisively (there's a pun in there if you know the Latin origin of *decisively*).

Named for **Joseph Ignace Guillotin** (1738–1814), a French physician who suggested its adoption to prevent pain in a candidate for execution. Readers of Charles Dickens's enduring novel of the French Revolution, *A Tale of Two Cities* (1859), remember its scenes of execution of members of the French nobility.

Gunter. See **according to Gunter.**

guppy A small West Indian freshwater fish.

Named for a Trinidadian clergyman, **R. J. L. Guppy** (1836–1916), who sent the first recorded specimens to the British Museum, in 1866. The **guppy**, first named *Gerardinus guppyi*, is now known as *Poecilia reticulata*.

Little more can be said about the poor fish, at this moment dying by the thousands in home aquariums everywhere.

Guy Fawkes From the name of the English conspirator **Guy Fawkes** (1570–1606), who plotted with several fellow Catholics to instigate an uprising against the English government in revenge for laws passed against their coreligionists.

The uprising, known as the Gunpowder Plot, was set to be launched at the opening of Parliament on November 5, 1605, and its immediate targets were the Protestant King James I, his ministers, and members of the House of Commons and House of Lords. Barrels of gunpowder had been stored in the cellar beneath the House of Lords, and Guy Fawkes had been selected to set off the explosives. But things did not go right for the Gunpowder Plot from then on.

One of the conspirators told his Catholic relative, a certain Lord Monteagle, about the plot. And he, as you may have guessed, passed word of the plot to the authorities, whereupon a search of the cellar uncovered the explosive cache, and Guy Fawkes was taken captive.

What followed for Fawkes was your garden-variety torture, trial, and hanging. But Guy Fawkes is recalled in England every November fifth, **Guy Fawkes Day**, when bonfires are set whose star fuel is an effigy of the hapless Fawkes. English official memory being what it is, before Parliament opens each year the cellar beneath the Houses is searched—just in case another Gunpowder Plot is in the offing.

H

hansom   Also given as **hansom cab**, originally a light two-wheeled, covered one-horse vehicle for two passengers, in which the driver stood uncovered at the rear. Today, any similar horse-drawn vehicle, as well as, occasionally, an automobile with a folding top.

From the name of **Joseph Aloysius Hansom** (1803–1882), an architect who invented the Patent Safety (Hansom) Cab (1834). Since horse-drawn vehicles are no longer a common sight in modern cities—though you may see a few making their way around New York City's Central Park—**hansom** and hansom cab are terms needed primarily by writers and readers of historical novels.

Hayflick limit   The hypothetical limit on the number of times a human cell can divide before dying. A portentous number.

Named after **Leonard Hayflick** (born 1928), an American microbiologist who asserted in 1961 that he had discovered this limit. Because of the accelerating progress being made by geneticists and their cohorts, the **Hayflick limit** is probably worth your attention.

Human cells in a culture normally will not divide and grow after a more or less fixed number of divisions, no matter how well they are treated. The number at which cell division stops varies from twenty for some cells taken from adults to an upper limit of about sixty for fetal cells.

Early in 1998 scientists announced they had found a gene-engineered way to circumvent the Hayflick limit, thus possibly helping to reduce aging in tissues, although probably not in entire human bodies. We'll see. (Also see **HeLa cell**.)

hector As a verb, meaning intimidate, bully, treat with insolence. As a noun, meaning a bully, a blustering and domineering person.

From **Hector**, a Trojan hero in Homer's **Iliad** (which see) who was killed by Achilles (see **Achilles heel**). Achilles, after killing Hector, lashed the body behind his chariot and dragged it in triumph three times around the walls of Troy.

Thus Hector, who started out in Homer's *Iliad* as a Trojan hero, ended up in English as a bully so remarkable that his name also came into English as a verb meaning intimidate or bully.

How the mighty have fallen.

HeLa cell Also given as **Hela cell** and **hela cell**, any of a strain of human cells maintained in a culture and used widely in cancer research.

From the name of *Henrietta Lacks*, the woman whose cervical cancer provided the original cells. Before Ms. Lacks died, she had been a patient at Johns Hopkins Hospital, in Baltimore, Maryland, where a sample of her tissue was taken on February 8, 1951. The cells—**HeLa cells**—descended from her original cells are still alive *in vitro* and contributing to science.

Biologists have for many years worked with this strain of human cells, immortalized by the mutation of cancer. Along with some other strains of cancer cells, the HeLa cells are said to be immortalized because they do not obey the **Hayflick limit** (which see) on continued cell division. It must quickly be added that individual HeLa cells are not themselves immortal without cell division.

But hey! You never can tell.

Hepplewhite A light, delicate, and graceful style of furniture of the latter part of the eighteenth century, much prized by collectors.

Named for **George Hepplewhite** (died 1786), the English cabinetmaker who originated the design. Later, the English firm A. Hepplewhite and Company continued to design and produce furniture in the **Hepplewhite** style, characterized especially by use of inlaid ornamentation and heart- and shield-shaped chair backs.

Herculean   Pertaining to the great strength of Hercules. As **herculean**, meaning as strong and courageous as Hercules; also, as difficult to perform as the labors of Hercules.

Quite a guy, this **Hercules**. In classical mythology a celebrated hero, whose superhuman strength and courage are best illustrated by considering the twelve formidable tasks of great difficulty and danger that were imposed on him.

It happened this way: Eurystheus, king of Argos in southeast Greece, punished Hercules by ordering him to perform the twelve tasks as penance for having murdered his wife and children—his insanity plea was unsuccessful. (For the details of one of the tasks, see **Augean**.)

His other tasks included bringing Cerberus up from hell, and to do so without using weapons. Cerberus was the three-headed dog that guarded the entrance to hell—as in Milton's *L'Allegro*:

> *Hence, loathed Melancholy,*
> *Of Cerberus and blackest midnight born,*
> *In Stygian cave forlorn,*
> *'Mongst horrid shapes, and shrieks, and sights unholy.*

Well, this did not stop Hercules, nor did the problem of catching the horses of the Thracian Diomedes, or the nine other great labors.

hermaphrodite   A person or animal with indeterminate sexual organs or with the reproductive organs of both sexes; also, a plant in which this same physical characteristic is normally present.

From **Hermaphroditus**, son of Hermes and Aphrodite. Hermes was the ancient Greek messenger of the gods as well as god of commerce, invention, and more. Aphrodite was the Greek goddess of beauty and love.

The handsome youth, while bathing in the fountain of the nymph Salmacis, became united with her and so combined male and female characteristics.

When a sign says "No Swimming Today," obey!

hertz   The basic unit of frequency for any sort of wave; it is equal to one period, or cycle, per second.

Named after the German physicist **Heinrich Rudolf Hertz** (1857–1894), who was the first, in 1886, to show that radio waves exist. As a result, radio waves are sometimes called **Hertzian waves**.

But back to our Hertzian primer: The *period* is the length of time it takes for one complete waveform to pass a given point, so the period is closely related to the wavelength. For electromagnetic waves, which all travel at the same speed in a vacuum—known as the speed of light—the same information can be reported either as a *frequency* in **hertz** or as a *wavelength* in some unit of length, such as the meter.

Thus, a wave with a frequency of 1 hertz would have a wavelength about 300,000 kilometers long. More often, we encounter frequencies of thousands of hertz, the **kilohertz** of AM radio; or we encounter frequencies of millions of hertz, the **megahertz** of FM radio.

This definition excludes the so-called permanent wave.

Hobson's choice   No choice at all; take it or leave it.

From the name of **Thomas Hobson** (c.1544–1631), of Cambridge, England, an innkeeper and carrier of goods and passengers who also rented out horses. It was his policy not to give any rental client a choice of horses, but always to rent the horse standing nearest the stable door—**Hobson's choice**.

Better read the fine print in the rental agreement.

Hodgkin's disease   A type of cancer characterized by swelling of lymph tissue; also described as a special type of lymphoma, a tumor arising from any of the cellular elements of lymph nodes.

Named after an English physician, **Thomas Hodgkin** (1798–1866), who described the condition in 1832.

When detected early and treated properly, **Hodgkin's disease** usually can be cured completely today, although formerly it was nearly always fatal. It should also be pointed out that lymphomas other than Hodgkin's disease are generally called **non-Hodgkin's lymphomas**.

Homeric   Large-scale, of heroic dimensions; imposing. Also meaning pertaining to or suggestive of Homer or his works.

From the name of **Homer**, the great Greek epic poet, author of the **Iliad** and the **Odyssey** (both of which see), about whom nothing is known for certain, not even his authorship of the two **Homeric** epics.

Almost any action or trait can be magnified by referring to it as Homeric. Thus, the phrase **Homeric laughter** is taken to mean loud, hearty laughter, worthy of the gods.

Hooke's law   The physical law stating that the amount a spring stretches is directly proportional to the force stretching it; in high school physics classes (c.1936), given as *Within the elastic limit, strain is proportional to stress.*

Named after **Robert Hooke** (1635–1703), an English physicist and chemist, who first formulated this law. It is interesting to note that when Hooke first enunciated it, in 1676, he expressed it as a Latin anagram, *ceiiinosssttuv*, which was deciphered two years later as the Latin *Ut tensio sic vis.* This translates in Hooke's own words as "The Power of any Spring is in the same proportion with the Tension Thereof." A closer translation in high school English is "As the tension, so the force."

A word must be said about Hooke's coded message above, called an *anagram* by science historians. They report that scientists of time past were interested in protecting their discoveries against conflicting announcements by competitors. By embedding a discovery in an anagram—*anagrammatizing* it—they would gain time needed to thwart the claims of other scientists. Even Galileo is known to have done this.

Hooke was a brilliant scientist who unfortunately was inclined to think he was even better than **Newton** (which see). His claims to have anticipated Isaac Newton as well as other insulting taunts he came up with are considered by some to have contributed to Newton's nervous breakdown. Others say Newton was hit on the head by apples too often while not wearing a helmet.

The main practical result of Hooke's investigation of springs was the development of the spring-driven balance that powered wristwatches until Timex came along with battery-powered, quartz-timed watches. But Hooke had actually invented the balance spring almost twenty years before he announced his famous law, and it is believed he expressed it as an anagram as a means of guaranteeing his priority over Newton and other possible contenders for the invention.

It is also thought that Hooke discovered his famous law way back, c.1650, when he was developing the balance spring.

Hoyle.   See **according to Hoyle**.

I

ignoramus   An utterly ignorant person.

From **Ignoramus**, the name of an ignorant lawyer in the play *Ignoramus* (1615) by G. Ruggle, an English playwright about whom little is known. As you might expect, the play exposes the ignorance of lawyers.

If you recall your Latin, *ignoramus* means "we do not know," in legal parlance it is taken as "we take no notice of it." Thus, a grand jury once might have returned a finding of *Ignoramus* in rejecting an indictment.

Modern grand juries rejecting an indictment use the words "no bill" or "not found" or "not a true bill." Anything to avoid writing "ignoramus" on the back of an indictment, since the public often construed the word as an admission that the grand jury was stupid.

What grand jury would want to admit that?

Iliad   A long story or account; a long series of disasters. Also, a poem describing martial exploits.

From the title of Homer's **Iliad**, his great epic—and bloody—poem of the siege of Troy, also known as Ilium. The poem focuses on events of a few days toward the end of the Trojan War, particularly the withdrawal of Achilles (see **Achilles heel**) from the action and the catastrophic effect his withdrawal had on the outcome of the Greek campaign. (See **Trojan**.)

Ishmael   An outcast; a person at war with society.

From **Ishmael**, in Genesis the son of Abraham and his Egyptian concubine Hagar, an arrangement Abraham's wife, Sarah, consented to because she was barren and any progeny resulting from the arrangement would be considered hers.

Before Ishmael was born, however, Sarah and Hagar had a falling-out, proving that families—extended or otherwise—are not always easy to manage. The result was that Hagar was sent off to the desert to have her baby. Mother and son might have starved and died there had it not been for the happy intervention of an angel.

Now, it was prophesied of Ishmael in Genesis that "he will be a wild man; his hand will be against every man, and every man's hand against him." Whence the definition of Ishmael as an outcast, a person at war with society. But it was also prophesied that Sarah would bear a child, and so—even though Abraham and Sarah were thought too old to produce children—Isaac was born, making Ishmael a half brother of Isaac.

In time Ishmael became a famous archer and the father of twelve sons—the Arab peoples are said to be their descendants. Notwithstanding, the name Ishmael, in Hebrew meaning "God will hear," continues in English to have pejorative meanings.

Perhaps this encouraged Herman Melville in his great novel *Moby-Dick* (1851) to use Ishmael as the assumed name—"Call me Ishmael"—of the novel's narrator.

J

jackanapes An insolent fellow, a whippersnapper; an impudent child. Perhaps from **Jack Napes**, nickname of **William de la Pole, Duke of Suffolk** (1396–1450), whose badge was an ape's clog and chain, a clog being a block of wood intended to hamper an animal's movement.

It is worth pointing out that **jackanapes** once had the meaning, now archaic, of ape or monkey.

But back to the Duke. He served his government from 1445 on but made such a mess that he was slated to be banished to Flanders, across the English Channel. Banishment became moot when the ship carrying him was intercepted off Dover and the duke was beheaded.

Left behind is the word **jackanapes** with its various meanings. And if by chance you do not see that Jack Napes can lead to jackanapes, try pronouncing Jack Napes as though it were spelled Jacken Apes.

Jacob's ladder On ships, a rope or chain ladder with wooden or metal rungs.

From **Jacob's ladder** in Genesis, a ladder seen in a dream by Jacob, reaching from earth to heaven. Jacob saw angels going up and down the ladder.

Various plants of the phlox family are called **Jacob's-ladder** because their flowers and leaflets have a ladderlike arrangement.

jacquard   Also given as **Jacquard loom**, a loom for weaving an elaborately patterned fabric, called **jacquard**.

From the name of its inventor, **Joseph Marie Jacquard** (1752–1834), a French silk weaver. It is interesting to note that M. Jacquard was not popular with experienced silk weavers, who were accustomed to spending many hours at their looms on a length of fabric that an inexperienced workman with a Jacquard loom could produce in much less time. Vital to this new weaving technique were the so-called **Jacquard cards**, a series of perforated cards fitted to a loom to guide the weaving. (These were the direct progenitors of the punched cards used in computers before about 1970.)

The experienced weavers could easily see their jobs vanishing into thin air because of this technological advance. It is said that M. Jacquard faced such hostility that on one occasion he narrowly escaped with his life. (Does this sound familiar?)

At approximately the same time, English workers were also unhappy with what they perceived as occupational displacement. (See **Luddite**.)

Nothing like downsizing to organize labor.

Jacuzzi   A large bath equipped with underwater jets to massage the body.

Named for **Candido Jacuzzi** (1903–1986), an American engineer born in Italy, who invented and manufactured the **Jacuzzi**, protected by trademark.

Mr. Jacuzzi initially wanted to devise a pump that would produce a whirlpool effect in a bath in order to provide his arthritic infant son with the benefits of hydrotherapy.

Search for a way to help a child and stumble upon a million-dollar idea. Talk about serendipity.

Jehu   A driver, especially one who burns up the road; also, a cab driver.

From the name of **Jehu** in 2 Kings, who was famous for driving his chariot at a furious pace. In a scene described therein, Jehu is spotted from afar when he and his fellow charioteers set out across the Plain of Jezreel—today in northern Israel—to take their king by surprise and "depose" him, meaning assassinate him. At any rate, they accomplished their mission and, by the by, killed more than two hundred others. (See **Jezebel**.)

We remember Jehu not as a regicide but as a reckless driver.

Jekyll and Hyde   A person in whom two personalities alternate, one good and the other bad.

From the names of the protagonist in *The Strange Case of Dr. Jekyll and Mr. Hyde* (1886), by Robert Louis Balfour Stevenson (1850–1894). **Dr. Jekyll**, a physician, is a generous man who is concerned with problems of good and evil and ponders the possibility of separating good and evil into two distinct personalities. He succeeds in accomplishing this, with the result that the demonic **Mr. Hyde** gets all the latent evil inherent in Dr. Jekyll.

Everything goes downhill from then on, as every moviegoer and a few modern readers know.

jeremiad   A lamentation or mournful complaint about one's troubles.

From the name of **Jeremiah** in the Old Testament. Jeremiah (c.650–c.585 B.C.) was a major prophet of the Hebrews who witnessed the conquest of his country first by Egypt and then by Babylon, and witnessed the destruction of Jerusalem.

Thus, to no one's surprise, his prophecies and his reflections on events of his time were unrelentingly dire, giving English the splendid word **jeremiad**.

jeroboam.   See **rehoboam** and **Methuselah**.

Jezebel   Also given as **jezebel**, a profligate, shameless woman; a prostitute.

From **Jezebel**, in 1 and 2 Kings a woman who was said to have painted her face—not half the condemnation today that it was in biblical times.

But there was more to her story. Elijah decided she had introduced the worship of Baal into Israel, and **Jehu** (which see) ordered her killed after he triumphed over King Ahab, Jezebel's husband.

How did Jehu have her killed? She was thrown from the window of the tower from which she had watched Jehu's chariots approaching. When it was time to bury her, the grave diggers found that wild dogs had been at her carcass. All they found were her skull, feet, and the palms of her hands.

Maybe painting your face is not such a good idea after all.

Job's comforter   A person who magnifies—whether unwittingly or intentionally—the distress of a person he or she is supposed to be comforting.

From the name of **Job**, the central figure in an Old Testament parable of the righteous sufferer. Job, a wealthy man, has his piety tested by undeserved misfortunes that are brought on him. Despite his bitter lamentations in the face of a multitude of troubles, Job remains steadfastly confident in the goodness of God. That's the good part of the story.

The bad part is that during Job's ordeal, three friends—**Job's comforters**—come to console him, but say not a word for three days. Scarcely the way to help a friend.

Maybe they were hoping he'd work out his own problems, or maybe they were practicing client-centered psychotherapy. But couldn't they at least have told him a few jokes?

John Hancock   A person's signature.

From the name of **John Hancock** (1737–1793), an American Revolutionary statesman who was the first person to sign his name to the Declaration of Independence, an act of defiance not without some risk to the signer. Hancock also had the advantage of an especially large and clear signature, forcing others to write around his name.

Some speakers use **John Henry** in the same way that most of us use John Hancock, for example, "Just put your John Henry right here." John Henry, hero of a cycle of tall tales and ballads that originated in the nineteenth century, was a powerful man who could work harder and faster than most. There is no evidence, however, that he ever signed his name, so why John Henry would be used to mean a signature is not clear.

A pretty good guess is that persons who remember the name John Henry from folk songs confuse it with the name John Hancock, which they do not know. Except, perhaps, as the name of an insurance company.

Jonah   A person believed to bring bad luck.

From the name of **Jonah** in the book of the Old Testament that bears his name. His well-known story begins with God's telling him to go to Nineveh, the ancient capital of Assyria, today in northern Iraq, to preach repentance for its great evil. He disobeys God and boards a ship bound elsewhere.

A mistake. When a storm comes up—brought on by you know who—and threatening the lives of everyone aboard, Jonah is thrown overboard by the crew, to whom he has confessed his disobedience of God's order. Behold, Jonah is swallowed by a great fish. Not to worry. During the three days Jonah spends in the belly of the fish, he prays continually. With the result that Jonah is vomited up by the fish and lands unharmed on dry land. He then proceeds to Nineveh to fulfill the mission God had given him. And Nineveh does some big-time repenting.

joule   The basic unit of energy in the International System of Units.

The **joule** replaces not only the *erg*, but also the *calorie*, the *foot-pound*, and the *Btu*, the British thermal unit. Notice that some of these units are associated with work, some with heat, and one—the calorie beloved of the dieter, which is 1/100 the calorie of the engineer—with food energy.

It is fitting, then, that the joule was named in honor of the English physicist **James Prescott Joule** (1818–1889). Considered one of the great experimental scientists of the nineteenth century, he was the first to demonstrate accurately that every form of mechanical energy turns into heat, and that heat and work are both to be treated as forms of energy.

For the record, the joule is the same as the work done when a force of 1 newton produces a movement of 1 meter, which translates to 1/1,356 of a foot-pound, while a Btu is 1,055 joules.

Although Joule also worked as a brewer all through his life—surely a tribute to the quality of the British brew—he was from the beginning obsessed with careful measurement and with the idea that heat and energy were exactly equivalent. Even on his honeymoon he used a specially designed thermometer to check the water going over the scenic falls he and his bride were visiting. He wanted to show that the water must gain in heat to make up for the energy it lost in falling.

Calling to mind the observation that Niagara Falls is the American bride's second greatest disappointment.

Judas   An infamous traitor who will stop at nothing; a betrayer of his friends.

From the name of **Judas Iscariot**, in Mark the disciple who betrayed his friend Jesus to the chief priests for thirty pieces of silver. While the priests were watching, Judas signaled his betrayal by kissing Jesus' cheek. This act gives us the expressions **Judas kiss**, meaning a show of courtesy or kindness that masks deceit, and **Judas hole**, meaning a peephole.

No one seems to have anything good to say about Judas, even though he did the right thing when he saw that Jesus had been condemned because of Judas' act of betrayal. He hanged himself.

Julian calendar. See **Gregorian calendar**.

Juliet cap A skullcap, often decorated with pearls, worn by a bride.

From the name of **Juliet**, the tragic heroine of Shakespeare's *Romeo and Juliet*. Actresses playing the role of Juliet on the stage often wear a **Juliet cap** as part of their costume.

Junoesque Resembling Juno in stately beauty.

From the name of **Juno**, in Roman mythology the wife of Jupiter, the god of all gods, and the queen of heaven, protector of women and goddess of marriage.

Painters and sculptors represent Juno as a beautiful woman of **Junoesque**, that is, ample, proportions. As older people among us are wont to say, Juno is full-figured.

No half-starved supermodel, Juno.

Kafkaesque   An adjective describing a situation or literary work that evokes an uneasy response.

From the name of **Franz Kafka** (1883–1924), an Austrian novelist whose work centers on the problems of existence of modern man and portrays an enigmatic reality. As he described it, the individual person is anxious, lonely, perplexed, and tormented.

A **Kafkaesque world**, thus, is marked by paradox, futility, and grotesque unreality—all delineated by Kafka in a literary style that is remarkably precise and clear.

Kelvin scale   An absolute scale of temperature, beginning with absolute zero—determined to be the coldest possible temperature.

The basic unit of temperature in the International System of Units is the **degree kelvin**, which is measured on the **Kelvin scale**.

Named after **William Thomson, 1st Baron Kelvin** (1824–1907), who proposed the absolute temperature scale in 1848. In this scale, a degree kelvin—by International System diktat uncapitalized in this usage—is identical with a degree Celsius (See **Celsius scale**).

So what is the difference between the Kelvin scale and the Celsius scale? Kelvin has no negative temperatures. Absolute zero on the Celsius scale would be given as –273.15°C, on the Fahrenheit scale as –459.7°F. And on the Kelvin scale? 0K (zero K). That's all.

Notice the absence of a degree symbol with K. Another convention established by the International System gurus.

But how was it that William Thomson—not Lord Kelvin until 1892—established his absolute zero? He proposed that since heat results from the motion of molecules, and since motion appears to stop at about –273°C, that temperature could be used as a basis of an absolute temperature scale.

For some time scientists referred to Thomson's proposed absolute scale as the Absolute scale, but eventually it was renamed in Thomson's honor. When Thomson was created 1st Baron Kelvin in 1892, all the scientific work he had conducted in the first sixty-eight years of his life was from then on reattributed to Lord Kelvin.

Perhaps in consideration for his entire body of work—including collaboration in establishing the second law of thermodynamics and invention of many useful scientific instruments—Lord Kelvin is buried in Westminster Abbey beside Sir Isaac Newton.

People on this side of the Atlantic seeking to honor the great man named a line of refrigerators the **Kelvinator**.

Keynesian   As an adjective, pertaining to economic theories or policies regarding governmental control of an economy through taxes and money supply. As a noun, a person who subscribes to **Keynesian** theory.

From the name of **John Maynard, 1st Baron Keynes** (1883–1946), an influential English economist and pioneer of the theory of full employment. Keynes argued that full employment and control of inflation are achievable through regulation of interest rates, tax rates, and public expenditures.

In the final years of his life, Keynes played a leading role in the Bretton Woods Conference, which led to establishment of the International Monetary Fund and the World Bank.

Klein bottle   In mathematics, a closed surface that has only one side, which may be thought of as either the outside or inside. It is formed by passing the neck of a bottle through the side of the bottle to join a hole in the base of the bottle.

Named for its inventor, the great German geometrician and algebraist **Felix Klein** (1849–1925). Klein is best known today for proposing that geometry be built on a foundation of group theory, a goal to which he was one of the main contributors.

The **Klein bottle** is closely related to the **Möbius strip** (which see). Indeed, it can be formed by gluing two Möbius strips together at their edges, provided that the two Möbius strips are made so that both strips have half twists in opposite directions. The result is that the strips are mirror images of each other.

The Klein bottle itself has no edge at all. In practice, however, the Möbius strips must pass through each other to make it possible to glue their edges together, and this can only be accomplished in four or more dimensions.

Imagine an ant crawling into the apparent opening at the larger end of a Klein bottle and moving along the tube until it finds itself back where it started.

And we don't have to concern ourselves with the poor befuddled ant.

klieg light The brilliant light often used to illuminate scenes for moviemaking; also used to make daylight scenes brighter.

Named for its inventors, two German-born American brothers who were lighting engineers and businessmen: **John H. Kliegl** (1869–1959) and **Anton T. Kliegl** (1872–1927). In 1896, they organized the Kliegl Brothers Universal Electric Stage Lighting Company.

A **klieg light** is a variety of carbon-arc light, the type of electric lamp that preceded the incandescent lightbulb. The light is produced by a continuing spark, called an arc, between two carbon rods connected to a powerful electric current. The bright light comes from the carbon that is on the receiving end of the arc, which glows with brilliance as it is gradually vaporized. The same brilliant light can be seen in arc welding, which uses a similar arc to melt metal.

knickerbockers Usually given as **knickers**, loose-fitting trousers gathered at the knees; formerly worn only by boys—now, goodness knows, by girls as well.

From the name of **Diedrich Knickerbocker**, the fictitious author of Washington Irving's *A History of New York* (1809), a send-up of the old Dutch settlers of New York, back when real men wore **knicker-**

bockers. Irving's full title for the book is an indication of its tone: *A History of New York from the Beginning of the World to the End of the Dutch Dynasty*.

Maybe the city would have turned out better if the Dutch hadn't lost their grip.

Köchel listing   Also given as **Köchel number**, the chronological number of a Mozart composition, assigned in a catalog of the composer's music.

From the name of the original cataloguer, **Ludwig Ritter von Köchel** (1800–1877), an Austrian musicologist. While the catalog has been revised since Köchel's time to reflect new information and new discoveries, Köchel's name has not been displaced, and we are reminded of him each time we see the abbreviation *K* before a Köchel number.

L

laconic As an adjective, meaning brief, concise; saying much in few words. And from it the noun **laconism**, meaning brevity; also, an instance of laconic speech.

From the Latin name *Laconicus*, translated as **Laconian**, pertaining to ancient Laconia in southern Greece, capital Sparta (see **Spartan**), and to its people. We can claim the name of this people as progenitor of the English word **laconic**.

The Laconians, and therefore the Spartans, were known for their terseness, best exemplified by an incident in the career of Philip of Macedon (fourth century B.C.), who wrote threateningly to the magistrates of Sparta: "If I enter Laconia, I will level Lacedaemon [Sparta] to the ground." The magistrates' reply was given in one word: "If."

But other peoples are also known to prefer brevity under the correct circumstances. For example, a U.S. Army general, Anthony McAuliffe (1898–1975), almost matched the Spartan "If" in brevity when he replied to a German commander's demand that he surrender his forces at Bastogne, in World War II. As reported in the press—to the delectation of all Americans—the message he sent in reply to the German commander consisted of one word: "Nuts."

It has reliably been reported, however, that in fact McAuliffe sent a two-word message. The first word was unprintable, and the second was *you*.

Lady Bountiful   A woman of exemplary generosity.

From **Lady Bountiful**, a character in *The Beaux' Stratagem* (1706), a play written by the Irish playwright George Farquhar (c.1677–1707). (See also **boniface**.)

Lady Bountiful's hobby, would you believe it, is tending the sick. She takes Thomas Aimwell, who is broke and feigning illness, into her home to recuperate, and he falls in love with the generous woman's daughter and marries her.

Things were a lot simpler in the old days, weren't they?

Lamarckian evolution   The theory that a trait acquired by a parent as a result of experience in life can be inherited by a child.

The classic example given to illustrate **Lamarckian evolution** is the idea, mistaken, that the giraffe developed a long neck as a result of stretching to reach leaves high in trees.

From the name of **Jean Baptiste Pierre Antoine de Monet, Chevalier de Lamarck** (1744–1829), a French naturalist. In his *Philosophie zoologique*, published in 1809, he advanced the idea that acquired characters are inherited by future generations. Although he was and is considered incorrect in his thinking, he is said to have facilitated acceptance of the generally believed theory of evolution.

This theory is of course Darwinian evolution, in which, for example, the giraffe's neck has grown long because giraffes with longer necks lived longer and healthier lives than their short-necked pals. The result is that long-neckers produced more offspring than short-neckers, and long necks came to prevail as generation succeeded generation.

Of greatest interest in Lamarck v. Darwin—fully decided after generations of dispute—is that Lamarck was not the first to advance the idea of inheritance of acquired characteristics. Actually, his idea was commonly accepted throughout most of history. Lamarck's name became associated with the idea for two reasons: originally because he was the first to construct a theory of evolution of species based on inheritance of acquired characteristics; then because Darwin and followers of Darwin chose to argue specifically against Lamarck's argument.

Darwin's supporters might have chosen instead to conduct their argument against a theory of inheritance of acquired characteristics advanced by Charles Darwin's physician grandfather. In that case, Darwin v. Darwin might have sounded like a case headed for divorce court, or it might have been called Charles Darwin (1809–1882) v. Erasmus Darwin (1731–1802).

In either case it would have been messy for science historians.

lazar   A poor person infected with a loathsome disease, especially leprosy.

From the name of **Lazarus** in Luke. Lazarus was the diseased beggar—a **lazar**—in the parable of the rich man and the beggar. Lazarus is laid daily at the gate of the rich man's home, and he is not taken in by that man. As you might expect, when Lazarus dies, he is carried to **Abraham's bosom** (which see).

And when the rich man dies, he is tormented in Hades.

Have you made a charitable donation lately?

Lecher wires   A pair of parallel taut wires for measuring the frequency of a high-frequency electric oscillation by means of a sliding conductor so placed that it can bridge the wires.

Named after **Ernst Lecher** (1856–1926), an Austrian physicist, whose fascinating surname guaranteed his **Lecher wires** a place in this book.

By no means should it be suspected that it was his name that gave rise to the words *lecherous* and *lechery*.

leishmaniasis   A tropical and subtropical disease known also as sand-fly fever, kala-azar, Oriental sore, Aleppos button, Delhi boil, and chiclero ulcer.

From *Leishmania*, the name of the genus of parasites that cause **leishmaniasis**. The genus was named for **Sir William Boog Leishman** (1865–1926), a Scottish bacteriologist who was the first to identify the parasite that causes the disease.

Note that leishmaniasis was originally a prime suspect in the investigation of the so-called Gulf War syndrome that struck thousands of American soldiers who served in Kuwait or Iraq during the brief United Nations action against Iraq in 1990.

Although leishmaniasis was cleared of suspicion in the search for the troubling syndrome, it remains a significant disease in many parts of the tropics.

Different members of the same family of parasites, all transmitted to humans by the bites of sand flies, cause a variety of symptoms, one affecting the skin, another the nose and mouth, and yet another the internal organs, particularly the spleen.

In case you wonder, the parasites are related to the trypanosomes that cause African sleeping sickness and **Chagas' disease** (which see).

leotard   A skintight one-piece garment worn by ballet dancers, trapeze artists, exercise fanatics, and others.

From the name of **Jules Léotard** (1830–1870), a French trapeze artist.

Levi's   Also given as **Levis**, a brand of blue jeans or overalls reinforced with rivets, protected by trademark.

From the name of the clothing manufacturer **Levi Strauss** (1829?–1902), who was born in Germany and immigrated to the United States early in life. He left his home in New York City in 1850 for California, where the great gold rush was in progress. At first he sold tent canvas to the gold prospectors, but soon established the firm of Levi Strauss & Co. in San Francisco to manufacture the sturdy jeans that made him rich as well as a household name.

Like Scotch whisky, blue jeans carry a higher price when aged or when represented as aged. The beneficial effect of age on whisky cannot be denied, but what can be said for newly manufactured jeans that are made to appear old?

People will buy anything.

Lewis gun   Also given as the **Lewis machine gun**, a light, air-cooled machine gun with a circular magazine, operated by gas from its firing.

From the name of its American inventor, **Isaac Newton Lewis** (1858–1931), an artillery officer in the U.S. Army. The **Lewis gun** was adopted by the army in 1902, and when Lewis retired from military service in 1913, he went to Europe and manufactured his gun in Belgium and England.

Munitions Dealers Without Borders?

lewisite   A term of interest because it has two distinct meanings: an obscure mineral and an artificial blister gas developed in 1918, near the end of World War I.

The mineral **lewisite**, described as yellow to yellowish brown in color, was named in honor of an English mineralogist, **William J. Lewis** (1847–1926), about whom little is known except that he encouraged the study of mineralogy.

Also given as **Lewisite**, the blister gas **lewisite** was named for its inventor, **Winford Lee Lewis** (1878–1943), a U.S. chemist who served as a captain in the U.S. Army Chemical Warfare Service in World War I.

The gas, known to raise painful blisters, causes serious damage to eyes and lungs. It must be added that it has not thus far been used in anger, although many veterans of World War I will say otherwise.

However, if you hear that an army is using lewisite, you can be sure nobody is spreading little yellow minerals over a battlefield.

lindy hop   Also given as the **lindy** and the **Lindy Hop**, a popular and energetic jitterbug dance that originated in New York's Harlem during the Great Depression and is still revived from time to time.

When the **lindy hop** was at its height of popularity, it was something to behold. The lindy was performed by energetic young couples, with the male partner holding the female in one or both of his arms, or at least holding one of her hands while they danced—a dance posture rarely seen in recent years.

Named for no apparent reason after **Lindy**, full name **Charles Augustus Lindbergh** (1902–1974), the daring young U.S. aviator, often called Lucky Lindy. He flew solo across the Atlantic in his *Spirit of St. Louis* Ryan monoplane, from New York to Paris in thirty-three and one-half hours in May 1927.

And captured the hearts of people everywhere.

Linnaean   Also given as **Linnean**, meaning of or pertaining to **Linnaeus**, the great taxonomist; also, pertaining to the system of botanical classification he established.

From **Carolus Linnaeus**, the Latinized name of the Swedish naturalist and physician **Carl von Linné** (1707–1778), whose interest in botany led to his pioneering work in botanical classification.

The **Linnaean species** are those assigned a binomial scientific name by Linnaeus himself in various scientific publications from 1735 on. The efforts of Linnaeus resulted in the establishment of binomial nomenclature—genus name followed by species name—as the official system of nomenclature for all plants and animals. Names not based on this system are called *common names*.

The official, or Linnaean, name for the lion, for example, is *Felis leo*, and lion is its common name.

load line. See **Plimsoll line.**

Lothario A lady-killer, a rake; a man who obsessively seduces and deceives women.

From the name of a young libertine in *The Fair Penitent* (1703), a tragedy by Nicholas Rowe (1674–1718), an English poet and playwright. Rowe was England's poet laureate from 1715 to 1718, but his character **Lothario**, a fashionable rake, lives on as an English word, while Rowe and his plays are all but forgotten.

All the world loves a lover. Even a promiscuous one—see also **Casanova**, another big-time lover.

Lucullan Said especially of banquets, parties, and the like, also given as **Lucullian**, meaning lavish, exceptionally luxurious, sumptuous.

Named after **Lucius Licinius Lucullus** (c.110–57 B.C.), a Roman general and epicure.

Lucullus managed to acquire enormous wealth during his military career and, after retirement, lived the high life so openly that his name became synonymous with fine food and drink.

A frequently repeated story has it that Lucullus, one day while an outstanding supper was being prepared for him, was asked who the guests were to be at his table. He replied, "Lucullus will sup tonight with Lucullus." So English adopted **Lucullus sups with Lucullus** as an unflattering remark that is employed to denigrate a glutton who enjoys sitting alone and stuffing himself.

In fairness to Lucullus, in addition to being known for throwing spectacular banquets, he was also a patron of artists and writers.

But the English adjective **Lucullan** is reserved today for describing the indulgences of the rich and famous. As long as they are free of digestive problems.

Luddite A person who destroys someone's manufacturing machinery in an attempt to halt production; also, a person who is opposed to change, especially change stemming from advances in technology.

The **Luddites** were members of bands of English workers who, from 1811 to 1816, organized riots for destroying machinery, which they saw as depriving them of employment. Leaders of the bands were referred to as **Captain Ludd**—perhaps an entirely imaginary figure— and band members called themselves Luddites. (See also **jacquard**.)

A possible source of **Luddite** is the name of an Englishman, **Ned Ludd** or **Lud**. Ludd is said to have been a farm laborer of weak intellect who lived about 1779 in Leicestershire, a center of the hosiery industry in England. He is reported to have broken into a neighbor's house and destroyed two stocking frames, machines used for making hosiery.

We all know people who see their chances of finding a good job and living the good life slipping away. They long for the good old days—however mistakenly they construe them—and may identify the dizzying pace of technological change as the root cause of their employment problems. They may even contemplate, ever so fleetingly, the possibility of destroying all electronic equipment. Such persons may be thought of as **Luddites**, even though they never intend to act out their destructive impulses.

lynch law   Mob law; especially the infliction of punishment, usually death, by an illegal, self-constituted court.

From the name of **Captain William Lynch** (1742–1820), a magistrate of Virginia, who wrote the so-called **Lynch laws**. These allowed the organizing of self-created judicial tribunals, at about the time of America's declaration of independence from England.

As time went by, particularly in frontier regions, where courts and judges usually were not to be found, **lynch law** became the order of the day, and **lynch mobs** did not conduct any kind of trial at all.

Soon enough the phrase **Judge Lynch** became the personification of hanging or of the rope used in the procedure.

M

macadam   A paving material of broken stone of nearly uniform size, crushed or rolled into position; later, such material improved by adding tar or hot asphalt to the stone.

From the name of **John Loudon McAdam** (1756–1836), a Scottish inventor and engineer, who lived in New York City from 1770 to 1783. While there he made his fortune and, after his return to Scotland, began experimenting with various means of road building, and succeeded in devising the scheme that took its name from McAdam, **macadam**.

Today it might be named potholing.

macadamia   An evergreen tree native to Australia; **macadamia nut** or **macadamia**, the edible seed of this tree, said to have been introduced to Hawaii at the end of the nineteenth century.

Named after **John Macadam** (1827–1865), an Australian chemist, who was secretary of the Philosophical Institute of Victoria, in southeast Australia.

Tourists still prefer Hawaii's macadamia nuts to its less expensive fresh pineapples.

McCarthyism   The practice of openly accusing political or ideological opponents of disloyalty—usually without justification—and especially accusing them of membership in the U.S. Communist Party.

From the name of **Joseph Raymond McCarthy** (1909–1957), a Republican senator from Wisconsin who struck fear in the hearts of State Department employees with irresponsible charges that the department was riddled with Communist spies. When McCarthy conducted public hearings on alleged subversion of the U.S. Army, television coverage of the proceedings brought him into disfavor with many citizens, and the U.S. Senate formally censured him.

His failed efforts still render **McCarthyism** synonymous with the use of unsubstantiated charges to destroy reputations. A **McCarthyite** is a person who endorses the despicable practices that were espoused by the late senator.

Which does not mean that some politicians and journalists have given up intimidation and destruction of reputations by innuendo, lying, and exaggeration. After all, what's life without the occasional well-organized *ad hominem* attack?

Machiavellian   Also given as **machiavellian**, meaning deceitful; subtly or unscrupulously cunning, dishonest, perfidious.

All this from the name of **Niccolò Machiavelli** (1469–1527), an Italian statesman, political philosopher, and writer. Big Mac is principally known as the author of a book called *Il Principe*, in English *The Prince*. In it, Machiavelli offered practical comments on the relations between a prince and his subjects, suggesting, among other things, that deceit and terrorism were justifiable means of achieving a prosperous and peaceful nation.

It was this approach to government that made *The Prince* a practical textbook for dictators and made the adjective **Machiavellian** synonymous with deceitful and perfidious.

Mach number   Also given as **mach number**, a number indicating the ratio of the speed of an object to the speed of sound in the medium through which the object is moving.

Thus, the speed of sound at a given altitude, temperature, and humidity is called Mach 1, while twice that speed is Mach 2, and so on. Decimals are usually used to express speeds that are not exact multiples, so Mach 0.25 is one-fourth the speed of sound under the given conditions, while Mach 2.5 is two and a half times the speed of sound.

From the name of an Austrian physicist and philosopher, **Ernst Mach** (1838–1916), who conducted experiments on airflow in 1887. These experiments resulted in the recognition of disturbances caused by the interaction of the shock waves of an object moving faster than the speed of sound. Interference waves are still called **Mach waves**.

It was not until about 1925 that the concept of Mach number was introduced in conjunction with the effects of Mach waves on diving airplanes, the first mode of transportation enabling humans to reach speeds high enough to have to reckon with the problem. Mach's findings proved important in the study of projectiles and in aeronautical design.

Mach was also an influential philosopher of science, whose views have influenced virtually everyone since, whether or not they agreed with him. Einstein gave the name **Mach's principle** to the idea that properties of space all derive from the masses embedded in space, and Mach's principle became one of the basic ideas behind the general theory of relativity.

Good company to be in.

mackintosh   Also given as **macintosh**, a raincoat of rubberized cloth; also the cloth itself.

Named after **Charles Macintosh** (1766–1843), a Scottish manufacturing chemist who patented a method of waterproofing garments that had been developed by James Syme (1799–1870), a Scottish surgeon. Macintosh went on to manufacture garments that came to bear his name.

Syme was, of course, overlooked in the coining of **mackintosh**.

Maecenas   A generous patron or supporter, especially of art or literature.

Named after a Roman statesman, **Gaius Cilnius Maecenas** (died 8 B.C.), a man renowned for his luxurious habits and as a patron of the arts because he freely entertained and subsidized poets and writers, among them Horace and Virgil.

Of course, if you persist in sending small annual contributions to National Public Radio, you'll never make it as a **Maecenas**. But that doesn't mean you ought to forgo giving.

Mae West   An inflatable life jacket, used especially by sailors and by airmen flying over open water.

Named after **Mae West** (1893–1980), the playwright and Hollywood movie actress, whose ample bust bore a fancied resemblance to a fully inflated life jacket.

West was known for her steamy innuendos, delivered in a gum-chewing manner that can well be described as arch self-caricature.

Magellanic clouds   Two bright patches in the sky of the Southern Hemisphere that are actually companion galaxies to the Milky Way galaxy, whose center is our Sun. One is called the **Large Magellanic Cloud**, and the other is the **Small Magellanic Cloud**.

Named after the Portuguese navigator **Ferdinand Magellan** (c.1480–1521). The bright patches of light were first observed by his crew as his ships passed around South America in a historic circumnavigation of the globe.

For the next four hundred years no one knew exactly what the bright patches were, although with the help of good telescopes it was clear that the clouds contained a very large number of stars. Beginning in 1912, the U.S. astronomer Henrietta Swan Leavitt (1868–1921) began a study of the **Magellanic clouds** that revealed them to be too far away from Earth to be a part of the Milky Way galaxy. Later it was established that the Magellanic clouds are small companion galaxies that orbit our much larger galaxy.

The Large Magellanic Cloud is about one three-hundredth the size of the Milky Way. It is about 160,000 light-years away from the Milky Way at present, but will fall into the Milky Way some ten billion years from now. The Small Magellanic Cloud is about a hundred times smaller than the Large Magellanic Cloud and is still farther away.

Comforting news.

Maginot line   A system of fortifications built before World War II by France along its eastern border as part of its preparation against attack by Germany. Also, any elaborate line of defense.

Named after **André Maginot** (1877–1932), the French minister of war (1922–1924 and 1926–1931), who pursued a policy of military preparedness. The **Maginot line**, which M. Maginot launched, extended from the Swiss border to Belgium.

When Nazi troops invaded, however, they went through Belgium and into France like a sharp knife through ripe Brie.

The best laid plans . . .

malapropism A ludicrous misuse of a word, especially by confusing the word with another of similar sound.

Named after the character **Mrs. Malaprop**, in *The Rivals* (1775), by the Irish playwright Richard Brinsley Sheridan (1751–1816). It was Mrs. Malaprop who mangled the English language splendidly and gave English the word **malapropism**. Sheridan, of course, created her name from the adverb malapropos, meaning inappropriate, which is itself derived from the French *mal à propos*.

Two of Mrs. Malaprop's typical malapropisms are "headstrong as an *allegory* on the banks of the Nile" and "the very *pineapple* of politeness."

man Friday. See **Friday**.

mansard Also given as **mansard roof**, a type of hip roof that slopes up from the four sides of a building.

Named after the French architect **François Mansard**, also given as **Mansart** (1598–1666), who designed a wing of the Château de Blois, giving it the double-angled high-pitched roof we call a **mansard**.

marcel A noun, also used as an adjective in the phrase **marcel wave**, meaning an artificial wave produced in the hair through use of heated curling tongs. As a verb **marcel** means wave (the hair) in this way.

From the name of **François Marcel Grateau** (1852–1936), the Parisian hairdresser who devised this method. The subsequent introduction of a variety of chemical fixatives has written finis to the use of curling irons, once part of every hairdresser's armamentarium. These irons resembled the cables used by motorists to jump-start a car.

It is conceivable that **marcelling** will return one day, perhaps because the **marceller's** hot irons will be deemed preferable to the chemical sprays used by modern hairdressers, which stiffen the hair objectionably.

And cause distress to grandchildren attempting to kiss Grandma.

March In the modern calendar, the third month of the year.

From Latin *Martius mensis*, literally month of **Mars**, and Mars was the ancient Roman god of war and agriculture.

In Roman times, **March** was the first month of the year and began at the vernal equinox. Thus, it is clear that March was not named for Mars as the Roman god of war (see **martial**), but for Mars as the Roman god of agriculture.

But everything depends on which hat the god was wearing when March first came in like a lion.

Mariotte's law.   See **Boyle's law**.

martial   Of or pertaining to war or battle.

From the name of **Mars**, the Roman god of war. And because war and battle are so much a part of mankind's nature, **martial** has led to **martial arts**, meaning judo and the like; **martial law**, law imposed on a country during wartime, as well as law imposed on a conquered nation by the conquering nation; and **martial music**, music appropriate to warfare and played by military bands.

For another take on an important word related to Mars, see **March**.

martini   A **dry martini**, in the United States also called a **martini**, is a cocktail of gin or vodka and dry vermouth, usually served with a green olive, a cocktail onion, or a twist of lemon peel.

Perhaps derived from the name of **Martini & Rossi**, a long-established company that makes vermouth, both dry and sweet.

Which leads inevitably to consideration of the art of the **martini**. To begin, let it be understood that in the United States there is only the dry martini, which means a cocktail made almost solely with gin or vodka plus a grudging drop or two of vermouth. The olive, onion, or lemon peel is included only to give the drinker something to savor while the next martini is being prepared.

Any drink made with sweet vermouth or a large proportion of dry vermouth is not a true martini.

Be warned: If you order a martini in England, it will be a sweet abomination, consisting of two parts of gin to one part of Messrs. Martini & Rossi's dry vermouth, plus orange bitters.

Stick with a pint of lager.

masochism   In psychiatry, the condition in which sexual gratification depends on the subject's self-inflicted pain and self-humiliation.

From the name of Austrian short-story writer and novelist **Leopold von Sacher-Masoch** (1836–1895), who depicted persons showing this abnormality in many of his novels, including *The Legacy of Cain* (1870–1877) and *False Ermine* (1873). (See also **sadism**.)

Mason-Dixon line   Also called the **Mason and Dixon line**, the boundary between Pennsylvania and Maryland.

Named after two English astronomers, **Charles Mason** (1730–1787) and **Jeremiah Dixon** (died 1777), employed to survey part of the line. The Mason-Dixon line is taken as the historical northern limit of slave-owning states.

Mason and Dixon worked from 1763 to 1767 with the goal of ending an eighty-year-old dispute over the boundary between the two states. Their work was interrupted by local Indians, and it was left to others to complete the survey.

But, in U.S. schools the phrase Mason-Dixon line will always be taught and remembered.

maudlin   Foolishly sentimental, especially because of drunkenness.

From **Mary Magdalene**, the penitent sinner in Luke who is often portrayed with eyes swollen from weeping. If you wonder how English made **maudlin** of **Magdalene**, consider that the latter term made an appearance in Old French as *Madelaine*, pronounced mad-LAYN before going on to its English form, pronounced MAWD-lin.

Repeat the French *Madelaine* and the English maudlin a few times, and you'll get the hang of it.

maverick   A dissenter who stands alone in holding an unorthodox opinion; also, an unbranded calf or yearling.

From the name of **Samuel Augustus Maverick** (1803–1870), a pioneer Texas cattle rancher who, unlike most other ranchers, let his cattle (**mavericks**) run unbranded.

But there was more to Maverick than his ornery refusal to brand his calves. From 1835 on he agitated for independence for Texas from Mexico and served as a member of the convention that established the Republic of Texas in 1836. He held various offices in the state during the years after independence was declared.

Maxim gun   An early self-cocking, single-barreled, water-cooled machine gun.

Named after **Sir Hiram Stevens Maxim** (1840–1916), an inventor born in Maine. In England after 1880, he created the Maxim Gun

Company and perfected his **Maxim gun**. He also invented, among other things, smokeless powder and a flying machine.

Build a successful machine gun and the English will beat a path to your door, knightship in hand.

medusa   The free-swimming form of jellyfish, with a gelatinous body and stinging tentacles. A sessile form, such as a coral or sea anemone, is a polyp.

From the name of **Medusa**, in classical mythology the chief **Gorgon** (which see). The three Gorgons had serpents on their heads instead of hair. While Medusa was mortal, the other two were immortal, and a glance from any of the Gorgons turned their victims to stone.

Medusa was decapitated by a blow from Perseus, who used Medusa's head—it had not lost its terrible ability to turn victims to stone—to rescue **Andromeda** (which see).

Incidentally, in case you think Perseus was a fine fellow, you ought to know that he accidentally killed his grandfather with a discus.

Melba toast.   See **peach Melba**.

Mendelian   As an adjective, meaning of or pertaining to Mendel or his theory of heredity; as a noun, a follower of Mendel.

Named after the Austrian monk **Gregor Johann Mendel** (1822–1884), who was a biologist and botanist. Between 1857 and 1868, Mendel taught science in a small town in what was then part of Austrian Silesia. It was there he conducted the pea experiments that led to his discoveries in genetics.

Mendel was lucky not only in his choice of peas for study—peas have a simple inheritance pattern—but also in his choice of traits in peas, which for the most part are on separate chromosomes, minimizing complications.

There are some who think Mendel had an additional advantage, which was the knack of jiggering his data if they did not match his theory. In any case, he had to stop his work in about 1868 because he not only had been appointed abbot of his Augustinian cloister but also had gained weight and could not bend to garden.

Mendel discovered the laws of genetics that concern inheritance of dominant and recessive traits, aspects of heredity that are labeled **Mendelian**. For example, consider the calculation that there is a certain chance that the offspring of pea plants with a dominant gene for red flowers and a recessive gene for white flowers will have all red flowers in the first generation but a one-in-four chance of having white flowers in the second generation. Mendel was employing **Mendelian genetics** to explain a **Mendelian ratio**.

At any rate, even though Mendel in his lifetime was able to publish his findings only in a local science journal, in 1900 three different biologists came across his report and proclaimed him correct in his explanation of heredity.

Proving that word got around even before the advent of the Internet.

mentor   An experienced and trusted advisor, a guide; an influential senior sponsor. Also used as a verb, meaning act as **mentor** to (someone).

From the name of **Mentor**, in the *Odyssey* an old man who was a loyal advisor of Odysseus, entrusted with the care of Telemachus, the only son of Odysseus, when Odysseus left to fight in the Trojan War. As things turned out, Telemachus returned home when his father returned after his twenty-year absence. When Telemachus found Odysseus, he helped him kill the suitors of Penelope, his mother and the wife of Odysseus.

Which in some way proves the value of proper **mentoring**.

Mercator projection   In cartography, Mercator's representation on a plane surface of the curved surface of the earth.

Named for **Gerardus Mercator**, the Latinized name of the Flemish geographer **Gerhard Kremer** (1512–1594), inventor of a system of map projection in which the globe is projected onto a cylinder. The meridians of longitude are all straight lines perpendicular to the equator, and the parallels of latitude are all straight lines parallel with the equator.

In studying a map of the earth, few students can appreciate the task facing the geographer who made the map. Mathematicians have proved that it is impossible to make a map of a sphere on a flat surface that preserves both shapes and distances. So mapmakers are forced to make choices, and unwanted distortions are inevitable.

The method used by Mercator preserves directions exactly, so it is good for navigation along straight lines. Shapes are also preserved, but size and distance are lost. Thus, in the **Mercator projection**, regions near the poles, such as Greenland, appear to be much larger than they should, while regions toward the equator, such as Brazil, are unrealistically small.

Mercator's work survives to this day, and schoolchildren of an earlier generation knew that the British Empire was almost everywhere on earth and was colored pink. (See also **atlas**.)

mercerization   Treatment of cotton to make it smooth and silky.

In **mercerization**, cotton yarn, cloth, or thread is treated with caustic soda (sodium hydroxide), giving it a shiny finish resembling that of silk.

Named by its inventor, **John Mercer** (1791–1866), an English textile manufacturer and self-educated dye chemist. Mercer made other important discoveries connected with dyeing and calico printing, but it was the process of **mercerizing** that made his name a household word.

Although not heard in many households today.

mercurial   Said of a person, meaning volatile; quick-witted. Of an alloy, of or containing mercury.

From Latin *mercurialis*, meaning of or pertaining to the god or planet **Mercury**. The god Mercury was the son of Jupiter, god of gods, whom he served as messenger.

See also **Galilean satellites** and **volcano**.

mesmerism   Hypnotism; a hypnotic state.

Named after **Franz** or **Friedrich Anton Mesmer** (1734–1815), an Austrian physician who founded **mesmerism**, based on what he said was an extraordinary power he called "animal magnetism." In Paris, he employed this so-called power to cure diseases at séances.

When Mesmer was denounced as an impostor by a learned group that investigated his cures, he did what any honorable impostor would do. He skipped town and from then on lived in obscurity in Switzerland. Where he apparently had stashed some money.

While mesmerism belongs to centuries past, the adjective **mesmeric** is still going strong, meaning hypnotic, compelling, fascinating. The verb **mesmerize** means fascinate, spellbind; hypnotize.

But mesmerism has been displaced by hours on end spent on an analyst's couch; eating nothing but you-name-it; pumping iron under the watchful gaze of musclebound personal trainers—and all the rest.

Methuselah   An extremely old man. Also, a very large wine bottle, holding six and a half quarts.

From the patriarch **Methuselah** in Genesis, of whom it was said he lived for 969 years, although Gershwin's "It Ain't Necessarily So" from *Porgy and Bess* (1935) puts his age at 900 years.

And we must not forget that no gal will give in to no man what's 900 years.

Vintners typically have gone to biblical sources in naming the bottles in which their wines are delivered: Think of the **jeroboam** (which see), the **rehoboam** (which see), and the **methuselah**. These designations have nothing to do with how long the wines are stored before drinking.

Metonic cycle   A period of 19 years, more specifically 235 lunar cycles, after which the new and full moons—and the eclipse pattern of the moon—return to the same day of the year as at the beginning of the cycle.

Named after **Meton**, an Athenian astronomer (fifth century B.C.) who, according to Greek sources, discovered the cycle in 432 B.C. It is thought by some, however, that the cycle was known earlier to Babylonian astronomers.

Regardless of who first made this interesting astronomical observation, the Greeks were so taken by the **Metonic cycle** that they based their calendar on it, and the Jewish calendar long in use is also based on this cycle. As a result, since Easter was originally dated from Passover, the method used by Christians in calculating Easter is to this day a hangover from the **Metonic calendar**.

And because old practices are difficult to shake, this method probably will continue for a long time.

Midas   Any person of great wealth; also, a person able to make a great deal of money in every venture undertaken.

From the name of **Midas**, in classical mythology a king of Phrygia in northwest Asia Minor, who asked the gods to grant that everything he touched be turned to gold. When the gods acceded to Midas's request, he found his new ability marvelous as a means of creating wealth for him, but catastrophic in that it turned to gold his corn flakes, his hamburgers, and everything else he wanted to nosh.

A classic example of the Law of Unintended Consequences in

action. But this untoward incident in the king's life gave us the **Midas touch**, meaning the ability of a person to make money in all his or her activities. Also expressed as *Everything he (or she) touches turns to gold.*

It is interesting to note that Midas's father, Gordius, was the king of Phrygia who was involved with the **Gordian knot** (which see).

Two memorable English phrases from one Phrygian family—not bad.

milquetoast Also given as **Milquetoast**, meaning any timid, spineless person, especially one who is easily cowed.

From the name of **Caspar Milquetoast**, also given as **Casper Milquetoast**, a character created by the American cartoonist Harold Tucker Webster (1885–1952) in *The Timid Soul*, a widely syndicated comic strip that ran for many years in U.S. newspapers. The name Milquetoast was a play on milk toast, a dish that real men do not order at the local diner or truck stop.

What Milquetoast lacked in assertiveness, he made up for by enabling many thousands of American men to realize they were not alone in struggling daily with life's problems. And to laugh at themselves.

Miltonic An adjective, also given as **Miltonian**, meaning pertaining to John Milton or to his writings; also, in a manner or style evocative of Milton. As a noun, a **Miltonian** means an admirer or imitator of Milton.

From the name of **John Milton** (1608–1674), the English poet who gave English its great epics, *Paradise Lost* (1667) and *Paradise Regained* (1671), both written after Milton had gone blind, in 1652. Afflicted with weak vision since childhood, Milton is said to have succumbed to blindness because of all the hours he spent writing.

Milton also wrote prose and is remembered especially for his eloquent pamphlet *Areopagitica* (1644) in support of a free press. Thus, to use **Miltonic** or **Miltonian** in describing a writer's style is to pay the writer so characterized the greatest of compliments.

Minotaur Any person or thing that destroys or eats one alive.

From the **Minotaur** in classical mythology, a monster with the head of a bull and the body of a man. The Minotaur was fathered by a bull sent by the god Poseidon to Minos, king of Crete. The

Minotaur's mother was Pasiphaë, the wife of Minos. Minos + *taúros* (bull) = Minotaur.

If you're curious about how this unusual coupling of the bull and Pasiphaë came about, here's the scoop: Poseidon had had it in for Minos ever since the king failed to sacrifice to Poseidon the white bull that Poseidon had sent him—you have to observe the rules of the game when you deal with gods. At any rate, as a result of this slight, Poseidon caused Pasiphaë, Minos's queen, to have a thing for the bull. Talk about godly revenge!

Daedalus, about whom more soon, built a wooden cow—a bovine pacifier?—inside which Pasiphaë was able to satisfy her passion for the bull. Please don't ask for details. Just understand that: (1) the Minotaur was not the only offspring of this strange union; and (2) mythological royalty, like some human royal lines, had its share of unusual behavior beloved of supermarket tabloids.

But back to the Minotaur, whose name was Asterius. It was kept confined in a labyrinth in Crete and fed on human flesh—accounting for the modern meaning of Minotaur. In every ninth year, Asterius's larder was stocked with fourteen youths and maidens. This practice continued until Theseus, in legend a Greek hero, finally killed the Minotaur.

Incidentally, it was Ariadne, the daughter of King Minos and Pasiphaë, who enabled Theseus to escape the Cretan labyrinth by supplying him with a thread he could follow to find his way out—the labyrinth had no signs pointing to the exit. In gratitude Theseus married her, but not for long. After Theseus deserted Ariadne, she married Dionysus, a swinging god. (See **Dionysian**.)

And now back to Daedalus, credited with many ingenious and useful inventions, who built the labyrinth, the mazelike building that served as the palace of Minos in Knossos, the capital of Crete. It was there, in the center of the maze, that the Minotaur would be imprisoned.

We remember Daedalus best in mythology for his invention of wings that he built of wax, enabling him and his son Icarus to fly. Icarus—a typical son in this respect—did not follow instructions and flew too close to the hot sun. Of course, he lost his wings, a fatal lapse.

Think about that when it's time to hand the car keys over to junior.

mithridatism A noun meaning an acquired tolerance of a poison obtained by taking gradually increasing amounts of it, beginning with an amount so small that it causes no harm. The verb **mithridatize** means achieve a state of **mithridatism** in (a person).

Named after **Mithridates VI** (120–63 B.C.), known as "the Great," who was the king of Pontus, an ancient country on the south side of the Black Sea. His expansionist policies led to three wars with Rome, two of them ending in victory, and the last in his final defeat by Lucullus (see **Lucullan**) and Pompey.

Mithridates inherited the throne of Pontus when he was still a boy, but court conspiracies caused him to flee and live in the woods in disguise. When Mithridates returned to court he was wary of possible conspiracies against him, so he took a little of each of the known poisons every day to protect himself against poisoning. He also investigated known antidotes.

All this interest in poison led to his writing a book on poison, which was translated into Latin by command of Pompey.

Mithridates was particularly fond of an antidote called theriac, which contained the pulverized flesh of snakes as well as at least sixty different drugs. He had it prepared daily to build up his immunity. As an indication that Mithridates was no mere natural remedy faddist, it should be pointed out that the Roman emperor and Stoic philosopher Marcus Aurelius (121–180) took theriac daily, and the influential physician Galen (129–199) strongly recommended theriac for all sorts of illnesses.

Mithridates is said to have died by his own hand because his troops revolted. Who knows how long he might have lived with his drug habit? Maybe snake flesh works better than snake oil.

Mitty. See **Walter Mitty**.

Möbius strip Also given as **Möbius band**, the figure formed when one end of a rectangle is given a half turn—rotated 180 degrees—and then connected to the opposite end.

The result is a figure that has only one side and one edge, which can easily be verified by running a finger around the edge. Among the unusual properties of a **Möbius strip** is that if you cut it in two lengthwise, it does not fall into two pieces but stays connected.

Named for the German mathematician **August Ferdinand Möbius** (1790–1868), who discovered the Möbius strip in 1858. In that same year, the same general idea was discovered independently by another German mathematician, Johann B. Listing (1806–1882). Although Listing published the discovery in 1858, and Möbius's description of it was not published until 1865, Möbius is usually given all the credit.

It's a matter of who gets the breaks.

Molotov cocktail   An incendiary grenade made of an inflammable liquid and a wick, in a glass bottle.

From the name of **Vyacheslav Mikhailovich Molotov** (1890–1986), a Soviet politician who played a prominent role in the October 1917 revolution and held various important positions in the Soviet government thereafter.

The **Molotov cocktail** was originally devised as an antitank weapon to aid the Republicans in the Spanish Civil War (1936–1939), which ended in victory for the anti-Republican forces.

You can't win 'em all.

Momus   Also given as **momus**, meaning a faultfinder, a nitpicker.

From the name of **Momus**, in classical mythology the god of ridicule, who was thrown out of heaven for his criticism of the gods. Momus even attacked **Venus** (which see) for the noise her feet made while walking.

But Momus had nothing critical to say about the naked body of the goddess. Maybe Venus wore combat boots.

Montessori method   Also given as **Montessori system**, a program of education for children three to six years old, based on freedom from restraint and encouragement of spontaneous expression.

From the name of **Maria Montessori** (1870–1952), an Italian physician and educator. She opened the first school based on her methods in Rome in 1907, and today Montessori schools are still found almost everywhere in the world.

Moon type.   See **Braille**.

Morris chair   A large armchair with an adjustable back and loose cushions.

Named after **William Morris** (1834–1896), English poet, craftsman, painter, and socialist writer. He designed and furnished his home, and soon thereafter the pieces he manufactured began to influence the design of English furniture.

He always found time to do more than make furniture. He wrote many books, was active as a leader in various socialist societies, and founded a publishing house. Yet he is known today primarily for his comfortable **Morris chair**.

Morse code   The code invented for use first in telegraphy, consisting of dots and dashes in combinations that represented the letters of the alphabet.

Named for its American inventor, **Samuel Finley Breese Morse** (1791–1872). He sent the first message ever employing **Morse code** from Washington, D.C., to Baltimore on May 24, 1844: "What hath God wrought."

Thereby setting a standard for first messages that were to follow— "That's one small step for a man . . ." "Mr. Watson, come here . . ." and all the others—regardless of which PR specialist wrote them. (See also **baud** and **Wheatstone bridge**.)

Mrs. Grundy.   See Grundy, Mrs.

Münchausen, Baron   An outrageously untruthful storyteller.

From the name **Baron Münchhausen**, hero of a book of fantastic adventures written in English, and published in 1785, by Rudolph Erich Raspe (1737–1794), a German scientist and author who lived in England when he wrote the stories. They were based on the exaggerated anecdotes told by a German soldier and hunter, **Baron Karl Friedrich Hieronymus von Münchhausen** (1720–1797), who was given to recounting his exploits in the Russian campaign against the Turks.

As a result, the name **Baron Münchausen** from then on was inextricably associated with absurdly exaggerated stories and later was to become the basis for a comedy routine on radio. The comedian Jack Pearl played the role of Münchausen and achieved a national reputation. The program, aired well before World War II, featured Pearl's tall tales told in a burlesque German accent. When his straight man, a person he called Charlie, would say he did not believe a story the Baron told, Münchausen would invariably reply, "Vas you dere, Sharlie?"

"Vas you dere, Sharlie?" became a national tag line. Ask your grandfather about this.

myrmidon A person who obeys unquestioningly and remorselessly the orders of a superior. Also, a hired ruffian; a hit man.

From the name **Myrmidon**, in classical mythology one of the warlike people of Thessaly in ancient Greece. The Myrmidons, known for their fierceness in battle and blind devotion to a leader, followed **Achilles** (which see) to Troy to prosecute the ultimately successful siege by the Greeks.

So though we recall the ancient Myrmidons admiringly for their devotion to their leaders and their prowess in warfare, paradoxically we implicitly denigrate anyone we refer to as a **myrmidon**, thinking of him or her as a henchman, someone who will follow any order, no matter how unscrupulous or illegal.

Which becomes an ethical issue when a war criminal, for example, offers the classic justification for heinous acts: "I was only following orders."

N

namby-pamby Insipid, wishy-washy; weakly sentimental.

From the label attached to the English poet **Ambrose Philips** (1674–1749) by rivals envious of the praise accorded Philips in a newspaper review of his work. The nickname **Namby Pamby**, a play on the first syllable of Ambrose, was used in the title of a poem by Henry Carey (c.1687–1743) that ridiculed Philips. The poem offers two unmemorable lines:

> *Namby Pamby's little rhymes,*
> *Little jingle, little chimes.*

This quotation surely disabuses one of the notion that Henry Carey was a second Milton. And if this quotation is not enough, consider that "Sally in our Alley" is his best-known poem:

> *Of all the girls that are so smart,*
> *There's none like pretty Sally.*
> *She is the darling of my heart,*
> *And she lives in our alley.*

Memorable.

Napier's bones   In mathematics, a predecessor of the slide rule, consisting of a pair of rectangular shafts—called **bones** because they often were made of bone or ivory—and marked with numerals. By aligning a pair of numerals, one from each shaft, a product or quotient could be read directly.

This was the first type of calculating device to operate on a principle different from that of the abacus.

From the name of **John Napier** (1550–1617), a Scottish mathematician known particularly as the inventor of logarithms, in 1614. Napier invented logarithms as a way of simplifying arithmetic, and his **Napier's bones** as a way of simplifying logarithms.

Along the way he also invented the decimal point. Now, there's something anyone can understand.

napoleon   Also given as *mille-feuille*, in English, thousand-leaf, a type of puff pastry split and filled with custard, cream, and cholesterol.

In French given as **napoléon**, from the names of a string of nineteenth-century French emperors.

narcissism   In psychoanalysis, excessive admiration of oneself; vanity.

From the name of **Narcissus**, in classical mythology a beautiful youth who saw his reflection in a pool and fell in love with it. Two plot twists are given to explain what happened next. In one, he wasted away from unsatisfied desire, whereupon he was transformed into the flower **narcissus**, which bears his name. In the other, much more interesting version, he jumped into the pool to join his reflection, and there he died.

The moral of the story is clear: Join the YMCA to learn how to swim before you go around plunging into pools.

negus   A drink of port or sherry wine with hot water, sugar, spices, and lemon.

From the name of **Colonel Francis Negus** (died 1732), the Englishman who invented it. The name of the drink should not be confused with **Negus**, the title of the ruler of Ethiopia, which has its roots in an Amharic word for king.

nemesis   An opponent or rival one cannot best; also, inevitable retribution.

From the name of **Nemesis**, a goddess in classical mythology, the embodiment of divine retribution. Everybody, whether we recognize it or not, has a **nemesis**. He, she, or it makes life uncomfortable to a small degree but can also hamstring us, sometimes throughout life.

For example, there was a boy who sat in front of me in third grade who always . . .

nereid   A long sea worm.

From **Nereid**, any of the daughters of **Nereus**, whose daughters numbered fifty. (See **andromeda**.) Nereus, an old sea god, was also noteworthy for his ability to change his shape whenever he wished. (Especially when his daughters were all dining at home?)

In astronomy, **Nereid** is one of the moons of Neptune. On the whole, wouldn't you rather be a moon than a sea worm?

Or be childless rather than the father of fifty daughters?

Nesselrode   A mixture of nuts, preserved fruit, and the like, used as a sauce or in pies, ice cream, etc.

Said to have been invented by a chef who worked for **Count Karl Robert Nesselrode** (1780–1862), a Russian diplomat who played an important role in the negotiations leading up to the Peace of Paris (1814).

But he still had time for fine dining. Anybody who has tasted **Nesselrode pie** knows the Count must have had a fine palate.

Nestor   A wise old man; also, the senior member of a firm, university department, or the like, valued for his wisdom.

From the name of **Nestor**, in classical mythology the oldest and wisest of the Greeks in the Trojan War, and the king of Pylos, in southwest Greece. He was widely known for his wisdom and eloquence.

Nestor is not to be confused with the noun **Nestorian**, meaning a follower of **Nestorius** (died A.D. 451). Nestorius, a patriarch of Constantinople, advanced the doctrine that Christ had distinct human and divine persons.

newton   The basic unit of force, about the same force as exerted in lifting a Quarter Pounder without cheese. More formally the amount of force needed to accelerate a mass of 1 kilogram by 1 meter per second per second.

If you recall the famous physics formula $F = ma$, Force equals mass times acceleration, you can see why the **newton** involves both mass and acceleration.

Compare this with the acceleration caused by gravity, which is 9.8

meters per second, in pre-metric times given as 32 feet per second per second. Thus, a newton is the force produced by a mass of 1 kilogram divided by 9.8 when subjected to Earth's gravity. Returning to somewhat more familiar terms, a newton is the force exerted on your hand by the weight of two large, fresh eggs—about 3.6 ounces.

It is appropriate that the newton was named for **Isaac Newton** (1641–1727). Among Newton's many accomplishments, he was the first to state clearly that F = ma, which is also known as Newton's second law of motion. (See also **Newtonian**.)

Newtonian   An adjective applied to anything explained by Newton's laws of motion or of gravity. In contrast especially to other theories of gravitation, such as the Cartesian theory, advanced by René Descartes but later discredited by physical evidence, and the Einsteinian theory of general relativity, which is considered to have superseded Newtonian gravity.

Sometimes, any physics of force and motion that does not use relativity, special or general, is called **Newtonian physics**. Again, a fluid that does not change viscosity with its rate of flow is called a **Newtonian fluid**.

Just one more example: The simplest kind of reflecting telescope is called a **Newtonian telescope** because Newton was one of the first to propose that a telescope based on a curved mirror would be superior to one based on light passing through a lens. Newton was the first to actually build such an instrument.

What would he have thought of the Hubble telescope?

nicol prism   A device made of two pieces of Iceland spar, also known as calcite crystals, that have a transparent layer of a suitable material between them so that the combination can produce a ray of light that is completely polarized in one direction.

From the name of its inventor, **William Nicol** (1768–1851), the Scottish geologist and physicist who first demonstrated it, in 1828.

Several different properties of light's interaction with materials are used to get the effect of the **nicol prism**. The polarized light that results was very helpful in the development of organic chemistry, since it provided the first evidence that the shape of molecules is important, not just their chemical composition.

nicotine A poisonous alkaloid extracted from tobacco as an oily liquid.

Ultimately from the name of **Jacques** or **Jean Nicot** (1530–1600), a French diplomat who is said to have introduced the tobacco plant into France from Portugal, where he was the French ambassador. The plant was named **nicotiana** after M. Nicot, and today *Nicotiana* is the generic name for the ornamental flowering tobacco plant.

Do you suppose M. Nicot transported the plant in his diplomatic pouch?

Nimrod Also given as **nimrod**, any daring or outstanding hunter or sportsman.

From the name of **Nimrod**, in Genesis called "a mighty hunter before the Lord." Nimrod was the son of Cush and great-grandson of Noah.

Niobe A weeping woman, the personification of maternal sorrow.

Named for **Niobe**, in classical mythology the wife of Amphion, king of Thebes. Niobe made the classic woman's error: She taunted the goddess Leto, reminding her that Leto had only two children while she had fourteen. While an ordinary woman might have responded by not speaking to anyone who behaved in this way, Greek goddesses usually did more . . .

In this case, much more.

Leto commanded her twin sons, **Apollo** (which see) and **Artemis** (see **artemisia**), to kill Niobe's children. When Niobe heard the news of what these dutiful young men had done, she wept inconsolably. By some accounts Niobe wept herself to death, and Zeus turned her into stone.

Whereupon the stone continued the weeping. A marvelous image.

Nissen hut A prefabricated tunnel-shaped shelter made of corrugated iron with a cement floor.

From the name of **Colonel Peter Norman Nissen** (1871–1930), the Canadian Army engineer who invented the structure, much used during World War II as an inexpensive and easily erected shelter.

But an uncomfortable one in the memories of an older generation.

Nobel Prize One of the annual prizes awarded from funds originally established by **Alfred Bernhard Nobel** (1833–1896), a Swedish chemist, manufacturer, and philanthropist.

The prizes, first distributed in 1901, are given for outstanding achievement in the promotion of peace, and for outstanding achievement in physics, chemistry, medicine or physiology, literature, and, from other private funds since 1961, in economics. These prizes now have a value of more than $1 million each, and the recipients of the prizes are known as **Nobelists**.

Where did all that money come from? Nobel made his vast fortune as inventor and manufacturer of dynamite and smokeless gunpowder.

Nostradamus A person who professes knowledge of future events; a prophet.

Named after **Nostradamus**, the Latinized version of the name of **Michel de Nostredame** (1503–1566), a French astrologer and physician who published a collection of prophecies in 1555 entitled *Centuries* in English.

Nostradamus wrote his predictions in rhymed quatrains employing enigmatic and ambiguous language, which encourages ingenuous readers—as well as unscrupulous translators—to see what they wish to see in the oracular predictions.

O

. . . .

Occam's razor   Also given as **Ockham's razor**, the maxim traditionally stated as "Entities are not to be multiplied beyond necessity." Which means that when conducting an analysis, unnecessary facts or elements must be eliminated to the extent possible.

Named after **William of Occam** or **Ockham** (c.1285–c.1349), an English philosopher and theologian, considered the most influential of late medieval philosophers.

It's easier to cite Occam's maxim than to put it to work. It would sure help if we had a razor to cut away superfluous details.

odyssey   A long adventurous journey, especially one filled with hardships.

From the title of the great epic poem *Odyssey*, attributed to Homer and relating the adventures of the Greek leader **Odysseus** as he makes his way home to Ithaca after the end of the ten-year Trojan War. The journey, unfortunately, also takes ten years, ending only when, with the help of his son Telemachus, he slays the evil suitors of Penelope, his faithful wife. Along the way Odysseus has to deal with a number of fabulous monsters, including **Scylla and Charybdis** (which see) and the Cyclops.

Odysseus, we blush to relate, also has amorous encounters with

Calypso and Circe and receives first-class hospitality from the Phaea-
cians, a pleasure-loving bunch. All the while, his ever-loving wife is
weaving by day and unraveling by night, because she has promised
she will remarry only when she has finished the weaving.

But let's not rush to judgment on this marriage. Odysseus only
stayed away from home for twenty years, after all.

Oedipus complex   In psychoanalysis, the unresolved desire of a child
for sexual gratification through the child's parents, especially the
attraction felt by a son for his mother. (See **Electra complex**.)

From the name of **Oedipus**, in Greek legend the son of Laius, king
of Thebes, and Jocasta, his queen. As was prophesied at his birth,
Oedipus unwittingly kills his father and marries his mother. When
this terrible state of affairs is revealed, he goes mad and puts out his
own eyes. As for his mother, she hangs herself.

No wonder the psychoanalysts conjured up the **Oedipus complex**.
They certainly couldn't have done much with an Oedipus simplex.

ohm   The amount of resistance produced when 1 ampere of electricity
is driven by a force of 1 volt.

Named for the German physicist **Georg Simon Ohm** (1787–
1854), who was the first to work out, in 1827, the laws governing
resistance of electric currents.

The **ohm** may be more clearly explained by saying that the potential difference from one end of a wire to another, which is measured in
volts divided by the amount of current passing through the wire, is
called the resistance of the wire to the flow of electricity.

A length of copper wire, a good conductor, which is not especially
thick or thin, may have a resistance of a score of ohms over the length
of a mile. By contrast, the filament of a lightbulb, selected to have a
high resistance so that the current will heat it to glowing temperatures, may have a resistance of a hundred ohms or so.

Ohm's ideas met with so much scientific resistance (irony!), possibly because he was a lowly high school teacher, that he lost his job.
While he lived in abject poverty, his theory was becoming known in
England, however, and he was honored by the Royal Society. At that
point the Germans began to accept him, and eventually, in 1849, he
became a university professor in Munich. But that was twenty-two
years after he first explained resistance.

Ohm actually had two units named for him. In addition to the ohm, which measures resistance, its reverse, the unit of conductance, is whimsically named the *mho* (see **siemens**).

You could look it up.

Old Man of the Sea. See **Achilles heel**.

orrery A clockwork model of the planetary system; also, a planetarium.

From the name of **Charles Boyle, 4th Earl of Orrery** (1676–1731), for whom one of the clockwork models was made. The inventor of the **orrery** was George Graham, who was big in the history of clockmaking, but not big enough to have it named after him.

All for the best. Imagine calling an orrery a grahamry.

Orwellian An adjective with two meanings: resembling the literary work of George Orwell, and resembling the totalitarian world of the future that Orwell described.

From **George Orwell**, pen name of **Eric Arthur Blair** (1903–1950), English novelist and essayist, who taught readers in his novel *1984* (1949) the language of propaganda he called "Newspeak," which enables people to hold simultaneously two conflicting views.

In this work Orwell described a world that people soon were calling **Orwellian**. Such a world is characterized by complete thought control and political slavery.

Ossianic Bombastic, magniloquent.

From the name of **Ossian**, in Gaelic legend a bard and warrior and the son of Finn, also known as Fingal, who was himself a leader of the Fenian warriors. Son and father are supposed to have lived during the third century B.C.

Ossian's name became widely known in the eighteenth century when the Scottish poet James Macpherson (1736–1796) claimed to have found an ancient epic poem written by Ossian and dealing with Fingal's exploits.

In 1762 and 1763, Macpherson created a sensation when he published two volumes of what he said were his English translations of the ancient work. In fact, except for a few fragments, he was unable to produce the original manuscripts and, like other literary hoaxes, the publicity bubble soon burst.

Predictably, the jackals gathered and moved in on the unfortunate Macpherson, criticizing the language of his purported translations, which they saw as bombastic. And that's where the adjective **Ossianic** was born.

Ossian retreated into legend and Macpherson into business, at which he is said to have excelled. The *Cambridge Biographical Dictionary* of 1990 reports ironically that Macpherson "was buried, at his own request and expense, in Westminster Abbey."

Otto cycle The sequence of operation of the four-stroke internal combustion engine.

Named after a German engineer, **Nikolaus August Otto** (1832–1891), who read a newspaper description in 1862 of a theoretically superior four-stroke engine that existed only on paper and decided to build one, in 1876. The four-stroke engine is based on the repetition of four basic operations: fuel and air intake, compression of the mixture, ignition, and exhaustion.

Otto's model worked so well that he formed a company to build engines and in the first year sold 35,000 of them.

Today, almost all automobiles and propeller-driven airplanes use **Otto cycle** engines, though lawn mowers and chain saws are built with simpler two-stroke engines. Maybe Otto scored so big he hired gardeners to mow his lawn.

The Otto message is clear: Read your daily newspaper from beginning to end, and get on the Internet. You never know what you'll come up with.

out-herod Herod Also given as **out-Herod Herod**, meaning outdo a tyrant in violence or wickedness; also, outdo anyone in evil or extravagance.

The tyrant in this instance, of course, is **Herod** (c.74–4 B.C.), known as Herod the Great, a ruler of Palestine in Roman times.

At the faintest suspicion he was being hoodwinked, Herod ordered wholesale proactive slaughter. For example, there was the slaughter of the innocents—the babes—at Bethlehem, as reported in Matthew.

But take note of the second definition of **out-herod Herod**, which enables you to create your own "outdo sundae": "He surely is *out-scrooging Scrooge, out-steinbrennering Steinbrenner . . .*"

Get the idea?

P

Pandora's box A source of unforeseen and unmanageable problems that, once activated, cannot be stanched. Also, a gift that seems valuable but is really a curse.

From the name of **Pandora**, in one version of classical mythology the first woman. She was sent to earth by Zeus with a box containing all the evils that could trouble mankind. This was **Pandora's box**, and it was intended by Zeus as a counterbalance for the fire that Prometheus had stolen from heaven. Inevitably, Pandora opened the box, and when she did, all the evils flew forth.

Ever since, all these evils have continued to afflict mortals. Yet, in some interpretations of the legend, there were blessings in the box as well, so Hope remains trapped in the box.

If cliché wins out in the long run, hope springs eternal. But don't count on it.

Panglossian As an adjective, given to unmitigated optimism, especially in the face of extraordinary hardship. As a noun, a person given to such optimism.

From the name of **Dr. Pangloss** in the novel *Candide, ou l'optimisme*

(Candide, or Optimism) (1759), by François-Marie Arouet, or Voltaire (1694–1778). The pedantic Dr. Pangloss, tutor of Candide, believes along with the contemporary German philosopher and mathematician Gottfried Wilhelm Leibniz (1646–1716): "All is for the best in this best of all possible worlds." The result of this **Panglossian** outlook is that Pangloss and the young Candide spend almost all their time together undergoing harrowing misadventures.

Voltaire succeeded in his intention to satirize the extreme optimism of Leibniz, and English benefited directly. It acquired Panglossian as a new term, along with Dr. Pangloss, the embodiment of foolish optimism.

paparazzi Freelance photographers who pursue celebrities to take candid photographs for publication.

The Italian singular form, **paparazzo**, is almost never seen in English outside unabridged dictionaries. Newspapers facing the problem of how to characterize a paparazzo will usually say he was "one of the **paparazzi** in pursuit."

From **Paparazzo**, the name of a fictional freelance photographer in the 1959 film *La Dolce Vita* (The Sweet Life). Federico Fellini (1920–1993), while directing the film, happened to be reading an Italian translation of a travel book, *By the Ionian Sea* (1901) by George Gissing (1857–1903).

Fellini was struck by the name of a hotelier Gissing mentioned, Paparazzo. He immediately adopted it for the energetic tabloid photographer in his movie.

And tabloids all over the world promptly took to a new way to describe their photographers.

Parkinson's disease Also known as **Parkinsonism**, a serious disease of older persons that is caused by the death of certain brain cells responsible for controlling movement of muscles.

Named after **James Parkinson** (1755–1824), an English physician, who was the first to describe the disease, in 1817, when it was described as "shaking palsy."

Parkinson's disease may produce such symptoms as a noticeable tremor of the head, hand, or leg, although not all patients develop such tremors. As the disease progresses, it may cause muscle stiffness and rigidity on one or both sides of the body. More severe cases make walking difficult, and the disease sometimes completely restricts a patient's mobility.

If anything good can be said about this progressive disease, it is that mental capacity is not affected until later stages, and even then this occurs in only a third of all people who contract the disease.

Parkinson's law

> Work expands so as to fill the time available for its completion, and subordinates multiply at a fixed rate, regardless of the amount of work produced.

A seriocomic observation made by **Cyril Northcote Parkinson** (born 1909), an English historian and journalist. This dig at bureaucracy gone amok, first made by Parkinson in his *Parkinson's Law, the Pursuit of Progress* (1958), has for many years been celebrated as **Parkinson's law**, and collected avidly by editors of quotation books, who implicitly salute its acceptance in the great English language.

pasteurize A verb meaning heat (a material, most often a food) to a temperature high enough to kill bacteria or other microbes that might cause spoilage or disease. Thus, the noun **pasteurization** may be thought of as a kind of partial sterilization.

Named for **Louis Pasteur** (1822–1895), the French chemist sometimes called the father of modern bacteriology, who invented the process.

Pasteur was not directing his efforts toward preventing spoilage or disease when he invented his process, but was working on a different problem entirely. In the early 1860s, French vintners were in trouble. Their wines were souring in the bottle, and restaurant diners were sending their wine back. Pasteur found there were two kinds of yeast in wine and beer, one that produces alcohol and one that sours by producing lactic acid. His remedy was to heat the wine or beer enough to kill both kinds of yeast—**pasteurize** the wine and beer—and then bottle them in sterile bottles.

A year or two later, while studying a disease of silkworms, he discovered that the disease was caused by bacteria, which led him to think bacteria also caused disease in humans. A few decades later, when tuberculosis and undulant fever were found to be spread by bacteria in milk, pasteurization was applied effectively to milk as well as to wine and beer.

Other contributions made by Pasteur include development of vaccines against anthrax in cattle, cholera in chickens, and rabies in humans.

A great man.

peach Melba Also given as **peach melba** and in French as *pêche Melba* and *pêche à la Melba*, a dessert of cooked peach halves on vanilla ice cream, flavored with raspberry sauce, called **Melba sauce**.

Named in honor of the famous Australian operatic soprano **Dame Nellie Melba** (1861–1931), the stage name of **Helen Mitchell**, who chose the name **Melba** from Melbourne, the city of her birth.

To go from the sublime to the ridiculous, let it be known that **Melba toast**, the bread crime with a name but no shame, was also named for the great diva.

pecksniff A hypocrite who mouths moralizing lessons, commits horrid sins, and forgives only himself for such transgressions.

Named after the character **Seth Pecksniff** in the novel *Martin Chuzzlewit* (1843), by Charles Dickens. Pecksniff, a canting hypocrite, is a member of a greedy, grasping family of Chuzzlewits who mostly deserve one another.

Thanks again to Dickens for a name that has become an expressive English word in good standing. For other evocative names from Dickens, see **Fagin, gamp,** and **Gradgrind**.

peeler. See **bobby**.

Peter Pan A person who retains his youthful features, interests, and characteristics, seeming never to age.

Named for the hero of the play *Peter Pan* (1904), by Sir James Matthew Barrie (1860–1937), a Scottish novelist and playwright. *Peter Pan* is still performed regularly, to the delight of children and adults, and is shown on television as an example of musical theater at its captivating best.

The growing popularity of plastic surgery notwithstanding, eternal youth should not be encouraged except on the stage or movie screen. Agree?

Peter Principle

In a Hierarchy Every Employee Tends to Rise to His Level of Incompetence.

This satirical perception was advanced by **Laurence Johnston Peter**, an author born in Canada in 1919, in his book **Peter Principle** (1969). This first so-called law of organizational structure proved so popular and was considered to be so accurate that other **Peter Principles** followed in the same satirical vein. And with the same incisive wit.

petri dish A shallow, flat glass container with a loose-fitting glass cover, used for culturing microorganisms.

Named after the German bacteriologist **Julius R. Petri** (died 1921), who developed the **petri dish** so he could culture bacteria and observe the progress of the culture without lifting the lid.

pinchbeck As a noun, a goldlike alloy of 10 to 15 percent zinc and the rest copper, used especially in cheap jewelry; also, something sham, spurious, counterfeit; a knockoff. As an adjective, sham, spurious, counterfeit; also, made of **pinchbeck**.

The alloy is named for an English clockmaker, **Christopher Pinchbeck** (c.1670–1732), who invented it for use in making imitation gold watches.

Planck's constant Also given as **Planck constant**, the fundamental unit of quantum mechanics, a tiny physical constant that is measured as the product of energy and time.

Named after the German theoretical physicist **Max Karl Ernst Planck** (1858–1947), who formulated the quantum theory, which revolutionized physics.

Planck's constant is often described as the smallest unit of energy, although it is not energy exactly, but energy multiplied by time. The unit originated in the equation that calculates the energy of light from its frequency. Since frequency is measured as *times per second*, the equation works out as *the energy of light equals the frequency of light times Planck's constant*.

All of physics from before 1900 is known now as classical physics, while physics after 1900 is known as modern physics, because all physics since then must incorporate **Planck's constant**. Planck thought of the constant, in its original form for the energy of light, as a mathematical fiction, for it gives correct results by assuming that light must come in small packets. In 1905, Einstein established that light actually does come in small packets.

After Planck won the Nobel Prize for physics in 1918, he was honored by having the Max Planck Institute—still one of the great research centers of the world—named after him and was made director of the institute. In the 1930s, Planck tried to intercede with the German government on behalf of Jewish scientists and was dismissed from his post.

One of Planck's sons was executed in 1944 for plotting against Adolf Hitler.

Enough said.

Plimsoll line   Also called **Plimsoll mark** and load line, a distinctive mark on the side of a cargo ship indicating its maximum permissible load line under various conditions.

Named after **Samuel Plimsoll** (1824–1898), an English social reformer. While serving as a member of Parliament, he led a campaign against the overloading of cargo ships, which culminated in passage of the Merchant Shipping Act by Parliament in 1876.

So whenever you see a **Plimsoll line** on a cargo vessel, remember it was a social reformer, not a sailor or insurance company executive or bureaucrat in the U.S. Occupational Safety and Health Administration, who was responsible for putting it there.

Incidentally, in British English, a **plimsoll** is a canvas shoe with a rubber sole—what Americans call a sneaker—so called because the sole was thought to resemble a Plimsoll line.

poinsettia   A plant with variously lobed leaves and brilliant scarlet, pink, or white petal-like bracts.

Named in honor of **Joel Roberts Poinsett** (1799–1851), first U.S. minister to Mexico, who discovered the **poinsettia** there.

This plant, native to Central America, is raised by the thousands in hothouses, especially in time for Christmas blooming. So popular has it become that it ranks next to Christmas trees as a symbol of the season.

For houseguests, often the gift plant of last resort.

Pollyanna   As a noun, a cheerful, blindly optimistic person. As an adjective, also given as **pollyanna**, **Pollyannish**, and as the tongue-twisting **Pollyannaish**, meaning unduly cheerful and optimistic.

From the name of **Pollyanna**, the heroine of stories written for children by the American author Eleanor Hodgman Porter (1868–1920). Pollyanna was portrayed as expert in the "glad game," in which one is able to find cause for happiness no matter how ominous or disastrous the situation.

In life, of course, skill in playing the glad game derives ultimately from a person's proclivity for self-delusion. Not something most optimists would want to admit.

Better stick to Monopoly and TV game shows.

pompadour   A woman's hairstyle in which the hair is swept up in a wave above the forehead; also, a man's somewhat similar hairstyle. Also, a color between claret and purple.

While the color **pompadour** is taken to be related most closely to the name of **Jeanne Antoinette Poisson le Normant, Marquise de Pompadour** (1721–1764), who was one of a series of mistresses of King Louis XV of France, the hairstyle so named soon followed.

The status of the Marquise de Pompadour was so secure in the king's ménage that she was considered the reigning mistress, able to influence public affairs (no pun intended) of state. Her source of power lay not in her ability to manage royal policy, for which she showed little talent, but in her liberal attitude toward the king's debaucheries, even going so far as to procure young mistresses for him.

Twentieth-century democracies are beginning to bear some resemblance to eighteenth-century monarchies, don't you think?

Pooh Bah   Also given as **Pooh-Bah**, meaning someone who holds many public offices at the same time, usually from motives of self-interest; also, a VIP.

From a character of this name in *The Mikado* (1885), a light opera by Sir William Schwenk Gilbert (1836–1911) and Sir Arthur Seymour Sullivan (1842–1900). Their **Pooh Bah** is First Lord of the Treasury, Lord Chief Justice, Commander-in-Chief, Lord High Admiral, Master of the Buckhounds—a buckhound being a hound trained to hunt bucks—Groom of the Back Stairs, Archbishop of Titipu, Lord Mayor, and in case Pooh Bah forgets any of his titles, Lord High Everything Else.

But he was not Lord High Executioner—that post was held by Ko-Ko. Nor was he the Mikado.

And in case you have forgotten, Gilbert was the master librettist, and Sullivan was the composer. And both were English.

And a Pooh Bah is a Poo Bah no matter where we find him. Or her.

Portia A woman lawyer.

From the character of this name in William Shakespeare's *Merchant of Venice*. It is **Portia** who argues successfully in court against the claim of **Shylock** (which see) that he is entitled to a pound of flesh because he has not been reimbursed for his loan to Antonio, the merchant.

It is interesting that Shakespeare's Portia—unlike Portias ever since the great playwright gave us the word—was not actually a lawyer. She quickly prepares for her eloquent representation of her client, Antonio, and dresses as a lawyer. Her argument in court succeeds because it cleverly turns the case around, making it an attack against the accuser, Shylock, instead of a defense of Antonio.

Makes you wonder whether anyone ought to worry about an LSAT score.

Pott's disease A form of tuberculosis of the spine, usually recognized in a patient by marked spinal curvature.

Named after **Percival Pott** (1713–1788), the English physician who first described the condition, although he failed to recognize that what came to be known as **Pott's disease** was associated with tuberculosis.

Pott is best remembered today as the first physician to recognize, in 1775, that an environmental condition can cause cancer. Specifically, he observed that men who had worked as chimney sweeps tended to develop cancer of the scrotum and cancer inside the nostril, which Pott attributed to the heavy concentrations of soot they had encountered in their careers.

In medical circles, one still hears of **Pott's fracture**, which is any fracture of the lower fibula, especially such a fracture close to the ankle. Not only was Pott the first to describe it, in 1765, but he also suffered such a fracture.

Physician, heal thyself.

praline   A candy prepared in various ways, but especially how it has long been prepared in New Orleans: Pecans are browned in butter and then boiled in water flavored with molasses or brown sugar.

Named after **Marshal César de Plessis-Praslin** (1598–1675), a French soldier, whose name Praslin is pronounced as though it had no letter *s*. Plessis-Praslin did not invent **pralines**, but his cook did.

Nobody remembers the cook's name.

priapism   Prurient behavior or display; also, a pathological condition marked by persistent penile erection.

From the name of **Priapus**, in classical mythology a god of male procreative power who was the son of Dionysus (see **Dionysian**) and Aphrodite, goddess of love. The symbol of Priapus was, fittingly, the phallus. It must be noted that Priapus was also a god of gardens, and a statue of Priapus—sculpted as a misshapen little man with genitals of exaggerated, even heroic, proportions—is sometimes seen in gardens.

Making gardening even more fun.

Prince Albert   A man's long, double-breasted frock coat.

Named after **Prince Albert Edward** of Great Britain, eldest son of Queen Victoria and Prince Albert and later crowned King Edward VII (1841–1910) of Great Britain and Ireland.

As a young man, Prince Albert cut quite a figure in European café society. His legacy to the English language is the name of the **Prince Albert**, the coat he wore, which became fashionable among his society contemporaries. Alas, it is no longer worn except, it is said, by English Hasidim who enjoy the warmth afforded by a long coat.

What would he have thought if he had lived to see not only his coat fall from fashion but his portrait adorning cans of tobacco?

Now that this brand of pipe tobacco is no longer available, young wiseacres no longer can ask a tobacconist if he has "Prince Albert in a can" and then, when answered in the affirmative, ask the salesclerk to let the prince out.

Prince Charming   Every young girl's dream man.

From the name of **Prince Charming**, a fairy tale hero first in a seventeenth-century French story, where he appeared as King Charming, and later in English stories as Prince Charming.

procrustean   An adjective meaning seeking to produce uniformity by violent means. Also given as **Procrustean**, meaning suggestive of **Procrustes**.

In Greek legend Procrustes was a robber of Attica, a region in southeast Greece, who placed his victims on a metal bed and made them conform to the length of the bed—the infamous **Procrustes' bed**. If a victim was longer than the bed, he would cut off any overhanging parts; if shorter, he would stretch the victim until he fit the bed.

Procrustes has given English his name to apply to any person who insists on reducing people to a single way of thinking or behaving. And such a person is said to *place them on Procrustes' bed*.

To help you feel better, Procrustes died at the hands of Theseus, in Greek legend the chief hero of Attica, the area surrounding Athens, which he unified.

New York State, perhaps aware that some bad as well as some good things happened in Attica, placed one of its penitentiaries in a town called Attica. As far as is known, the inmates there sleep in metal beds.

But with mattresses supplied.

protean An adjective meaning taking many forms; also, variable, versatile.

From the name of **Proteus**, in Greek legend represented as an old man and servant of Neptune. Proteus was known for his ability to escape capture by assuming different shapes at will.

psyche The mental or psychological structure of a person, especially seen as influencing and affecting the entire person; also, the human soul or spirit.

From the name of **Psyche**, in Greek mythology the soul personified as a beautiful girl, beloved of **Eros** (which see), the god of love.

Roman mythology identifies Cupid as the counterpart of Eros and gives us the legendary love story of Cupid and Psyche, in which Cupid visits his beautiful Psyche every night but leaves at sunrise. Cupid thus can hide his identity from Psyche.

When Psyche lights a lamp to get a look at her sleeping beloved, a drop of hot oil falls on Cupid and wakes him up. Cupid flees, and Psyche from then on is impelled to search for him everywhere. When the lovers are eventually reunited, Psyche becomes immortal.

Which is how every love story should end.

Ptolemaic system A conception of the universe in which Earth is considered its fixed center, with the Sun and planets moving about it.

This so-called **Ptolemaic system** takes its name from the Egyptian astronomer and geographer **Ptolemy**, also called **Claudius Ptolemaeus** (c.90–168). So powerful were Ptolemy's ideas that he dominated scientific thinking up to the seventeenth century, and the geocentric Ptolemaic system was part of Catholic Church doctrine until the late Renaissance.

Ptolemy based his ideas on the work of Hipparchus (fl.160–125 B.C.), a Greek astronomer who is considered one of the world's all-time greatest astronomers. Hipparchus used a system of small circular orbits imposed atop a main circular orbit to explain the apparent motions of the planets—sometimes it appears as if a planet reverses motion for a while and then returns to the original direction. Thus, the actual Ptolemaic system is this complex circles-on-circles system.

Now see **Copernican system** to get closer to how things really work.

Pulitzer Prize   One of thirteen highly revered annual awards, also known as **Pulitzers**, for achievement in American journalism, literature, drama, music, etc., and administered by Columbia University.

Named for **Joseph Pulitzer** (1847–1911), a U.S. journalist and publisher, who left Hungary in 1864 and served for a year on the Union side during the Civil War. Afterward, penniless, he worked first as a reporter but soon began to acquire newspapers and build them up. His publishing empire blossomed when he acquired the St. Louis *Post-Dispatch* and the New York *Evening World*.

His accumulated wealth enabled him to endow the Columbia University School of Journalism and, in his will, to establish the **Pulitzer Prizes**, first awarded in 1917.

Pullman car   A railway sleeping car, its name protected by trademark.

Named after its designer, **George Mortimer Pullman** (1831–1897), an American inventor and businessman. Pullman also designed parlor cars and, most important, introduced railway dining cars, popularly known as diners. These travel amenities have all but disappeared, victims of the onslaught of faster, less comfortable air transportation. With poor food, alas.

Nothing could be finer than dinner in a diner.

Pyrrhic victory   A victory or goal achieved at too great a cost.

From the name of **Pyrrhus**, a king of Epirus, an ancient district in northwest Greece and southern Albania. Plutarch reported that in 279 B.C. Pyrrhus won a costly victory over the Romans at Asculum in Apulia, in southeast Italy. Taking note that he had lost many men and all his best officers, Pyrrhus said: "One more such victory and we are lost."

Thus, in time, bequeathing to English the phrase **Pyrrhic victory**, an implicit warning to all military and political strategists. (See also **Cadmean victory**.)

Pythagorean theorem

The squares on the legs of a right triangle are equal to the square on the hypotenuse.

Attributed by classical writers to one of their own boys, **Pythagoras** of Samos (late sixth century B.C.), this sentence is the famous **Pythagorean theorem**.

In ordinary language it might be stated as follows: The number that is the sum of the squares of the lengths of two sides of the right angle in a triangle with such an angle is the same as the square of the length of the remaining side.

One familiar right triangle, known to the ancient Egyptians and Babylonians, has sides of 3 units and 4 units for the right angle and 5 units for the side opposite the angle, known as the hypotenuse of the triangle. The Pythagorean theorem guarantees that 3 times 3 plus the product of 4 times 4 is the same as 5 times 5, which when worked out becomes $9 + 16 = 25$.

Recently, scholars have found versions of this theorem that were known to Mesopotamian scholars and to the Chinese well before Pythagoras. It seems possible, however, that Pythagoras was the first to propose a proof of the theorem, which subsequently has had many proofs. One of the most famous of these proofs is the one known as *Garfield's proof*, attributed to U.S. president James A. Garfield.

Pythias.   See **Damon and Pythias**.

python   A boa constrictor of very large size, sometimes reaching 20 feet in length.

From the name of the **Python** in classical antiquity, a huge serpent or monster slain by **Apollo** (which see) near the chasm at Delphi, enabling Apollo to establish his oracle at Delphi.

From then on true believers could visit the oracle to obtain wise, albeit cunningly ambiguous, advice from the gods.

Q

Queensberry Rules   A standard set of rules for modern boxing.

From the name of **Sir John Sholto Douglas, 8th Marquis of Queensberry** (1844–1900), in Britain also given as **Marquess of Queensberry**. This Scottish peer was known as a patron of boxing, which at one time was practiced as a gentlemanly art.

One might suppose that the use of Queensberry in **Queensberry Rules** or in **Marquis of Queensberry Rules**, as the rules are invariably called by sportswriters who need to fill up a generous space allotment, would indicate that Lord Queensberry drew up these rules.

Actually it was an English sportsman named John Graham Chambers (1843–1883) who formulated the rules for boxing as well as for other amateur athletic competitions. Queensberry's role was merely that of sponsor of the promulgation of the rules.

Ignoring Chambers's contribution to the rules of boxing might be considered hitting below the belt.

quisling   A traitor, especially one who betrays his country by collaborating with the enemies of his country. While a **quisling** may be a woman as well as a man, it was a man whose name was taken into English.

Vidkun Quisling (1887–1945) was a Norwegian diplomat who became a traitor to his country during the era of Fascist ascendancy in Europe, which began during the Spanish Civil War (1936–1939).

By 1933 he had founded the *Nasjonal Samlung*, the Norwegian National Party, in imitation of the German National Socialist Party.

In 1940, during World War II, this admirer of Hitler and Mussolini acted as advance agent for the successful German invasion of Norway. His collaboration facilitated the takeover and occupation of his country, and he served as prime minister in occupied Norway. After he gave himself up in May 1945, he was tried by a Norwegian court and hanged.

After Quisling's traitorous activities became widely known, **quisling** became a synonym for traitor, denoting any official who acts against the interests of his country.

It is interesting that the Spanish Civil War also gave us *fifth column*, another label for traitors. In this case, the traitors were the supporters of General Francisco Franco in Madrid, who were said to be a fifth column operating within the capital city and ready to rise up and join the four Franco columns known to be marching on Madrid. Their combined strength was thought correctly to be sufficient to defeat the Loyalist supporters who were fighting Franco.

Today, fifth column is used to denote any group of people who act covertly and subversively out of a secret sympathy for the enemies of their country. And quisling is the personification of this tendency.

quixotic   Also given as **Quixotic**, an adjective meaning impulsive, rashly unpredictable; also, visionary, lofty, and idealistic, but impracticable.

From the name of **Don Quixote**, hero of Cervantes's great novel (1604–1615) of the same name. (See also **rosinante**.)

Incidentally, *quixote* in Spanish means "thigh armor."

R

Rabelaisian An adjective meaning characterized by broad, coarse humor and keen satire; also pertaining to the work of **Rabelais**.

From the name of **François Rabelais** (c.1490–1553), the French satirist and humorist, whose works still impress the reader with their astonishing bounty of wit, common sense, and satire. (See also **gargantuan**.)

raglan A type of men's overcoat with sleeves, called **raglan sleeves**, extending to the neck without a shoulder seam.

Named for **Fitzroy James Henry Somerset, 1st Baron Raglan** (1788–1855), an English soldier who eventually attained the rank of field marshal. He was the officer at Balaclava, in the Crimea, who gave the infamous order—said to have resulted from a misunderstood message conveyed by a superior officer—that led to the heroic but disastrous charge of the Light Brigade.

Not the first or last time information was screwed up in war.

Yet another article of clothing, the **balaclava** or **balaclava helmet**, is associated with the battle for the Crimea in 1854, in addition to the **cardigan** (which see) and the raglan. The balaclava was originally a woolen covering for the head, neck, and shoulders, which was worn by soldiers on active service in areas beset by low temperatures.

Nowadays it is typically seen on mountain climbers, skiers, snow shovelers, and bank robbers.

Ramos gin fizz   An iced cocktail made of gin, raw egg white, lime and lemon juice, sugar, and cream, often topped with soda.

Named after the inventor of the drink, **Henry C. Ramos**, a bartender who worked in a New Orleans hotel bar, about whom little else is known.

His popular drink is well worth sampling, especially in New Orleans.

Rasputin   A person who exercises a corrupting influence over another; also, a miracle man.

From the name of **Grigoriy Efimovich Rasputin** (1871–1916), a Siberian peasant monk and religious fanatic said to have hypnotic eyes who was very influential in the court of the Russian czar Nicholas II and czarina Alexandra during World War I.

Rasputin was a libertine and mystic who claimed to have miraculous powers that could heal the hemophiliac heir to the Russian throne, and he apparently was able to ease the crown prince's bleeding. His resulting magnetic influence over the royal couple was responsible in large measure for the czar's failure to respond to the growing public discontent that eventually resulted in his abdication and the outbreak of the Russian Revolution of 1917.

Rasputin was assassinated in 1916 by a group of Russian noblemen who opposed the reigning monarch. As for Nicholas and Alexandra, in 1917 they and their entire family were assassinated by troops of the Revolution.

And their bones were reburied in 1998.

rehoboam   A large wine bottle, equivalent to six regular bottles and holding five quarts, twice the size of a **jeroboam** (which see). **Rehoboams** are used especially for champagne.

From the name of **Rehoboam** (tenth century B.C.), who succeeded his father, **Solomon** (which see), as king of Israel. When northern tribes broke away from Rehoboam's rule, they set up a new kingdom, under Jeroboam. Rehoboam continued as king, but from then on as the first king of Judah. All this is related in 1 Kings.

Just how two wine bottles came to be called Rehoboam and Jeroboam is a matter of conjecture. Note that a wine bottle intermediate in size between jeroboam and rehoboam is called a **methuselah** (which see).

Please don't ask why.

Reynard Any fox.

Also given as **Renard**, from a medieval fable of French, Flemish, and German literature. Today's students know **Reynard** best from the fables of Aesop and La Fontaine, in which a wily Reynard outfoxes (!) a vain crow who is holding a piece of cheese in his craw. By praising the crow's singing voice, Reynard is able to seize the cheese, which the crow drops as soon as he opens his mouth to sing.

The moral of the tale: Beware of flatterers. As though we didn't know. And don't talk to foxes you haven't been introduced to properly.

Rhodes scholarship Any of a large group of scholarships at Oxford University, in England, awarded each year for students from the British Commonwealth, the United States, and Germany.

The scholarships were established by terms of the will of **Cecil John Rhodes** (1853–1902), a South African statesman born in Britain. Rhodes made his fortune at the Kimberley diamond mines, where he organized the De Beers Consolidated Mines Company.

Over the years since the death of Rhodes, American **Rhodes scholars** have usually found their time spent at Oxford to be a springboard for career success, whether in business, academia, government, or the Oval Office.

rickettsia The smallest one-celled creature known, genus *Rickettsia*, plural **rickettsias** or **rickettsiae**, placed by some authorities among the bacteria and by others in taxonomic limbo, between bacteria and viruses.

The rickettsias were named for the American pathologist **Howard Taylor Ricketts** (1871–1910), who discovered them while he was investigating Rocky Mountain spotted fever. Rickettsias are best known as the cause of this disease and of typhus.

Like viruses, rickettsias live within cells and seem unable to live anywhere else, but otherwise rickettsias appear to be tiny bacteria, similar to the rod-shaped bacilli. Among the most recently discovered diseases caused by rickettsia is ehrlichiosis—no relation to the author of this book—which is transmitted by the bite of a tick.

When Ricketts completed his work on Rocky Mountain spotted fever, he turned his attention to typhus, which he demonstrated was transmitted by the bite of a louse—others were making the same finding at that time. But Ricketts had the misfortune of contracting typhus, and he died of it.

Many of his colleagues considered him a martyr to science and, to honor him, named for him the group of organisms he had discovered.

ritzy   Also given as **Ritzy**, a colloquial adjective meaning luxurious, ostentatiously smart, swanky, usually intended in a derogatory sense. As a noun, **ritz** means an ostentatious display and is used primarily in the phrase **put on the ritz**, also given as **put on the Ritz**.

Whichever way the noun is spelled, anyone who **puts on the ritz** is guaranteed to do a reverse Dale Carnegie, losing friends while influencing people. After all, few of us admire persons who flaunt their wealth.

From **Ritz**, a name used for various sumptuous hotels established by **César Ritz** (1850–1918), a Swiss hotelier and restaurateur. The hotels became synonymous with wealth.

In the unlikely event that the various Ritz hotels, whether in London, New York City, or Paris, ever go out of business, the name Ritz will still survive and be understood correctly. F. Scott Fitzgerald took care of that when he entitled one of his best short stories "A Diamond as Big as the Ritz" (1922).

robot   An automaton, a person who responds and acts automatically without showing initiative.

From the mechanical men in the science-fiction drama *R.U.R.*, an abbreviation for Rossum's Universal Robots, written in 1920 by the Czech playwright and author Karel Čapek (1890–1938).

Čapek coined **robot** from the Czech word *robota*, meaning forced labor.

roentgen   In physics, the international unit for measuring ionizing radiation, described as the amount of radiation—usually **X rays** or gamma radiation—that will ionize a cubic centimeter of dry air to the level of one electrostatic unit.

The **roentgen** was named in honor of the German physicist

Wilhelm Conrad Röntgen (1845–1923), in English often spelled **Roentgen**, who discovered X rays. He made his discovery quite by accident when he was using black paper to coat a **Crookes tube** (which see). He found that an invisible radiation had penetrated the paper and caused a phosphorescent substance he had been planning to study to begin glowing.

Roentgen did not let the moment pass, but began to test substance after substance to see which were transparent to the radiation. He found, for example, that flesh was transparent, but bone was not. Without knowing it, Roentgen had launched the enormously valuable medical specialty of radiology, or **roentgenology** as it first was called.

But Roentgen also is credited with adding the word *X ray* to the English vocabulary. When at first he did not know he had encountered an electromagnetic radiation of higher frequency than light, he called the new radiation X rays, taking his *x* from the common algebraic usage of *x* as the unknown. Other persons at first called them **Roentgen rays**, after their discoverer.

Any first-class unabridged dictionary, such as *The Random House Dictionary*, 2d edition, edited by Stuart Berg Flexner, deceased, offers at least twenty terms stemming from the name Roentgen, but most are scarcely ever used. One term in almost constant use, particularly by health physicists employed at atomic energy plants, is *rem*, an acronym of *r*oentgen *e*quivalent in *m*an. A rem expresses the damage potential of exposure to radiation, defined as the biological effect produced by human exposure to one roentgen of high-energy X rays.

This is why **Geiger counters** (which see) are used to measure rem exposure—listen for the clicks!

Rorschach test A test in which ten standardized inkblots are successively presented to a subject, who is asked to state what they represent. The responses given are said to reveal much about underlying personality structure.

Named after the Swiss psychiatrist and neurologist **Hermann Rorschach** (1884–1922), who devised the test as a diagnostic procedure for mental disorders.

Roscian An adjective meaning of or involving acting; also, eminent as an actor.

From the name of **Quintus Roscius** (c.134–c.62 B.C.), considered the greatest comic actor in Rome. He also was author of a treatise on acting and eloquence.

rosinante   A worn-out old nag.

From the name of **Rocinante** (in Spanish, worn-out nag), the bony steed ridden by Don Quixote in Miguel de Cervantes's novel *Don Quixote* (1605, 1615).

Dazzled by stories of feats of chivalry, Quixote sees himself as a knight-errant setting out to redress injustice wherever he finds it, and sees his mount as splendid and worthy of its distinguished rider.

We are left with **Rosinante** as the name in English for Quixote's horse, and **rosinante** as an English word for a tired old horse.

Roy Rogers.   See **Shirley Temple**.

Rube Goldberg   Fantastically complicated; intentionally and deviously complex.

Named for the American cartoonist **Reuben (Rube) Lucius Goldberg** (1883–1970), widely syndicated and never successfully imitated by other cartoonists. Rube Goldberg had the unique gift of being able to devise ingenious and unnecessarily complex means of accomplishing the easiest of mankind's daily routines, and then draw them in rib-tickling detail.

For example, rising from bed in the morning, brushing your teeth, and dressing—all with the assistance of an alarm clock that rouses a mouse, that tickles a cat, that jumps on your chest, that . . . you get the idea.

Understand, however, that describing someone's proposal for a new device as a **Rube Goldberg** idea is a criticism of the idea's excessive complexity and in no way is intended as a compliment.

S

. . . .

sadism In psychiatry, sexual gratification obtained through the infliction of humiliation or pain on another person or on an animal; also, the morbid pleasure experienced in being cruel or in observing acts of cruelty.

From the name of the infamous French writer the **Marquis de Sade**, more correctly **Donatien Alphonse François, Comte de Sade** (1740–1814). While serving as an officer in the French army, Sade was condemned to death for acts of cruelty and unspecified unnatural sexual practices. He escaped, but later served time in the Bastille, and it was there he wrote his books describing sexual perversions and fantasies.

He died in a mental institution at Charenton, France, but is remembered almost everywhere for the word **sadism**—not his invention—and all its spinoffs, including but not limited to **sadist, sadistic**, and **sadistically**. (See **masochism**.)

You never can tell where a hobby will lead you.

St. Valentine's day. See **valentine**.

St. Vitus's dance Also given as **Saint Vitus's dance** and **Saint Vitus dance**; in medicine, a common name for chorea, a childhood condition in which damage to the nervous system results in involuntary movements—a dance—of the limbs and facial muscles. (The word *chorea* is derived from a Greek word meaning *dance*.)

St. Vitus was an early-fourth-century Sicilian martyr. He is regarded as the patron saint of comedians, and his name is invoked as protection against childhood diseases, especially chorea, and against sudden death. In Germany in the seventeenth century, it was a matter of faith that good health for the coming year could be obtained by dancing before a statue of the saint on his feast day. It was such dancing, carried to excess, that is said to have led to naming **St. Vitus's dance**.

In modern times, St. Vitus's dance is better known among physicians as **Sydenham's chorea**, since it was an English physician, **Thomas Sydenham** (1624–1689), who was the first to describe the condition. In addition, Sydenham was the first to identify measles as a separate disease and also wrote extensively on gout.

Incidentally, one good thing about Sydenham's chorea is that it tends to disappear after two or three weeks. But there is the much more serious **Huntington's chorea**, a hereditary and progressive disease. It was named for the U.S. physician **George S. Huntington** (1850–1916), who first described it, in 1872.

Salk vaccine A preparation of inactivated poliomyelitis viruses that produces immunity against polio.

From the name of the U.S. bacteriologist and physician **Jonas Edward Salk** (1914–1995), who became an international hero when he developed the vaccine that stopped a polio epidemic in its tracks in 1954.

A word must be said about the situation in the United States in 1952, when the country was in the grips of the polio epidemic. It had killed nearly 50,000 persons, many of them children, and had caused lifelong paralysis in many more—including Franklin D. Roosevelt, who was stricken in 1921 yet went on to become president in 1932. Newsreel images of patients in iron lungs frightened parents everywhere, and people avoided theaters and beaches lest they be exposed to the disease. As a result, when the polio vaccine was announced in 1954, Jonas Salk was looked upon as a saint.

A few years later, much to the relief of children who were uneasy about taking shots of any kind, the Polish-born U.S. microbiologist

Albert Bruce Sabin (1906–1993) developed an oral polio vaccine, which uses a live attenuated strain of the virus and has been the mainstay of the fight against polio for the past forty years.

Notwithstanding the Sabin accomplishment, the immediate and dramatic effect of the introduction of the **Salk vaccine** makes most people remember Salk better. Recently, because a small number of people contract polio from the **Sabin vaccine** when it is used alone, the Salk vaccine has been reintroduced.

A double boon to humankind.

sally lunn In England, a teacake, slightly sweet, served hot with butter.

Named after a pastry baker, **Sally Lunn**, who lived at Lilliput Alley, in Bath, England, in the late eighteenth century. It is known that she peddled her popular teacakes on the streets of Bath, but little else is known about her. We do know a bit more about her pastry business.

For one thing, if you happen to visit Bath, you may still try a **sally lunn**. Another thing we know is that **Sally** eventually tired of her business and sold it to a baker named Dalmer. He turned out to be knowledgeable in the ways of capitalism, using advertising and a song he wrote about the sally lunn to publicize his product.

Could Dalmer's song have been the first singing commercial? And was Sally Lunn the eighteenth-century prototype of the twentieth-century Sara Lee? Which, in keeping with an American tradition, has become part of a huge conglomerate.

salmonella Any of several members of the bacteria genus *Salmonella* that may enter the digestive tracts of humans and cause food poisoning, characterized by abdominal pains and violent diarrhea.

In the popular mind, **salmonella** is a synonym for food poisoning—which it is not. It is a bacterium. Physicians use the term **salmonellosis** when conferring with colleagues or when filling out forms for health maintenance organizations. Ordinary people are known to correctly call the condition **salmonella poisoning**.

Salmonella is named for the U.S. pathologist **Daniel Elmer Salmon** (1850–1914), who discovered that injection with an inactivated virus could provide immunity to a viral disease. He was one of several scientists whose work led to creation of the **Salk vaccine** (which see).

Salmonella can infect almost any raw animal product, including raw meat and poultry as well as unpasteurized milk and milk products. The bacteria are also found in the feces of humans, farm animals, cats, dogs, and pet turtles. Hens infected with salmonella lay eggs with the bacteria in the egg yolks, and all the chickens in some northeastern flocks are infected.

So it comes as no surprise to learn that outbreaks of salmonellosis occur regularly in the United States. In fact, many cases go unreported because the symptoms typically are mild, but the elderly, the ill, and those with compromised immune systems can be seriously affected.

Thorough cooking of meat, poultry, and eggs and use of pasteurized milk and milk products thwarts most food-borne salmonella.

So be thorough.

Samaritan   Also given as **samaritan**, a person who comes forward to offer assistance to a person in distress who has no claim upon the person who comes forward; a philanthropist.

From the name of the **Samaritans**, inhabitants of ancient Samaria; especially from the unnamed Samaritan described in Luke, in the parable of the **good Samaritan**. This person assisted a man who had been attacked by robbers while on his way to Jericho from Jerusalem.

To show that there is life in the happy phrase, various states have proposed or enacted so-called **good Samaritan laws**, exempting from legal liability persons who give reasonable aid to strangers in severe physical distress.

This is another sign of how far society has progressed: We need to help helpers lest they be sued by those whom they help.

Help!

Sam Browne belt   Formerly a sword belt worn by U.S. Army officers, with a supporting strap over the right shoulder. Now seen occasionally as part of the dress uniform of members of various organizations, usually without a sword.

Named for **Sir Samuel James Browne** (1824–1901), a British soldier, to whom invention of the **Sam Browne belt** (1852) is attributed.

Samson   Any man of outstanding physical strength.

From the name of the Old Testament **Samson**, an Israelite leader famous for his strength, whose story is told in Judges.

Unfortunately, Samson fell under the spell of a certain Delilah, a seductress who betrayed him to the Philistines. The events that followed ended in his untimely death, a great hero brought down by the woman he loved too well.

For a fuller account of the story of Samson and Delilah, see also **Delilah**.

sandwich   One of the great contributions to civilized cuisine: slices of meat, fish (preferably smoked), cheese, and virtually anything you can imagine served in a roll or between two or more slices of bread.

Named after **John Montagu, 4th Earl of Sandwich** (1718–1792), an English politician whose name was attached to the **sandwich** perhaps because of his passion for gambling. In fact, **sandwiches** had been eaten for many centuries before the eighteenth, but nobody had thought to name them.

Notwithstanding, John Montagu is said to once have passed twenty-four consecutive hours in gambling, his only refreshment being slices of cold beef between two slices of toast, which collation enabled him to eat without holding up play.

For those who know how skimpy sandwiches are in England, France, and some other foreign parts, the occasional sandwich would scarcely keep body and soul together. Now, if the Earl had ordered pastrami on rye or a BLT, his hunger would surely have been contained.

Hold the mayo!

Sapphic   An adjective whose first meaning is pertaining to **Sappho** or to verse written by her or written by others in imitation of her style.

The second meaning of **Sapphic** is lesbian, with the noun **sapphism** meaning lesbianism and with the noun **sapphist** meaning a lesbian. The plot thickens.

Sappho was a Greek lyric poet (c.620–c.565 B.C.) born on the island of Lesbos. She married and had a daughter, but in the fragments of her poetry extant we know she showed affection and love for young girls in her circle, and in one love poem showed passion for a certain girl and was condemned for this.

Traditionally, therefore, Sappho has been represented as the famous poetess of Lesbos, the greatest woman poet of antiquity, exceptionally immoral, and a lesbian. Her name, with its connotations, has contributed richly to the English language.

Sardanapalian   Excessively luxurious or sensual; decadent.

From the name of **Sardanapalus** (669–626 B.C.), legendary last king of Assyria, in what is now northern Iraq. The king was notorious for his luxury and effeminacy. Hence the meaning of **Sardanapalian**.

Sardanapalus was the grandson of Sennacherib, the Assyrian king who destroyed Babylon and captured many of the cities of Judah. Jerusalem was spared when an angel of God came in the night and brought down a plague that destroyed Sennacherib's army. You may recall Lord Byron's poem of 1815 called "The Destruction of Sennacherib":

> *The Assyrian came down like the wolf on the fold,*
> *And his cohorts were gleaming in purple and gold.*

Without Byron many of us would never have heard of Sennacherib or his army.

But also recall 2 Kings: "The angel of the Lord went out and smote in the camp of the Assyrians an hundred fourscore and five thousand"? That's a lot of Assyrians.

When Sennacherib returned to Nineveh from Judah, two of his sons murdered him. Nice family. With values yet!

But back to Sardanapalus. When the wicked city of Nineveh (see **Jonah**), capital of Assyria, was subjected to a long siege by the Medes, whose empire included much of modern Iran, Sardanapalus fought bravely but finally chose death and sacrificed himself on a funeral pyre. Myrra, his favorite concubine, along with all his vaunted treasures, went into the flames right after him.

At least the king enjoyed himself while things were going his way. Beats putting your money into germ warfare and poison gas.

saturnalia   Unrestrained revelry; an orgy.

Derived ultimately from the name of **Saturn**, the ancient Roman god of agriculture. His festival, **Saturnalia**—plural Saturnalia or **Saturnalias**—was celebrated for seven days, a period of unrestrained freedom, merriment, riot, and debauchery. During this week, criminals went unpunished and the law courts and schools were closed.

Sounds like heaven on earth, but see **saturnine** to find out that the influence of **Saturn** could also be quite different.

saturnine   Gloomy, forbidding of temperament; grave, phlegmatic; taciturn.

Qualities markedly different from those exhibited by people during a **saturnalia** (which see).

From the name of the planet **Saturn**, named for the ancient Roman god of agriculture, father of Jupiter. Astrology credits those born under Saturn's influence with being cold and sluggish in temperament.

How can this be? The ancient astrologers and alchemists called lead by the name **Saturn**, so the planet Saturn was an evil planet to be born under. Today we have established that lead poisoning can result in anemia, muscle weakness, blindness, coma, and other unwelcome conditions that may be perceived as **saturnine**.

Once again we see that the ancient practitioners may have been on to something.

saxophone   A keyed brass wind instrument having a reed like that of the clarinet.

Named after **Antoine "Adolphe" Joseph Sax** (1814–1894) and his father, **Charles Joseph Sax** (1791–1865), both Belgian makers of musical instruments. They invented and named such instruments as the **saxophone, saxhorn, saxotromba,** and **saxtuba,** only one of which was played by a U.S. president.

As far as we know.

scheelite   A mineral, calcium tungstate, that was formed by metamorphic action and is one of the main sources of tungsten, so useful in incandescent lamps.

Named after the Swedish chemist **Karl Wilhelm Scheele** (1742–1786), who discovered many acids and made other important finds. But he is best known as a careful scientist who *almost* discovered no fewer than seven elements—barium, chlorine, manganese, molybdenum, nitrogen, oxygen, and tungsten—but through one accident or another missed gaining credit for any of them.

One of Scheele's near misses came when he investigated, in 1781, a mineral called *tung sten*, Swedish for "heavy stone," and proposed that it must contain a new element. Two years later, however, other chemists, working with a different mineral, wolframite, became the first to find the element Scheele had predicted. As a result, the names wolfram and tungsten were both used for this element.

Today, while wolfram has lost out to tungsten as the name of the element, tungsten retains the chemical symbol W. The original *tung sten* that Scheele investigated has become known as **scheelite**.

A compromise worthy of Congress at its most devious.

scopolamine   Various preparations of an alkaloid of several uses; for example, as a sedative and for dilation of eye pupils, but known by readers of spy fiction especially as truth serum.

Although **scopolamine** may reduce one's defenses somewhat, it cannot in fact guarantee that a person under its influence will speak the truth.

The drug's name derives from *Scopolia*, the generic name of the plant whose dried rhizomes are the main source of the alkaloid. In turn, the genus is named for the Italian physician and naturalist **Giovanni Antonio Scopoli** (1723–1788).

Scylla and Charybdis   A formidable, double-barreled threat to personal safety.

From the names of **Scylla** and **Charybdis** in Greek mythology, a pair of sea monsters. **Scylla**, female, devoured men from ships that tried to navigate the perilous channel between her cave and the whirlpool Charybdis. According to Homer, Scylla had twelve feet and six heads, each equipped with ferocious teeth. In later legend Scylla became a dangerous rock located on the Italian side of the Strait of Messina. (Location was everything, even in Greek mythology.)

Charybdis, spoken of as male, was a dangerous whirlpool located in a narrow channel of the sea, which came to be identified with the Strait of Messina, opposite Scylla's cave. According to Homer, Charybdis dwelt under a huge fig tree on a rock and thrice daily swallowed the waters of the sea and thrice daily disgorged them (the original bulimic?).

Unfortunately, the Strait of Messina has no whirlpool, but verisimilitude has never been a barrier to widespread acceptance of a good story.

Whatever the story, when you find yourself **between Scylla and Charybdis**, or between the devil and the deep blue sea, as we also say, you are in deep trouble indeed. And when you **fall from Scylla into**

Charybdis or **by avoiding Scylla, you fall into Charybdis**, you are getting out of the frying pan only to fall into the fire.

Better to avoid sea voyages.

Shavian   An adjective derived from the name of **George Bernard Shaw** (1856–1950), meaning after the manner of the great Irish dramatist, essayist, and critic and especially descriptive of his ideas on morality, self-discipline, integrity, and, of course, his wit.

The noun **Shavian** denotes a specialist in the study of Shaw's work, as well as an admirer of Shaw.

Sheraton   A style of furniture of elegant Neoclassical design.

From the name of **Thomas Sheraton** (1751–1806), an English furniture designer. Unlike his contemporary, **Hepplewhite** (which see), he did not manufacture the pieces he designed. (See also **Chippendale**.)

The name **Sheraton** today is more synonymous with a hotel chain known more for functional than elegant design.

sherlock   Also given as **Sherlock** and as **Sherlock Holmes**, a person adept at solving challenging mysteries; a private detective.

From the name of **Sherlock Holmes**, the fictional amateur detective created by Sir Arthur Conan Doyle (1859–1930), the Scottish writer known especially for his detective stories. Holmes, along with his sidekick, the good-natured Dr. Watson, has entertained generations of readers, especially the Holmes devotees known as the Baker Street Irregulars, named for the gang of street urchins the detective used to gather information.

Holmes, given to playing the violin and indulging his cocaine habit, solved mysteries by ingenious deduction, based on meticulous interpretation of minute details and strict attention to apparently insignificant circumstances—invariably to the astonishment of Dr. Watson and the never-flagging admiration of Doyle's readers.

The name of the great detective has also given English the noun **Holmesian**, meaning a devotee of the Sherlock Holmes stories, which is also used as an adjective, meaning pertaining to Sherlock Holmes.

Elementary, my dear Watson.

shigella   Any of several bacteria, genus *Shigella*, plural **shigellas** or **shigellae**, some of which are toxic to humans and other warm-blooded animals.

Named after the Japanese bacteriologist **Kiyoshi Shiga** (1870–1957), who discovered in 1898 the bacillus that causes one form of dysentery. This acute intestinal infection, called **shigellosis**, is caused by a toxin produced during infection by **shigella**.

The shigella toxin is actually produced by a small ring of DNA called a plasmid, which can be passed on to other species of bacteria. This toxin is the poison that has moved into one strain of **E. coli** (which see) and made that bacterium notorious.

The things we have to worry about!

Shirley Temple A nonalcoholic drink of ginger ale and grenadine, served in a cocktail glass and garnished with a maraschino cherry.

A **Shirley Temple**, in appearance not unlike a Manhattan cocktail, is intended to occupy a child, particularly a girl, who might otherwise feel deprived and have to sip ice water or Diet Coke while staring envyingly at parents swilling their favorite aperitifs in a restaurant before their food arrives.

Named after the quintessentially American child movie star **Shirley Temple** (born 1928), who not only could sing and dance but could also act until, alas, maturity overcame her. At that point, the good ship Lollipop sailed into the sunset, leaving her at the mercy of marriage and the rest of what we call adult responsibility. Her career from then on lacked tinsel, but included serving for a time as U.S. representative to the United Nations and later as ambassador to Ghana. Why not? U.S. voters elected another movie star president.

But back to the little girl sipping her Shirley Temple. What was her young brother doing while she sipped? He was concentrating on imbibing a **Roy Rogers**, which is what real boys drink. A Roy Rogers, named for the memorable Singing Cowboy, is identical with the Shirley Temple.

But we never let the children know.

shrapnel A noun with two meanings: the fragments of exploded artillery shells or bombs; an artillery shell containing metal pieces that is designed to explode above a target and scatter these pieces, known as **shrapnel**.

With devastating effects, as millions of war veterans can attest.

From the name of **Henry Shrapnel** (1761–1842), the English artillery officer who invented the artillery shell c.1806.

Shylock   As **Shylock**, a grasping, hard-hearted moneylender; also, a pawnbroker. As a verb, **shylock,** to lend money at usurious rates.

From the name of the character **Shylock**, a vengeful moneylender in Shakespeare's *Merchant of Venice* (c.1595). Shylock makes a loan to Antonio, a Venetian merchant, with the stipulation that if Antonio defaults on the loan, Shylock may cut a pound of flesh from the merchant's body. After Antonio does default—through no fault of his own—and the remaining plot intricacies are unraveled, the merchant manages to keep his flesh intact.

Shakespeare gave us a timeless play that added Shylock to English and the phrase *a pound of flesh*, meaning any legal but morally offensive demand; the whole of a bargain down to the last unconscionable detail. By creating Shylock as Jewish, Shakespeare also gave English a name that helped fuel ageless ethnic and religious stereotypes. As though any help were needed.

On a lighter note, remember that Antonio was just trying to help a friend who needed cash for a trip to win the hand of his lady, **Portia** (which see).

Maybe we'd all be better off if we did not cosign loans or borrow money for anyone.

sibyl   A fortune-teller; a female prophet or witch. Also, any of certain women of antiquity said to possess oracular powers, who uttered their prophecies under the inspiration of a god.

From the name of classical mythology's **Sibylla**, an Asian maiden whose lover, **Apollo** (which see), gave her the gift of prophecy and long life. In the past, there were **sibyls** all over the place, the most famous the sibyl of Cumae, in southern Italy, who guided Aeneas through the underworld. (See **Achates**.) A real challenge, but this sibyl was up to it.

The noun **sibyl** led naturally to the adjective **sibylline**, meaning oracular and mysteriously prophetic, as well as meaning issuing from a sibyl, as in the phrase *sybilline powers*.

Beats putting your faith in **Nostradamus** (which see) or in those tabloid tip sheets for sale at your supermarket checkout.

sideburns.   See **burnsides**.

siemens   The standard international unit of electrical conductance, which replaced the mho (see **ohm**).

Named after the German inventor and electrical engineer **Ernst**

Werner von Siemens (1816–1892). A word must be said about the extraordinary Siemens brothers. Ernst, among other achievements, developed electroplating. Karl Wilhelm Siemens (1823–1883) developed the open-hearth steel furnace. Friedrich Siemens (1826–1904) applied the principles of the open-hearth process to glassmaking. But only Ernst entered the English language, with **siemens**.

A trap for the unwary: *siemens* looks plural but must be treated as singular.

silhouette   As a noun, a picture of a person in profile; an object in outline. Also, a person or object seen against the light so only the outline can be perceived. As a verb, meaning show in or as if in **silhouette**.

From the name of **Etienne de Silhouette** (1709–1767), a French minister of finance known for his parsimonious ways in authorizing public expenditures. As a result, his name was applied to cheaply made things, especially to blacked-in shadow outlines.

Please don't talk about me when I'm gone.

Simon Legree   Any cruel boss or, in an earlier time, any cruel master.

From the name of the fictional **Simon Legree**, a brutal plantation owner and chief villain of the novel *Uncle Tom's Cabin* (1852), by Harriet Beecher Stowe (1811–1896). See also **Uncle Tom**.

simon-pure   As an adjective, meaning real or genuine, pure or unadulterated, honest or upright. As a noun, **Simon Pure**, meaning the real or authentic person or thing.

Thus we say, "This stone is the real thing, a **simon-pure** amethyst" and "Will the real **Simon Pure** please stand up?"

From the name of a Quaker character, **Simon Pure**, in the comedy *A Bold Stroke for a Wife* (1717), by the English playwright Susannah Freeman Centlivre (c.1667–c.1723). During part of the play, Simon is impersonated by another character.

Sisyphean   An adjective characterizing labor or a task, and meaning endlessly laborious.

From the name of **Sisyphus**, the all-time loser in Greek legend, who was the son of Aeolus, god of the wind (see **Aeolian**), and in post-Homeric legend the father of Odysseus (see **odyssey**), a traveling man known also as Ulysses.

The details of the career of Sisyphus are in dispute, but one account is given here: Sisyphus had to pay a stiff price after Autolycus, a well-known thief, stole his cattle. While that may not sound right, the story is far from over; indeed this is just the first installment of our story.

In the second installment, Sisyphus retaliated by stealing Aegina, the daughter of Autolycus. A daughter for some cows? Could this have been the ancient Greek version of an eye for an eye?

In the third installment, Sisyphus indulged in a bit of mudslinging, letting it be known that Zeus had raped Aegina, and as a result of this misdeed Aegina had borne a son of Zeus. And it was for this damaging revelation that Zeus, god of gods, condemned Sisyphus to Hades.

In Hades Sisyphus was condemned forever to roll a boulder to the top of a steep hill. It was an ornery boulder that kept slipping out of his grasp every time he was about to reach the summit, and then rolled down to the bottom of the hill. Thus, his task would never be done, making clear just what is meant by a **sisyphean** task.

Maybe Sisyphus would have been better off if he had overlooked the cattle rustling. The rest of us must recognize that whistle blowing does not always have the expected beneficial result.

smellfungus A carper, a faultfinder; a grumbler; a discontented person. Also given as **smelfungus** and **Smellfungus**.

From the nickname coined by Irish novelist Laurence Sterne (1713–1768) to ridicule Tobias Smollett (1721–1771), the Scottish novelist who wrote *Travels in France and Italy* (1766), a book that had little good to say of these countries.

Sterne, seeing Smollett as carping, wrote in his *A Sentimental Journey* (1768, unfinished):

The learned **Smellfungus** travelled from Boulogne to Paris . . . but he set out with the spleen and jaundice, and every object he pass'd by was discoloured or distorted.

We all know the type. And we thank Sterne for contributing what may be called an olfactory noun to English.

Socratic method A method of searching for definition, as in the mind of a student, or to impart information and the like by systematic use of questions and answers; dialectic.

From the **Socratic method** of the Greek philosopher **Socrates**

(469–399 B.C.). The method started with Socrates asking students for definitions of familiar concepts and, perceiving contradictions in the responses, demonstrating the ignorance of the students—which he would claim ironically to share—and the need for a deeper and more honest analysis.

This activity did not make him a popular figure in Athenian life— you can see why if you recall your freshman course in philosophy— and at age seventy he was accused of corrupting Athenian youth. Found guilty of the charge, he was given the option of paying a fine, which he rejected, and was sentenced to die by drinking hemlock.

He did so, without Dr. Kervorkian.

solander A carrying case for maps, drawings, botanical specimens, and the like, made to resemble a book.

Named after its inventor, **Daniel Charles Solander** (1732–1782), a Swedish naturalist.

Solomon Any extraordinarily wise man; a sage.

Named after **Solomon**, a king of Israel (c.970–930 B.C.), whose reign was seen as splendid for the unprecedented scale and magnificence of the temple and royal palaces that were built in his time. Solomon was credited with superlative wisdom, leading to the adjective **Solomonic**, taken to mean wise or reasonable in character.

We all know the wisdom shown by Solomon that is described in 1 Kings. He once had to rule on a dispute involving two women who both claimed parentage of the same baby. When he proposed to share the baby by cutting it in two, only one woman showed concern for the baby's life, whereupon Solomon gave her the baby.

Remember this if you come up before a **Solomon** in a paternity suit. But don't forget to hire a good lawyer.

Solon A wise lawgiver; also, a person who affects wisdom, a wise guy.

From the name of **Solon**, an Athenian statesman and sage (c.638–c.558 B.C.), the original wise lawgiver, considered one of the Seven Sages of Greece, who flourished in the sixth century B.C. The other six are Thales, Periander, Cleobulus, Chilon, Bias, and Pittacus.

It is Solon who is credited with originating the incontrovertibly helpful advice *Know thyself*, inscribed at the Delphic Oracle. These words alone would be enough to qualify Solon as a sage.

But **solon** is also used ironically, suggesting that a person so characterized is anything but a wise lawgiver. Thus the second meaning of solon: a wise guy, a person who affects wisdom.

See **Draconian** for more information about Solon.

sousaphone   A type of bass tuba, used especially in marching bands. Said by one wag to supply the low-pitched "oom" that precedes the higher "pa-pa" in Viennese waltzes.

The **sousaphone** is said to have been invented in 1899 by an American, C. G. Conn, who named his instrument after **John Philip Sousa** (1854–1932), American composer and bandmaster.

After serving for a time as director of the U.S. Marine Corps Band, Sousa organized his own band and went on to become famous as the composer of more than one hundred spirited marches, among them "Stars and Stripes Forever."

Many Sousa marches are played to this day and still are guaranteed to quicken the flow of blood through the veins of patriotic Americans.

Beats angioplasty.

Spartan   Also given as **spartan**, an adjective meaning frugal, austere; rigorously simple; disciplined. As a noun, a person showing **Spartan** frugality, austerity, and discipline. Especially a person who can bear pain unflinchingly.

From the name of the inhabitants of the ancient city-state of **Sparta**, in Greece, famous for its strict discipline and arduous training of its soldiers. So marked has been the influence of Spartan on English that we see phrase after phrase built on this adjective. Just for starters, consider "Spartan diet," "Spartan life," "Spartan simplicity," "Spartan courage," and "Spartan furnishings."

A story read by every schoolchild relates how a Spartan mother proudly handed her son the shield he would carry into battle. Her final words to him? Come back either with your shield or on it. That is, either victorious or dead.

Talk about tough love.

Spode   A kind of fine china or porcelain made originally by the English potter **Josiah Spode** (1754–1827), protected by trademark.

His son, Josiah Spode II, followed in his father's footsteps, and the firm continues until today.

spoonerism   A transposition of the initial sounds of words, usually by accident or absentmindedness, with ludicrous result. Consider the following:

> *Half-warmed fish for half-formed wish.*
> *Blushing crow for crushing blow.*
> *Shoving leopard for loving shepherd.*
> *Hissed the mystery lecture for missed the history lecture.*
> *I was sewn to this sheet for I was shown to this seat.*

Named after the **Reverend William Archibald Spooner** (1844–1930), an English clergyman and Warden of New College, Oxford, who had a nervous tendency to transpose sounds in the manner shown above.

Stakhanovite   A person who is exceptionally hardworking and productive. Formerly, a worker in the Soviet Union who regularly surpassed his production quota and was duly rewarded with special privileges and rewards for assiduity.

Named after a Soviet coal miner, **Aleksei Grigorevich Stakhanov** (1906–1977), whose extraordinary productivity became the focus of a propaganda campaign intended to spur other workers to increase their work output. The noun **Stakhanovite** and its offspring, **Stakhanovism**, are now relics of the glory days of the industrial U.S.S.R., before Soviet citizens began to enjoy the era of perestroika and glasnost, followed by collapse into the joys of privatization.

stapelia   Any of various plants of the genus *Stapelia*, native to North Africa and having leafless stems and oddly colored flowers.

Named after a Dutch botanist, **Jan Bode van Stapel** (died 1636), about whom little is known.

Stapelia's most distinctive characteristic is that most species emit a fetid odor, characterized as carrionlike. It is pollinated by beetles and maggot flies that are attracted to the plant by what they perceive to be decaying meat, and one species, *Stapelia hirsuta*, is called the carrion flower.

Proving that even the worst-smelling flower in the world can be loved.

Sten gun   Also given as **Sten**, a type of lightweight submachine gun formerly manufactured in England.

Sten is an acronym formed from the names of the designers, R. V. Shepherd and H. J. Turpin plus its place of manufacture, Enfield, Greater London, England.

A marvelous source for a name.

stent   A noun with at least two medical meanings: The first is a coil inserted in an artery to keep it open, most often after angioplasty. Usually, alas, this is only a temporary palliative and some other way of keeping the artery open—even a second angioplasty—must be tried.

The second meaning antedates the first: A sort of plaster used for taking dental impressions and as a temporary brace in dentistry; also, the impression or cast made in this way.

The dental meanings are from the name of an English dentist, **Charles R. Stent** (died 1901), who invented the substance and developed techniques for using it. The coil inserted in an artery borrows its name from the temporary dental brace usage, not from Mr. Stent.

Incidentally, an enterprising person presumed to have been a relative of Charles R. Stent, named Caroline Stent, had offices on Coventry Street, London, in 1899. She offered **stent** tablets, protected by trademark for sale to dentists and others seeking to make good impressions.

But there is more to the meaning of stent. The substance became useful—until Teflon was invented—as a temporary tubelike structure or glue used to hold a skin graft in place.

stentorian   Said of a voice, an adjective meaning very loud and far-reaching.

From the name of **Stentor**, a Greek warrior in the Trojan War known for his loud voice. According to Homer in the *Iliad*, Stentor's voice was as loud as the voices of fifty men combined, today surely what would be called a **stentorian** voice.

Stetson   A man's felt hat with a broad brim and high crown, protected by trademark; especially such a hat worn by a cattle rancher or a cowboy.

Named after **John Batterson Stetson** (1830–1906), a Philadelphia, Pennsylvania, hat manufacturer.

Stradivarius   A violin made by **Antonio Stradivari**, also called **Stradivarius** (c. 1644–1737), of Cremona, Italy, or by his sons, **Francesco** (1671–1742) and **Omobono** (1679–1742). Musicians call his violins Strads.

Stradivari was a student of Nicolò **Amati** (which see) and is generally credited with improving the design of stringed instruments and bringing to perfection the so-called Cremona violin. It is believed that between 1666 and 1737, the year of his death, Antonio Stradivari made more than a thousand violins, violas, and violoncellos.

The busiest shop in Cremona.

Stroganoff.   See **beef Stroganoff.**

Svengali   A person who exerts a controlling influence on another person, often for sinister purpose.

From the name of the character **Svengali**, an evil hypnotist in *Trilby* (1894), a novel by British novelist George du Maurier (1834–1896). (See also **trilby**.)

sword of Damocles   A situation threatening imminent harm or disaster, especially in a time of apparent well-being.

From the name of **Damocles** (fourth century B.C.), a courtier given to excessive flattery of Dionysius the Elder, tyrant of Syracuse. After Damocles extolled the happiness of Dionysius, a banquet was arranged by Dionysius at which Damocles was seated with a sword—the **sword of Damocles**—suspended over his head by a single horsehair. All this by way of teaching Damocles a lesson important in life: a ruler's happiness hangs by a hair.

It is interesting to note that Damocles enters our language only as the name of a historical figure, not as a synonym for sweet-talker or flatterer. Yet, Damocles thrives in *sword of Damocles* and probably always will, and many of us in our speech and writings will use the related phrase *a sword hanging over one's head* to convey the same meaning, thus illustrating the power of one figure of speech to breed other ways of conveying the same meaning.

And many of us know you don't have to be a tyrant or even a benevolent ruler to profit from the lesson that Dionysius taught Damocles: It may not take much to disturb the comfort of our lives and bring us down—no matter what our station in life.

We also know we must always look up before taking a seat at a table—especially when place cards are used to seat the guests.

You never know.

sybarite   A person inordinately fond of comfort and luxury; in English it is common to see **sybarite** preceded by the word "pampered." The adjective **sybaritic**, of course, means inclined to love luxury or sensuous pleasure.

From the name **Sybarite**, an inhabitant of **Sybaris**, an ancient Greek city in southern Italy noted for its wealth and self-indulgence, somewhat comparable to the California city we fondly call La La Land.

Incidentally, Sybaris was destroyed in 510 B.C. Wouldn't you know it? Some folks just can't stand seeing anybody have a good time.

T

∙ ∙

Tammany Hall A symbol of wholesale and widespread political malfeasance, corruption, and abuse of power. Also, the name of a once-powerful Democratic Party political organization in New York City.

Named after **Tammany Hall**, the building housing the organization's headquarters, which took its name from the late-seventeenth-century Delaware Indian chief **Tammany**, also given as **Tamanen** and **Tammenund**.

Tammany Hall, founded in 1789, was originally a New York City fraternal and benevolent society, but once it became associated with the Democratic Party in the nineteenth century, its name became synonymous with corruption.

Incidentally, the Indian chief Tammany is said to have welcomed William Penn, who founded Pennsylvania, and Tammany was regarded as the patron saint of Pennsylvania and other colonies.

But what happened to Tammany Hall? It was much reduced in power by President Franklin D. Roosevelt in the 1930s and is never in the news today, except when the *New York Times* is starved for nostalgic feature stories.

tam-o'-shanter   A round Scottish cap, usually woolen, with a pom-pom at its center.

From the name of the hero of **"Tam O'Shanter"** (1791), a narrative poem by Robert Burns (1759–1796), considered the greatest poet of his people. On a night when strong drink affects Tam's perceptions, he has to ride for his life to escape pursuing witches, including one called Cutty Sark, in English translated as "short shirt."

The popularity of Burns among his Scottish compatriots is such that his birthday on January 25 is celebrated each year with feasting and drinking.

Featuring haggis and Cutty Sark Scotch, one presumes.

tantalize   A verb meaning torment or tease by the sight or promise of something that is desired but is withheld or kept just out of reach.

From the name of **Tantalus**, in classical mythology a king of Phrygia, in Asia Minor. Tantalus may have been the original leaker of information, since he goes way back in time and is said to have been punished for revealing to mortals the secrets of the gods.

But it is the punishment, not the crime, of Tantalus that interests us. As a son of Zeus, he was himself a god and immortal, so any punishment he received would last forever.

Tantalus was punished by being sent to Hades, where he was plunged into a river. There he still remains, up to his chin in water. Above him are tree branches heavy with fruit. But whenever he tries to drink or eat, the water of the river recedes beyond his reach. As a result of this fiendish arrangement, Tantalus is perpetually thirsty and hungry. It must not be overlooked that he also is perpetually **tantalized**, that is, suffering the agony of unfulfilled anticipation.

The rest of us who may be inclined to **tantalize** someone must first think of poor Tantalus up to his chin in water. And anyone who considers leaking secrets must recall why and how Tantalus was punished.

Incidentally, we are indebted to Tantalus for two other English words. **Tantalum** is element 73, and **tantalus** is a rack holding wine or liquors in full view but under lock and key. Perhaps the inventor of this artifact of unalloyed temptation without fulfillment has a place in Hades next to that of Tantalus himself.

At least they could chat to help pass time.

Tartuffe   A religious hypocrite.

From the name of the title character in the comedy *Le Tartuffe* (1664) by Molière, stage name of Jean Baptiste Poquelin (1622–1673). Molière's **Tartuffe** pretends to a piety unsupported by his actions and, after the playwright has resolved various dramatic complexities, is taken off to jail.

Unscrupulous television evangelists, beware!

Tarzan   A person of extraordinary strength and agility.

From the name of the hero in a series of novels by Edgar Rice Burroughs (1875–1950) dealing with **Tarzan**, an Englishman who is abandoned in Africa as a child and is brought up by apes. As he matures, he becomes unusually muscular and athletic, learns to speak the languages of various animals, navigates the jungle as easily as the animals, and survives many hair-raising adventures, often with the help of animal friends—and the faithful readership of several generations of American boys and girls.

tattersall   A pattern of colored crossbars forming squares on a solid-color background. Also, a fabric made with this pattern.

Named after **Richard Tattersall** (1724–1795), an English auctioneer who set up shop at London's Hyde Park Corner in 1776. His auction rooms, Tattersall's, became a center of racing and a celebrated market for thoroughbred horses. The patterns of the horse blankets common in those times were made in the fabric that came to be called **tattersall**, which in time made its way to the vests of racetrack habitués and Connecticut homeowners.

teddy bear   A furry, stuffed toy bear.

From the name **Teddy**, a diminutive for Theodore, in this case of **President Theodore Roosevelt** (1858–1919), who was a dedicated big game hunter. When he went on a bear hunting expedition out west in 1906, the *New York Times* published a comic poem replete with cartoons concerning a pair of bears named Teddy B (B for Bear) and Teddy G (a sensible interpretation of which is yet unknown).

The two names were transferred to live bears given to the Bronx Zoo in that year, and soon enough were turned to commercial advantage by enterprising toy dealers who sold **teddy bears** imported from Germany. They were an instant success and still are sold in great numbers each year, although more likely produced by underpaid artisans in Asia.

Any large man who is sweet tempered and on the quiet side could be referred to as a teddy bear, too.

terpsichorean An adjective meaning pertaining to dancing. As **Terpsichorean**, meaning pertaining to Terpsichore. As a noun, **terpsichorean** means dancer.

From the name of **Terpsichore**, in Greek and Roman mythology the muse of dancing and lyric poetry.

Tesla coil A transformer that raises voltage—something all transformers do—and controls frequency of alternation for alternating current.

As a result, **Tesla coils** have been much used in various applications in radio and television signal generation and reception.

From the name of the coil's inventor, Yugoslav-born American electrical engineer and physicist **Nikola Tesla** (1856–1943). Although Tesla came up with many important inventions, the coil is the only one that carries his name. But the **tesla**, the unit of magnetic flux density, was also named in his honor.

It is generally recognized that Tesla's inventions made possible the modern distribution of energy over wires from central power stations. His chief contribution was the development of transformers that could raise alternating current to the high voltages needed for transmission over considerable distances, and then reduce the current's voltage to a level appropriate for homes and factories. He also invented an electric motor that would run on alternating current.

Ironically, Tesla's later work was met with skepticism from orthodox scientists, and there even have been suggestions that he epitomized the mad scientist of comic books. Why? He claimed he had communicated with other planets, invented a death ray that could destroy airplanes at a distance (Star Wars?), and come upon great electric currents coursing through Earth.

Further, he enjoyed demonstrating electrical phenomena, for example, lighting electric lightbulbs by using his body as a conductor, and creating lightning flashes as much as 135 feet long.

Today, he is honored by the Tesla Memorial Society, a group whose sole aim is to perpetuate Tesla's reputation and work.

And why not?

Thespian   Also given as **thespian**, an adjective meaning pertaining to tragedy or drama. More often a noun, given with or without a capital *T*, meaning an actor; formerly meaning an actor or actress.

From the name of **Thespis**, a sixth century B.C. Greek poet regarded as the father of Greek tragedy.

Thompson submachine gun.   See **Tommy gun**.

thrasonical   Boastful.

From the name of **Thraso**, a braggart soldier in the *Eunuchus*, written by Terence (c.190–159 B.C.), a Roman playwright, actual name **Publius Terentius Afer**.

titan   A person of great strength, intelligence, or influence. The adjective **titanic**, also given as **titan**, means of enormous strength, size, and power.

Suggesting how the ill-fated British luxury liner *Titanic* and **titanium**, element 22, got their names.

From the name of the **Titans**, in Greek mythology the six sons and six daughters of Uranus and Gaea. They were all enormous, with strength to match their size. Gaea, their mother, encouraged them to overthrow their father Uranus. Not only did they do so, but in the course of eliminating Daddy, they emasculated him.

Things didn't go the Titans' way for too long, and they all ended up in Hades.

So don't get any fancy ideas about kicking your old man around.

Titian red   Said of hair, variously described as bright golden auburn, reddish brown, and golden brown. What could be better?

From the name of **Titian**, the greatest of the Venetian painters and called by some the founder of modern painting, real name **Tiziano Vecellio** (c.1488–1576).

As a Michelin Guide might say, well worth a visit to the Uffizi Palace, in Florence, Italy, where some of Titian's paintings hang, and **Titian red** explains itself.

Tom Collins   A long drink of gin, lemon or lime juice, and soda water, sweetened and served over ice.

American lexicographers guess that the source of this drink was a bartender named **Tom Collins**. Reasonable enough.

The British use the name **John Collins** for a drink much like the American one, except that whisky may be substituted for the gin.

Could there have been a pair of Collins brothers, both pioneering bartenders, who divided the world market for drinks between them? Sounds like restraint of trade.

Tommy gun More formally known as the **Thompson submachine gun**, a .45-caliber short-barreled submachine gun, designed to be fired from shoulder or hip.

Named after **John Taliaferro Thompson** (1860–1940), an American soldier and inventor. Manufacture of Thompson's weapon began soon after he invented it in 1920, and Prohibition's bootleggers and gangsters proved unanimous in their endorsement of the **Tommy gun**, known fondly for a time as a "Chicago typewriter," for its chattering sound when firing.

tontine An insurance scheme in which subscribers to a common fund receive annuities that grow in value as subscribers die, until the last survivor inherits the entire fund. Also, the share of each subscriber.

From the name of **Lorenzo Tonti** (1620–1690), a French banker born in Naples, Italy, who introduced **tontines** into France in 1653. They were intended initially to float government loans, later to raise large sums for public projects.

Tony Any of the medallions awarded annually by the American Theater Wing for excellence in some aspect of theatrical production or performance.

Named after **Antoinette "Tony" Perry** (1888-1946), a founder, in 1941, of the American Theater Wing, a professional school in New York City for the performing arts. Ms. Perry, an American, had a long and successful stage career as actress and director.

The **Tony** awards were established about a decade after the Oscars, the statuettes awarded annually by the Academy of Motion Picture Arts and Sciences. It is not known how the Oscars got their name.

toxophilite A devotee of archery.

From an imaginary proper name, **Toxophilus**, used as the title of a 1545 treatise on archery written by Roger Ascham (1515–1568). Ascham, an English scholar, coined the term to mean an archer from Greek roots, literally translated as a "bow lover."

The term is rarely used and almost useless, along with **toxophily**, meaning archery.

trilby   A soft felt hat with narrow brim and indented crown, worn by men and women. Also given as **trilby hat**.

Named for the heroine of the novel *Trilby* (1894), by George du Maurier (1834–1896), in which Trilby O'Ferrall, a young artist's model living in Paris, falls under the spell of a hypnotist named **Svengali** (which see) and becomes a great singer.

In the stage version of the novel, the heroine wore a hat that came to be known as the **trilby**, once commonly called a slouch hat.

Triton   The largest moon of the planet Neptune. As **triton**, any of various marine gastropods, often having a large spiral shell; also, the shell of a triton.

Both words are from the name of **Triton**, in classical mythology the son of Neptune and Amphitrite, and represented as a bearded merman—the male counterpart of a mermaid—always shown in drawings and paintings as holding a shell. When Triton blows through his shell, one hears the roar of the sea.

Since Neptune is the god of the sea, the satellites of the planet Neptune have been named after less eminent sea gods or other sea-related creatures. Thus, in addition to Triton, there are the moons called Nereid and other Nereids as well. One of them was Amphitrite, another Galatea—both of them Neptunian moons. Galatea is best known because Pygmalion—a legendary king of Cyprus and a sculptor—made an ivory statue of a beautiful woman. When Pygmalion fell in love with his statue, named Galatea, it came to life.

Giving rise, much later, to the captivating play by George Bernard Shaw called *Pygmalion* (1913) and to the musical comedy *My Fair Lady* (1956), by Alan Jay Lerner and Frederick Loewe.

Another of Neptune's moons is Proteus, named after Neptune's herdsman. Thalassa, yet another of Neptune's moons, is not a god at all; her name in Greek means sea.

Mythology aside, the moon Triton is one of only three places in the solar system that are known to have active volcanoes or geysers. Earth and Jupiter's moon Io are the others, although it is expected that the planet Venus will be added to that list one day. But it is noteworthy that the geysers of Triton probably emit liquid nitrogen, because Triton is just about the coldest place in the solar system.

An interesting mental image for anyone who has visited Yellow-stone National Park.

Trojan A person who works energetically, fights with determination, or endures courageously.

From the name **Trojan,** an inhabitant of Troy, an ancient ruined city in Asia Minor. In Homer's *Iliad*, Troy was described as under siege for ten years by the Greeks in their effort to recover the kidnapped Helen, the beauty we know as Helen of Troy. (See **Achilles heel**.)

In the *Iliad*, the Trojans are characterized as brave, truthful, and patriotic. So when we speak of someone today as **a real Trojan**, we are complimenting him or her as a person who works energetically, no matter what the task assigned.

The ancient Trojans were also people who knew how to fight and endure, so see **Trojan horse**.

Trojan horse A person or device introduced to undermine an institution or destroy it from within.

From the **Trojan horse** of antiquity, a hollow wooden horse of some size left behind by the ancient Greeks when they pretended to abandon their long siege of Troy (see **Trojan**). When the besieged Trojans dragged the horse into their city, Greek soldiers hidden inside emerged during the night and opened the city gates so their countrymen could enter Troy and conquer it.

Surely this clever trick should have been called the *Greek horse*. After all, it was the Greeks who introduced the horse to destroy Troy from within.

But it has been called the **Trojan horse** in English since the sixteenth century, and it always will be.

trudgen A swimming stroke similar to the crawl, but employing a scissors kick.

Named after **John Trudgen** (1852–1895), a British swimmer.

Turing machine An imaginary device used to establish whether or not all functions capable of being described in mathematics can also be computed.

Named after the machine's inventor, **Alan Mathison Turing** (1912–1954), an English mathematician who was working at Princeton University when he designed his **Turing machine** in 1936.

Turing returned to England as World War II was about to begin and was soon recruited for the war effort. He served as a member of the team ordered to break the supposedly unbreakable German military code known as Enigma.

Turing applied his idea for a general-purpose computer to the team's specialized task, and together with other team members produced one of the first computers, called Colossus. The project was successful, and the knowledge of Germany's secret military plans gained through Colossus proved a key element in the Allied victory.

After the war, Turing continued his important work on computers, including the subject of artificial intelligence, but ran afoul of England's homosexuality laws in the early 1950s. After prosecution for alleged indecency, Turing died from eating a poisoned apple. It is not clear whether he was a suicide or the victim of a bizarre accident.

Society was the loser when Turing died at age forty-two.

U

Uncle Tom   A pejorative and offensive term applied to an African-American male, indicating that he is given to displaying chronic subservience to whites.

From the name of the hero in *Uncle Tom's Cabin* (1852) by the American novelist Harriet Beecher Stowe (1811–1896). **"Uncle Tom" Shelby**, an old slave cruelly treated by a Yankee plantation owner, **Simon Legree** (which see), is nevertheless devoted to his white master. Yet Tom dies as the result of a flogging inflicted by his white master when he refuses to reveal the hiding place of two runaway women slaves.

Uncle Tom's Cabin undoubtedly contributed to the success of the abolitionist movement, but Tom's fate—totally ignoring his heroism in not revealing the hiding places of the two slaves—was to suffer the disparaging use of the name **Uncle Tom**, particularly by modern black activists.

A bitter irony.

utopia   A perfect place or ideal state of things, sometimes given as **Utopia**; especially, a perfect social or political system.

From **Utopia**, the name of an imaginary island in the political romance *Utopia*, written by Sir Thomas More (1478–1535) in Latin in 1516 and translated by him into English in 1556. The island is a place where everything is perfect—laws, politics, morals, and the rest—in contrast to the situation More would confront in his life.

More, a principled English scholar, had the bad luck to be named Lord Chancellor by Henry VIII. After Henry had himself named head of the Anglican Church, More was imprisoned for a year and then beheaded because he recognized only the Pope as head of the Church. Henry VIII, as we all know, was not a man to be fooled with.

As might be expected, the noun **utopia** was so readily taken into English that it soon spawned the widely used adjectives **utopian** and **Utopian**, easily understood to mean visionary and idealistic, and the nouns **utopianism**, **utopism**, and **utopist**, also easily understood.

Incidentally, utopia is derived from Greek roots and literally means "not a place," making it quite clear that Thomas More was writing of a place that was not and would never be.

So don't get your hopes up.

V

valentine A card or message, often sent anonymously, avowing love but sometimes carrying a satirical thought, sent from one person to another on **Valentine Day**, also given as **St. Valentine's Day**. Also, a sweetheart chosen on this day.

Named perhaps after **St. Valentine** (died c.269), an Italian priest who was imprisoned for giving comfort to persecuted Christians and is said to have restored the sight of his jailer's blind daughter before Valentine was beaten to death.

Unfortunately for this St. Valentine, there was a bishop of Terni, who was himself martyred at Rome a few years later and also became **St. Valentine**. And both Valentines—wouldn't you know it?—are commemorated on the same day, February 14.

At any rate, **St. Valentine** is regarded as the patron of sweethearts, a tradition that may derive from an old belief that all birds, not only lovebirds, couple on February 14. The tradition may also be connected with the pagan fertility festival of Lupercus, an ancient Roman god of fertility. His celebration was held on February 15.

Whatever the correct origin of the custom of sending **valentines**, the principal beneficiaries of this annual outpouring of love are florists, greeting card companies, and manufacturers of chocolates.

Van Allen belts Also given as **Van Allen layers**, two doughnut-shaped regions of charged particles high above what we normally think of as the atmosphere, starting about 500 miles up and extending outward for thousands of miles.

The belts are formed when Earth's magnetic field bends the paths of incoming particles from the Sun—the solar wind—or the paths of less energetic cosmic rays so that the particles go into orbits around Earth or, at least, spiral around it a few times.

Named after their discoverer, the American physicist **James Alfred Van Allen** (born 1914), who had been using rockets to investigate the upper atmosphere since the end of World War II. Van Allen designed a small satellite, *Explorer I*, equipped with a **Geiger counter** (which see) and a radio, which was sent into orbit in 1958 to continue his investigation.

When the Geiger counter suddenly went dead, Van Allen knew enough from his other experiments to surmise that the cause of the interruption was high-intensity radiation. He subsequently proved this with another *Explorer* satellite later in the same year. Thus, it might be said that the **Van Allen belts**, also called the magnetosphere, became the first scientific discovery of the space age.

vandal A willful or ignorant damager or destroyer of something beautiful or valuable.

The noun **vandal** takes its name from **Vandalus**, the Latinized name of a Germanic people who ravaged Gaul and Spain in the fifth century. The **Vandals** are known especially in history for their sacking of Rome, in 455.

Thus, when we hear today of young ruffians **vandalizing** a neighborhood—by which may be meant nothing more than turning over a few trash cans—perhaps we ought to swallow hard and be thankful that modern vandals are just part of a long tradition and a pale imitation of early vandals.

Vandyke beard Also given as **Vandyke** and as **vandyke**, meaning a neat, short pointed beard.

Named after **Sir Anthony Van Dyck**, also given as **Vandyke** (1599–1641), the great Flemish portrait painter. Van Dyck sported a distinctive beard that was considered to be handsome and is the beard that has come to be known as the Vandyke.

Just right for any of the three musketeers. Completely wrong for Allen Ginsberg or Walt Whitman.

Venn diagram   A diagram consisting of two overlapping circles within a rectangle, used to determine or illustrate laws of logic or set theory by shading parts of the figure.

The portion of the circles that overlaps is termed the *conjunction* or *intersection*, while the portion outside a circle is termed the *negation* or *complement*.

Named for English logician **John Venn** (1834–1923), who used the idea to explain **Boolean algebra** (which see).

Venus   An exceptionally beautiful woman.

From **Venus**, the name of the Roman goddess of beauty and sensual love, who had an affair with Mars (see **March, martial**). Her name is attached to womanly figures of various configurations. Some are considered beautiful by modern standards, for example, the famous Venus de Milo and the Venus de' Medici.

Other **Venuses** demand a more relaxed conception of beauty, as seen in various paleolithic representations of the female figure, typically with exaggerated breasts, bellies, and buttocks.

But beauty is in the eye of the beholder, isn't it?

vernier   Also given as **vernier scale**, a small movable scale used to obtain a more precise measurement than attainable with the graduations on a larger scale.

This clever idea came, in 1631, to a French maker of scientific instruments named **Pierre Vernier** (1584–1638) and has been appreciated ever since by persons wanting precise measurements, not just of length but of any measurement. What's more, verniers are often attached to other precision instruments, such as micrometers, to give extra-precise measurements.

To understand the instrument better, suppose that a large scale is graduated in centimeters (cm) and millimeters (mm), which are tenths of centimeters. The **vernier** is a small scale with graduation marks at 0 millimeter, 1.1 mm, 2.2 mm, 3.3 mm, and so forth up to 9.9 mm. Now suppose that your measurement on the large scale is at a point between 5.6 cm and 5.7 cm.

The procedure is to line up the 0 on the vernier precisely with the measurement—between 5.6 cm and 5.7 cm—on the large scale and look to see where a line on the large scale most nearly matches a line on the vernier. The resulting reading gives a measurement accurate to the nearest tenth of a millimeter.

A truly versatile and valuable instrument.

Very lights   Signal flares fired from a special pistol for nighttime signaling or for temporarily illuminating part of a battlefield at night.

The special pistol is called a **Very pistol**. The flares were invented in 1877 by **Edward Wilson Very** (1847–1910), a U.S. ordnance expert and inventor.

vestal virgin   In ancient Rome, a virgin consecrated to **Vesta** and vowed to chastity.

The word **vestal** is an adjective meaning consecrated to Vesta. She was the goddess of the hearth and was worshipped not in a temple but in a round building that contained no images. It did contain a sacred fire that was kept burning continuously, and it was the responsibility of the **vestal virgins**, normally numbering six, to tend the sacred fire.

A vestal virgin who became unchaste would be punished by being entombed alive. Though not for very long. The quality of Roman construction being as good as it was, the unfortunate woman would soon die of asphyxiation.

Victorian   The safest way to define the adjective **Victorian** is to say it means designating or typical of the reign of **Queen Victoria** (1837–1901). And the safest way to define the noun **Victorian** is to say it means a person, especially an author, who lived during the queen's reign.

And go no further.

Although, when tweaked a bit, one might speak of the supposed prudishness of the Victorian period and its observance of conventionalities.

But if one were willing to court trouble, a definer might borrow freely from *The Oxford Reference Dictionary* (1986) and its highly respected editor, Joyce M. Hawkins. In paraphrasing Ms. Hawkins's entry for *Victorian*, one might speak of the Victorians' high standards of morality and decency; their self-satisfaction engendered by the great increase of wealth they saw; their rapid scientific and industrial development; and, finally, their unquestioning acceptance of authority and orthodoxy, accompanied by a conscious rectitude and deficient sense of humor.

Unfortunately, however, recent scholarship has upset much of our thinking about the Victorians, and we have been given a picture of them as living a life not nearly as conventional and prudish as we have believed.

This is not to say that Ms. Hawkins had it all wrong. But if you are asked what Victorian means, you would do well to go back to the third paragraph of this entry and capture "prudishness . . . and observance of conventionalities," even though that is how the Victorians were *perceived*, not what they *were*.

See **Caesar's wife** for further insight into the difference between how things are and how they appear to be.

volcano An opening in the earth's crust through which lava, steam, ashes, and the like are or have been expelled; also, a hill or mountain formed by ash and lava around such an opening.

From the name of **Vulcan**, the ancient Roman god of volcanoes, fire, and metalworking.

He had an interesting lineage. He was the son of Jupiter, the all-powerful supreme god, and Juno, the queen of heaven. But unlike some sons born to privilege, Vulcan was no idler. He had workshops under Mount Etna, in eastern Sicily, as well as under other **volcanoes**, and there he worked with the assistance of the Cyclops making thunderbolts for Jupiter. When he sided with Juno, his mother, against Jupiter, his father threw him out of heaven.

Literally. Gods don't usually indulge in metaphor.

It took Vulcan nine days to fall all the way to earth. He did not burn up during reentry to the earth's atmosphere, but he did break a leg as a result of the fall.

One more item of interest: Vulcan's wife was the beautiful **Venus** (which see), and she had an affair with Mars. As a result, Vulcan came to be seen as the special patron of cuckolds.

Proving that adultery can have good outcomes?

volt The unit of measure for electric potential, which is related to the concept of potential energy.

First an analogy: We are most familiar with the potential energy of *position*, as when a rock is balanced on the edge of a cliff. If the rock is rolled off the edge, it gains energy of *motion*. If the cliff is not very high, the energy of motion might not amount to much, but a high cliff corresponds to a high potential energy.

The electrical analog to the height of a cliff is called **voltage**, which is measured in **volts**. Notice that voltage tells us nothing about total amount of energy, any more than the height of a cliff tells how much potential energy there is in the rock balanced on the edge of the cliff. We also need to know the size of the rock, or the amount of electricity.

For example, if we walk along a carpeted hall in winter, our bodies may build up an electrical potential that will be discharged when we touch another person or a doorknob. Yet the amount of energy is not great. Think of a piece of gravel falling off a high cliff. It might sting when it hits us, but it will not crush us, the way a falling boulder will.

The **volt** was named in honor of the Italian physicist **Count Alessandro Giuseppe Anastasio Volta** (1745–1827) who, in 1800, was the first person to produce a steady current of electricity. Earlier, Volta had developed devices that produced powerful jolts of static electricity, but his main fame rests on his invention of the **voltaic pile**, which was the earliest form of battery, a marvelous device that converts chemical energy into electrical energy. (Except sometimes in winter, when a car won't start.)

In Volta's voltaic pile, or chemical battery, the electrical potential energy accumulates at one end of the device. When a conductor connects the two ends, the electrical energy flows from one end to the other as a current. Thus, for example, in the 12-volt battery commonly used in automobiles, each bit of electrical energy produced at the negative terminal can be thought of as falling 12 volts to reach the positive terminal.

Next time you jump-start a car, remember to match your jumper cables to the correct terminals and always keep your terminals clean.

vulcanize Make rubber or synthetic rubber stronger and more elastic by mixing it with sulfur and then heating it to high temperature.

Named after **Vulcan**, the Roman god of volcanoes, fire, and metal-working, by the impecunious American inventor Charles Goodyear (1800–1860), who developed the process in 1844 after ten years of experimentation.

It happened this way. Goodyear found that adding sulfur to rubber helped stabilize its elasticity—other researchers had also come upon sulfur for this purpose—but not sufficiently to make rubber useful in commercial products. In 1839, in one of the best known and true scientific accidents, Goodyear spilled some of his sulfured rubber on a hot stove while he was mixing a batch in his kitchen. Eureka! It was the heat that did the trick.

So if you can stand the heat, stay in the kitchen. You never know what you may come up with.

Even though Goodyear patented his process and became famous, **vulcanized rubber** proved easy to make, and other manufacturers grew wealthy while Goodrich drifted deeper in debt trying to pay his patent lawyers. He even had to borrow money to travel to Europe to accept membership in the French Legion of Honor.

He died in debt as he had lived in debt. The only difference **vulcanizing** made in his life was that he died much in debt instead of just a little bit in debt.

By the way, **vulcanization** works because sulfur, when heated, creates additional chemical bonds between the long molecules that make up rubber. But if a great many bonds are created, the rubber becomes **vulcanite**, or ebonite, and may be useful for manufacturing bowling balls, but far too hard for making automobile tires.

An example of too much of a good thing.

W

Walter Mitty A timid person given to daydreaming of adventures that relieve the tedium of his everyday, humdrum life.

From the name of **Walter Mitty**, the outrageously daydreaming central character of the short story "The Secret Life of Walter Mitty," by James Thurber (1894–1961), the famous cartoonist and writer originally published in *The New Yorker*.

While almost all of us have a Walter Mitty as part of our secret lives, we seldom admit to it.

Wankel engine An internal combustion engine in which the cylinder rotates, so there is no need to convert back-and-forth motion to rotary motion.

Named after its inventor, **Felix Wankel** (born 1902), a German mechanical engineer.

Successful **Wankel engines** have been built, including some for Mazda automobiles, but the conventional piston engine has always won out in side-by-side comparisons.

Wassermann test A diagnostic blood test, or reaction, specific to syphilis.

Before the test was developed in 1906 by the German bacteriologist **August Paul von Wassermann** (1866–1925), laboratory technicians had found it almost impossible to separate syphilis from gonorrhea, especially since many people who had one of these diseases had the other as well.

The bacterium that causes gonorrhea had been known since 1879, but not until 1905 was the bacterium identified that causes syphilis. With the introduction of the **Wassermann test**, the several stages of syphilis were sorted out for the first time, and progress followed in the treatment of the disease. An improved medicine, Salvarsan, was introduced in 1910, and a cure, penicillin, followed in the 1940s.

But the story did not end there. The U.S. Public Health Service, in 1932, launched the Tuskegee Study of four hundred syphilitic African-American men to observe the effects of the disease with the passage of time. The Public Health Service provided the men no treatment—it did not even tell them they had syphilis—until 1972, by which time most of the original participants had died from the disease.

After a public outcry was raised at the disclosure of the infamous Tuskegee Study, President Bill Clinton in 1997 apologized to the survivors and to the families of participants who had died.

Onward and upward with science and government!

watt   The unit for measuring electrical power, defined as 1 joule per second.

The **watt** was named in honor of the Scottish engineer and inventor **James Watt** (1736–1819), whose work had nothing to do with electricity, but everything to do with power.

First for some terminology: power is the rate of work, and the **joule** (which see) is the standard International System of Units measure of energy or work. Although most international measurement units are relatively unfamiliar, nearly everyone knows that a lightbulb is rated in **watts**, and that our electric bills are computed on the basis of **kilowatts**—thousands of watts—used. A familiar unit for measuring power is *horsepower*, which is still used to rate automobile engines.

To tie power units together, consider that 1 watt equals .00134 horsepower or, equivalently, 1 horsepower equals about three-quarters of a kilowatt. No one, however, would try to buy a car that has a 150-kilowatt engine, or a lightbulb rated at 0.134 horsepower.

It is interesting to note that James Watt introduced the term *horsepower* into English to describe the amount of work that could be performed by one of the steam engines he invented.

Wedgwood A kind of fine ceramic ware, protected by trademark, especially china with an embossed white cameo design.

From the name of its originator, an English potter named **Josiah Wedgwood** (1730–1795). The company he formed is still in business in Staffordshire, England.

Wedgwood is especially known for its powder blue pieces, a color known as **Wedgwood blue**.

wellington Also given as **Wellington** and **Wellington boot**, meaning a type of riding boot and a type of water-repellent overshoe.

Named after **Arthur Wellesley, 1st Duke of Wellington** (1769–1852), a British soldier and statesman known in his time as the "Iron Duke." After a busy career as a soldier in the English army he finally won the great military victory over Napoleon at Waterloo in 1825, for which he is best remembered. By then Arthur Wellesley had been given the title **Duke of Wellington**.

The original versions of **Wellington boots** were high boots, over which the trousers were tightly fitted. But no matter what the styles of the next century or two, **Wellies** will always keep our kids' tootsies warm and dry.

Another Wellington phrase, **beef Wellington**, is well known as a steak fillet covered with pâté de foie gras before it is wrapped in pastry and baked. Unfortunately, however, why this dish bears the Wellington name is not known.

Wheatstone bridge A device used for measuring the electrical resistance of a circuit by comparing it with the resistance of three other circuits of known resistance.

The **Wheatstone bridge** had surprisingly many uses in the early days of electronics, radio, and telegraphy.

Named after the English physicist **Sir Charles Wheatstone** (1802–1875), who did not invent it but helped popularize it. Wheatstone did invent, or almost invented, a number of devices connected to the dawn of the electric age, including a telegraph that preceded the telegraph invented by Samuel F. B. Morse (see **Morse code**). It must be mentioned that the telegraphs of both Wheatstone and Morse owed much of their basic design to the work of Joseph Henry, the American scientist whose name is remembered in the *henry*, a unit of inductance.

But the spirit of Wheatstone has no doubt been assigned to a special corner of hell for his invention of the concertina, a type of miniature accordion.

XYZ

. . . .

Xanthippe A scolding wife; a shrew.

From the name of **Xanthippe**, the bad-tempered wife of the philosopher Socrates (469–399 B.C.) and the subject of much gossip in Athens, where her nagging was well known.

Maybe that was why Socrates drank hemlock.

X ray. See **roentgen**.

yahoo A noun with two meanings: a bestial person and a boorish person.

From the name of the **Yahoos**, a race of filthy, loathsome brutes in human form in Jonathan Swift's satiric masterpiece *Gulliver's Travels* (1726). The Yahoos represented mankind living in a degenerate state, but they were tamed by the Houyhnhnms, a virtuous and reasonable race of horses representing the highest attributes of mankind.

Yet it was the **Yahoos**, not the Houyhnhnms, whose name became a household English word. Maybe because it was easier to spell and pronounce.

Yarborough In bridge, a hand in which no card is above a 9.

Named after the **2nd Earl of Yarborough** (1809–1897), who is said to have offered to bet 1,000 to 1 against such an occurrence in any designated hand.

The mathematical odds against a **Yarborough** are 1,827 to 1, which suggests that even an earl can learn to play the odds.

Zener cards Cards used in experiments in mind reading and other psychic phenomena, each showing a circle, cross, rectangle, star, or pair of wavy lines.

Named after the American psychologist **Karl E. Zener** (1903–1961), who devised the cards. Zener worked at Duke University with the well-known psychic investigator Joseph Banks Rhine (1895–1980).

Rhine's experiments were designed to establish on a statistical basis the existence of the phenomena of extrasensory perception and telepathy. In his experiments, a deck of twenty-five **Zener cards**, five of each type, was dealt one at a time by the transmitter while hidden from view, and the receiver drew pictures to illustrate the messages received.

The name Zener entered English when an American physicist named **C. M. Zener** (born 1905) invented his **Zener diode**, a type of junction diode, but little else is known of him.

And did Rhine succeed? Well, not exactly.

zephyr A mild, gentle breeze.

From the name of **Zephyrus**, in classical mythology god of the west wind, also name of the west wind itself.

zeppelin Also called a **dirigible**, a rigid, propeller-driven airship in the shape of a cigar.

Its compartments could be filled with gas—either helium or hydrogen—to provide lift. The airship also had accommodations for passengers, cargo, and crew, and its framework was covered with metal.

The **zeppelin** took its name from its inventor, **Count Ferdinand von Zeppelin** (1838–1917), a German army officer who served as an observer in the American Civil War (1861–1865) with the Union Army, and in the Franco-Prussian War (1870–1871) with the German army.

In 1891 he retired from the military to begin work in Germany on motor-driven airships and built the first rigid airship in 1900, which flew successfully on July 2 of that year. Designers in other countries, especially in France, Great Britain, and the United States, were also at work on rigid airships.

Along with successful demonstrations of these airships there came a series of spectacular failures, including the horrible accident in 1937 involving the *Hindenburg*, a German zeppelin, as it drew near its mooring mast at Lakehurst, New Jersey, and burst into flame, killing all aboard.

Whether the fire was caused by a spark in contact with hydrogen or whether the spark caused the fire when it hit the coated metal skin of the airship is not known. Whatever the cause, this fatal accident was captured on newsreel film and, wherever it was shown, put nails in the coffin of the rigid airship.

But **zeppelin** had entered the English language and remains there until this day.

Zöllner illusion   Also given as **Zoellner illusion** or **effect**, an optical illusion created when parallel lines are made to appear not parallel by adding short diagonal lines. The lines crosshatched in this way are called **Zöllner lines**.

Named after the German astronomer and physicist **Johann Karl Friedrich Zöllner** (1834–1882), who invented the first way to accurately compare the magnitudes of stars.